Natural ...
The Beautiful 'N' Word

Natural ...
The Beautiful 'N' Word

❖

Breaking the Psychological Bondage of the American Standard of Beauty

Richard O. Jones

Edited by Jennifer C. Jones
Michelle Bryant, Sisterlocks advisor
Photo on cover Dr. JoAnne Cornwell

iUniverse, Inc.
New York Lincoln Shanghai

Natural ... The Beautiful 'N' Word
Breaking the Psychological Bondage of the American Standard of Beauty

iUniverse books may be ordered through booksellers or by contacting:

iUniverse
2021 Pine Lake Road, Suite 100
Lincoln, NE 68512
www.iuniverse.com
1-800-Authors (1-800-288-4677)

ISBN-13: 978-0-595-42895-3 (pbk)
ISBN-13: 978-0-595-87232-9 (ebk)
ISBN-10: 0-595-42895-9 (pbk)
ISBN-10: 0-595-87232-8 (ebk)

Printed in the United States of America

Contents

Acknowledgements

I acknowledge Youth Communication. Youth Communication (YC) is a program that helps teenagers develop their skills in reading, writing, thinking, and reflection, so they can acquire the information they need to make thoughtful choices about their lives. Some of the activities available through YC are:

• training teens in journalism and related skills;

• publishing magazines, books and other materials written and illustrated by young people;

• encouraging teens and the adults who work with them to use YC publications to stimulate reading, writing, discussion, and reflection.

Printed with permission in this book is a published article in chapter eight by a past member of Youth Communication, Keshia Harrell. Thank you Keshia. For more information about Youth Communication visit: www.youthcomm.org

I acknowledge Sisterhood Agenda. Sisterhood Agenda is a program headquartered in New Jersey that helps instill good self-esteem in young girls. Sisterhood Agenda teaches them about the beauty of their natural god-given attributes. The girls in the program learn not to be influenced by media images that shun away from natural beauty in favor of the superficial. Sisterhood Agenda encourages writing skills and publishes a quarterly magazine with articles by the youth. For more information on Sisterhood Agenda visit: www.sisterhoodagenda.com.

Special acknowledgement is extended to Linda L. Jones. Ms Jones is an award-winning journalist and owner of Manelock Communications, a professional writing and media consulting service. Linda L. Jones is the author of <u>Nappyisms: Affirmations for Nappy-Headed People and Wannabees,</u> and also founder of A Nappy Hair Affair, Incorporated, which promotes African-American culture and identity.

Special acknowledgement is extended to A Christian Corporation (ACC) Christian and Community Newspaper in Los Angeles. The ACC, a weekly Baptist newspaper, has published my poetry regularly since 1991, which has helped me develop spiritually and poetically.

Special thanks and appreciation to The Black Voice News of Riverside and San Bernardino, California, a newspaper that strives to educate and inform the community on relevant matters that directly affects African-Americans. Furthermore, I acknowledge the Black Voice News for providing me a forum of expression through my weekly column.

The Pasadena/San Gabriel Valley Journal is acknowledged for their steady encouragement of African-American youth. The Pasadena Journal publishes a weekly poetry page that attracts submissions for elementary, middle, and high school students. The publishers of the paper have a commitment to let the youth know that they can aspire to be something greater than the stereotypical aspirations of most urban youth. I also thank The Pasadena Journal for publishing book reviewers written by members of The Literary Soul Food Café.

To Michelle Bryant: Special thanks. I am deeply grateful. Your spiritual aura propelled me to a higher level of sensitivity.

Dedication

This book is dedicated to QUINN COMMUNITY OUTREACH CORPORA-
TION (QCOC) a 501 © 3 nonprofit organization, which is an auxiliary of A. K.
Quinn AME Church in Moreno Valley, CA. QCOC facilitates beneficial pro-
grams throughout the Inland Empire such as:

- The Southern California Witness Project, a breast cancer education and
  screening program for African-American and Latino women

- The Literary Soul Food Café, which is a writer's workshop mobilized to
  inspire, encourage, and train novice writers and poets to develop and self-pub-
  lish their work.

It is through the support and assistance of the Literary Soul Food Café that I
was able to write and publish this work. As a member of the Literary Soul Food
Café, I invite unpublished writers and poets to visit our website at: www.
literarysoulfoodcafe.com for assistance in your literary projects or information on
starting a Literary Soul Food Café chapter in your city. For information about
Quinn Community Outreach Corporation write: QCOU 25400 Alessandro
Blvd. # 101 Moreno Valley, CA 92443

This book is further dedicated to every person who has ever felt inferior in
regards to his or her mirror image. If you ever wished that you were of a different
race, color, or ethnicity this book is dedicated to you. If you ever prayed or
wished for a different texture of hair, skin a different shade, eyes a different color
or shape, a taller stature, a handsomer or prettier face, longer, straighter, wavier,
or curlier hair, this book is dedicated to you. If you ever envied a celebrity,
model, friend, neighbor, relative or stranger solely based on physical attributes
this book is dedicated to you. If you ever felt especially superior because of your
looks or especially inferior because of your looks, it is no coincidence that this
book is in your hands.

The premise of this book is universal because self-criticism crosses all borders.
While the experience of racial inferiority is evident on every continent this book
is more specifically dedicated to people of African descendants and/or those con-

sidered black or a member of a minority group by the litmus test of white America.

This book pledges an allegiance of support to the bold black female public figures, celebrities, entertainers, educators, political leaders, clergy, and professionals who wear their hair in a natural style in spite of the American standard of beauty. Furthermore, this book is dedicated to all men and women of African descent regardless of their hairstyle choice or station in life.

To the men and women that have ever experienced sores in their head from chemical hair relaxers, burns on their scalp or neck from a hot comb, itching, stinging and/or other negative side affects on their head days after the hairdo, this book is dedicated to you. Dedications are also extended to the woman whose good self-esteem and confidence in her attractiveness is based on the length, color or style of her hair weave and/or hair extension, whereas it is my earnest desire that her psychological bondage is someday broken. Most importantly, this book is dedicated to the resilience and invincibility of black heritage in body, mind, and spirit.

Prologue

This book is not exclusively about hair. It is about learning to accept your 'Natural' inherited psychical features and overcoming or avoiding the force-feeding of cosmetic beauty by the movie industry. From the bottom of the feet to the top of the head people are seeking various types of chemicals, harmful creams, toxic lotions, implants and/or surgeries to improve their appearance. The facts are overwhelming but yet have remained an insider secret. There is too much to be covered here. My fundamental concern is to expose the surface of these vain cosmetic atrocities. No race or nationality is exempt from this vanity. African-Americans have been conditioned to carry a burden regarding their hair and skin tone—but they are far from the only ones. Natural ... The Beauty 'N' Word journeys behind the closed doors of liposuctions, breasts implants, anorexia, and botox injections and discovers horror from statements given by the plastic surgeons themselves. Hundreds of thousands each year rush to have their eyes widened and legs stretched, while others seek noses jobs. The need for perfection has send patients into an early grave and/or permanent deformity as a result of botched cosmetic surgeries. The craze for beauty is so strong that many women have resorted to paying to be illegally implanted with so-called designer babies. This same craze and/or obsession have led many young females into the delusional world of drugs and being sexually exploited, as actual victims will discuss. However, primarily, this book looks into the history of the beauty dilemma for African-Americans and further venture into the bigger picture of the global epidemic to obtain the American standard of beauty.

Physical freedom is not enough. When slaves were emancipated in the U.S. in 1865, the government enacted no psychological or financial rehabilitation. General William Tecumseh Sherman's promise to give each former slave "forty acres and a mule" never materialized. The result was four million people dumped into a shattered economy without resources and with few legal protections. The only thing slaves knew about life was the life of a slave. This is the information they brought into a free world. These teachings were passed down through generations and are still with many African-Americans today. Whether we admit it or not, or even know it or not, is irrelevant to the fact that it exists. Psychological bondage is so ingrained in the psyche that it's almost undetectable—yet it is in the American names we carry and give our children, it's in the diet we select and call soul food, and in the way we discipline our children. Above all, the most hidden and sociably accepted forms of psychological bondage are our attitudes about our natural hair and African facial features, and our longing to be embraced by the American standard of beauty. People of all races are made to feel insecure from the bottom of their feet to the top of their head and every place in between. This book will help the reader realize that psychological bondage is based on unintentional misinformation and/or blatant lies that have been overly exposed to the human spirit. In either case, the introduction and acceptance of truth is the key that unlocks the cage door and offers emotional freedom.

Black women of antiquity were legendary for their beauty and power. During this time, the African woman with her typical African physiognomy was believed to be the standard of beauty in that part of the ancient world. Yet, today, with very few exceptions, it is very rare to see a black woman who is reflected in the media with pronounced African features; rather, she is portrayed with more European features (aquiline noses, thin lips and eyebrows). It is rare that black women are portrayed as a symbol of natural beauty in magazines and other forms of media. It seems that all over the world, African females are encouraged or better yet subtly pressured to follow the standards of lily-white beauty.

While there is nothing wrong with Eurocentric beauty, there is something wrong with presenting it as the standard, which all women must follow. There is something wrong with touting straight hair and lighter skin as the more acceptable ideal of beauty and therefore negating authentic African beauty. However, all is not loss. There are millions of African-American women that are ravishing. They are not deterred by the ongoing attempts of national and international magazines, including some black owned magazines, which encourage them to shun their natural beauty. I had the good fortune to happen upon a heavenly array of beautiful black women who were proud of their Afro-centric beauty and celebrated it without anyone's permission with the grace of angels spreading their wings.

As a performance poet, I often browse the calendar section of newspapers, magazines and other printed or electronic media in search of a possible gig. When I discover an upcoming event that sounds interesting, I call the telephone and offer my entertainment services. In June 2006, I spotted such an event. I went to their website. It was a July 2006 event called the *Annual Sisterlocks Homecoming*. The festivities were taking place in San Diego, California. Sisterlocks seemed to be a group of women who wore an especially designed and styled natural hairdo referred to as Sisterlocks. The gatherings appeared to be a celebration of naturally grown hair rather than press and curls, and chemically relaxed hair. On the website, I discovered that Sisterlocks was more than a hairstyle, but also a lifestyle. Dr. JoAnne Cornwell founded and trademarked Sisterlocks in 1993 and thousands of black women across the country wore her design as a statement of freedom and expression of their heritage.

Dr. Cornwell took on the bureaucracy in the 1990s and was victorious after a long court battle to decriminalize hairbraiders for practicing in California without cosmetology training and a cosmetology license, which was seen as an expensive, oppressive, and unnecessary regulation that forced hairbraiders into a dilemma; go out of business or work illegally.

On the website were many pictures of the women and their various Sisterlock hairstyles. I emailed my request to recite poetry at the event. In my message, I said that I was the author of a special poem called *The Liberation of Aunt Jemima* about the change in the Aunt Jemima image on the pancake box, which was a milestone for the black woman's new image.

A few days later, Dr. Cornwell returned my call and invited me to recite my poem at the Sisterlocks dinner. Upon entering the hotel lobby there were signs and arrows directing patrons to various areas of the hotel. I followed the directives to the banquet room designated for the Sisterlocks Homecoming. In the huge room of several vendor tables, I was immediately fascinated by the many displays of African clothing, handmade purses, jewelry, and lady shoes. As I wandered from table to table, I observed one lady doing facials, another giving massages, and yet another styling hair. Finally, I asked one of the vendors for JoAnne Cornwell and was told that she was conducting a seminar in another part of the hotel, but one of her sisters was available. The vendor pointed to a table of pamphlets, booklets, and other literature. I approached the table and introduced myself.

"Good afternoon," I said, "my name is Richard O. Jones and I'm here to meet Dr. Cornwell."

"Hi Mr. Jones," replied the light skinned woman with big brown eyes that seemed to smile, and with a hairstyle I rightfully assumed were Sisterlocks. "I'm Carol Jenkins, JoAnne's sister. JoAnne is teaching a workshop right now."

"How long do you think she'll be?" Carol looked at her watch.

"About thirty or forty minutes. She's expecting you. Just hang around."

I noticed that most of the women had hairdos similar to Carol's. It occurred to me that everybody were wearing Sisterlocks except for a very striking, bald woman who was styling hair on the other side of the room. "May I ask you a question, Carol?"

"Sure. What is it?"

"I admire your hairstyle," I said, "are they Sisterlocks?"

"Yes and thank you," she replied.

"How long have you worn them?"

"Over ten years. I'm also one of the Sisterlocks administrators."

"Oh good," I said. "So you and your sister run Sisterlocks?"

"In a way, but our other sister is also a partner."

"Three sisters! Wow! That's terrific. Your other sister wears Sisterlock too I imagine."

Carol smiled and said, "Of course she does."

While talking to Carol, I discovered that the foundation of Sisterlocks rested on three siblings; JoAnne, Carol, and Celeste. I briefly met Celeste as she came over to refresh her memory regarding the evening schedule where she was booked to conduct a workshop. Celeste possessed a warm spirit that made you feel comfortable without words. I think it was the warmth I saw in her eyes and smile. I learned through my conversation with the youngest sister Carol that they were a close family and had the same vision regarding helping African-American and other black women feel good about their appearance. As Carol spoke, I pondered the company name and imagined that Sisterlock derived from the three sisters being locked in a love bond, which happens to coincide with the name of locks as pertaining to the hairstyle—thus, came the idea of Sisterlocks. But that was just my imagination. I figured that I would reserve that question for JoAnne.

"My sisters and I share the same philosophy about sisterhood and business," Carol said. "We know that many black women are in emotional pain. They're systematically rejected by society because of their race but especially their hair."

"No one likes being rejected."

"Well if they're doing something that is offensive that's one thing but if their rejection comes solely because of their appearance, it's painful."

When Carol said that, I thought about my two sisters. I remembered how they spent hours and hours working on each other's hair before they went to a dance. I remembered thinking that I was glad I was not a girl because they were too concerned about their looks. I shared those memories with Carol.

"Your sisters were not alone. Millions of black females grew up disliking their appearance. That's what Sisterlocks is really all about. We teach women to love their natural selves."

"I think that's great! Every woman should embrace that," I said.

"Oh no!" Carol corrected. "There're thousands of black cosmetologists that feel that if black women began to adore their natural beauty their business would suffer."

"Yes but that'll never happen. Many black women must wear their hair pressed & curled for professional purposes, and then others do it by choice."

"But as long as you're ashamed, you really don't have a choice," Carol said.

◆   ◆   ◆

I stood near Carol's table for most of the forty-five minutes it took before I met her middle sister JoAnne, a light skinned woman with lovely long Sisterlocks hair. It immediately occurred to me that the warmth in her eyes and smile was a family trait.

I soon learned that the Sisterlocks Consultants at the homecoming came from all over the United States. I saw the most beautiful and creative natural hairstyles that I ever imagined. The weird thing was that I had seldom actually had a chance to see a room full of naturally beautiful women without wigs, hairweaves, hair extensions, and perms. All of the women present possessed an aura of pride and high self-esteem, which transcended physical beauty. Most were professional, articulate, friendly, and independent entrepreneurs with their own salons throughout the nation specializing in Sisterlocks.

The purpose of this seminar was to network, exchange ideas, upgrade their skills through more training and introduction to new techniques taught by Dr. JoAnne Cornwell and/or her trained Sisterlock representatives. I thought this was something that I could support because I never liked the idea of so many black people (women especially) being manipulated by the ethnic hair industry. This was not only an innovative style and expression of self, but all the women were earning money by promoting the natural beauty of their own hair. I kept looking around and thinking, "Okay, where's the token black representative from the big 'ethnic hair' corporation? When is she or he going to make their pitch?" None appeared.

My performance went well. I even recited a special poem called *Sisterlocks* that I composed for the occasion, which went over well with the audience of approximately two hundred. After the dinner and dance, I retired to my room feeling as if I was in the making of history. These Sisterlock women were going to have a great influence on the future of black business and good self-esteem because Sisterlocks was breaking psychological the bondage of American beauty standards plus creating entrepreneurs. Wow! What a concept? Root profit! Making profits by the roots of your heritage without compromising with chemical blends and hair extensions.

Several days later, I called Dr. Cornwell and asked if I could write a book about Sisterlocks and its role in the future direction of black hair. She offered her moral support for my literary endeavor. I began to imagine Dr. JoAnne Cornwell as a woman destined for great prominence as well as many of the women in her company because black women had a long history of making great strides using hairdressing as their platform.

One editorialist commented in 1919 that it was a "noteworthy fact that the largest and most lucrative business enterprises conducted by colored people in America have been launched by women—namely Madame Walker, Mrs. Annie Malone, and Madame Sarah Washington." All three black women became millionaires. I found that interesting, very interesting. The first three black millionaires in America were women and all in the same business—black hair products.

This book examines the various concepts of beauty from Africa to America in an effort to understand the persona of true beauty. It retraces the black hair industry to its roots and follows the path of the deterioration of the black beauty image to its revival in the 1960s, and its remission during the 70s. Readers are given the tools to recognize and combat any latent inferiority in themselves, friends or family members as it pertains to hair.

As a direct result of African-Americans being influenced by the media the black hair care industry is a multi-billion dollar a year business, monopolized by white and Asian conglomerates. African-Americans manufacturers barely receive the crumbs that fall from the corporate tables. *Natural: The Beautiful 'N' Word* suggests to women with a penchant for natural hair, whether a licensed cosmetologist or not, to become an independent entrepreneur in the black hair industry. Sisterlocks and other natural hair care services are the projection of the future.

The money women spend on overpriced ethnic hair products could add up to enough money over several years to make a substantial investment for retirement income. This would be money saved from a simple change in attitude regarding natural beauty. Every woman that I talked to in Sisterlocks has begun to invest in other ventures such as stocks, annuities, real estate, and other businesses.

Natural: The Beautiful 'N' Word presents the idea of returning to natural hair and states reasons why natural hairstyles are superior to all others. Throughout the book, I return to the wondrous escapades of Dr. JoAnne Cornwell as she defied authority to overturn the oppressive laws that restricted natural hair care stylists from earning a legitimate living without the cumbersome burden of a cosmetology license.

As a poet, I could not resist the temptation to insert poems, quotes, and affirmations of encouragement. As a Christian, I could not resist the temptation to insert relevant scriptures from the Holy Bible that can be useful in offering an expanded perceptive.

Chapters one and two—The beginning of racism in American is delineated. It is important to understand the history before we can truly understand our present condition. Read these chapters and take notes if necessary because what you learn there will aid your understanding in later chapters. Within these chapters, you begin to understand how the black man/white woman attraction was inbred and passed from generation to generation. It is this early indoctrination that partially explains why so many black men are drawn to white women and also why black women have an inbred instinct to shun white men, and why white men have an inbred instinct to sleep with, but seldom marry black women. It is this same mentally and early mindset that causes black women to subconsciously envy the magnetism that white women seem to have over black men, which helped pave the path to black women buying hair and skin products that are advertised to make them more like their rival.

Chapters three and four—The pioneers of ethnic hair products are introduced. This was the era that black barbers flourished. The black beauticians had not yet made their mark on the industry. Male barbers were the hair stylists of white men and women in fancy barbershops. However, the women came later on like a bolt of lighting and electrified the ethnic hair industry. Dr. Joann Cornwell enters the scene with Sisterlocks in the early 1990s and revitalizes the black hair revolution. Chicago played a major role in the history of the black hair industry and some of the pioneering companies are introduced.

Chapters five and six—The obsession with the American beauty standards is examined. The many subliminal signs of inferiority imposed on blacks and the rest of the world become apparent. The psychology of brainwashing a nation and creating unsuspecting participants are explored. The creation of the standards of the American beauty, as we know it today, are revealed and discussed.

Chapters seven and eight—The Jheri curl becomes a vital part of the African-American culture in the 80s and the Natural becomes obsolete. The decline of the Black and Proud era is explored. Sisterlocks Consultants and women that wear natural hairstyles share personal testimonies.

Dr. JoAnne Cornwell begins her battle with the court to legalize natural hair care and hairbraiding without a cosmetology license. Hairbraiding shops and stylists are harassed and fined. The State of California Board of Cosmetology is determined to stop Dr. Cornwell who has begun a thriving natural hair revolution.

Chapter nine and ten—The axiom *"When life deals you a lemon—make lemonade"* is applied to the plight of many African-Americans as they turn their dire circumstances into profit. Such miraculous recovery will be referred to as *Root Profit* throughout the book. There is a discussion about a documentary film that exposes the domination of the retail ethnic hair industry especially in urban communities. Revelations are revealed how the hair and cosmetic industry targets blacks with weaknesses in their self-esteem.

Chapter eleven and twelve—A close look is taken of the mega bucks African-Americans contribute to the ethnic hair industry. Reasons for becoming self-employed as a consultant are explored. A summary report from a major marketing firm highlights the ploys the ethnic hair industry uses to lure African-American consumers. A court document charging a major ethnic hair company with violations of antitrust laws for targeting African-Americans through unlawful means is revealed.

Epilogue—An introduction of people, websites, organizations dedicated to preserving the integrity of natural beauty. Finally there is a listing of the Sisterlocks Consultants worldwide.

1

The Plot to Create Racism

Foreigners from all over the world braved rough terrain and raging waters venturing to America for an opportunity to prosper. However, Africans, my ancestors, were brought to America as cargo, against their will, to insure the prosperity of others. It has been over four hundreds years since Africans came to America in chains, after being kidnapped, stolen and sold into slavery. Behind us was the continent of Africa where we left a culture that would soon be forgotten. We were taught by the kidnappers and slave owners to adopt new cultures and traditions. To further disconnect our desire for Africa, we were forced to regard our hair and physical features as obscene. Nevertheless, our desire never died, although faded further and further as decades turned into centuries. The schools in America taught little truth of Africa and its people. Africa became an abomination to the now called Negro, and any resemblance of Africa including the language, religion, dark skin and coarse hair was scorned. Decades turned into centuries.

It took the newly arriving slaves from Africa to teach the American Negroes, the few that dared to listen, that no other culture could match the unique hairstyles, and aesthetic charms wore by warriors, maidens, and royalty. Some of the Africans arrived wearing locked hair, which was strange to the Negroes. No slaves wore locs and the Africans were soon stripped of their long locked hair.

According to African Heritage Volumes, starting in the cradle of civilization, ancient Kemet, now known as Egypt, around 3500 B. C., locs are evident in drawings on Egyptian artifacts. Locs were worn by priests, and by the people of prominence and royal status within various villages and tribes. Locs were depicted as the hairstyles of some gods and goddesses. Isis (goddess of wisdom), Maat (goddess of law and justice), Nzingha Amazon Queen of Matamba West Africa (1582–1663), Tiye, Nubian Queen of Kemet (Ancient Egypt) (1415–1340 B.C.) During this time, Queen Tiye was believed to be the standard of beauty in the ancient world, and Yaa Asantewa of the Ashanti Empire, and countless other women and men, also were depicted in locs. It was a beauty feature.

In the Old Testament, there were Israelites who followed a specific spiritual path in which they dedicated themselves to God. They were called Nazerenes. One of their practices is described in the book of Numbers 6:5: "All the days of his vow of Naziriteship there shall no razor come upon his head; until the days be fulfilled, in which he consecrateth himself unto the LORD, he shall be holy, he shall let the locks of the hair of his head grow long."

Early Relations Between Black Slaves and Indentured Whites slaves ∝ poor whites

Initially, some free blacks came to colonies as indentured servants, the same as poor whites. They were workers contracted to serve particular people for a stated number of years. For the first 40–50 years, both black and white indentured servants gained their freedom at the end of their contracts. Early black-white relations in North America are usually defined by the racial divide and conflict. However, historical records reveal quite a different relationship: one in which both African-Americans—those in servitude and those who had earned and won their freedom—and poor whites—the overwhelming majority of the white population—shared trial and tribulation. The idea of whiteness and white people, separate and apart from blackness and black people did not as yet exist. This was to come later as a direct product of the development of racist ideology, not just to justify slavery, but also to drive a wedge between black and white.

Historian Lerone Bennett, Jr. in his acclaimed work <u>Before the Mayflower: A History of Black America</u> poignantly summed up this early relationship:

"Working together in the same fields, sharing the same huts, the same situation, and the same grievances, the first black and white Americans ran away together, played together and revolted together. They mated and married, siring a mixed population. In the process, the black and white servants—the majority of the colonial population—created a racial wonderland that seems somehow un-American in its lack of obsession about race and color. There was to be sure prejudice then, but it was largely English class prejudice, which was distributed without regard to race, creed, or color."

Perhaps the most powerful feature of this early era is, as Bennett notes, "the equality of oppression" between white and black. Indeed, in the first years of slavery indentured white servants were often treated as badly as enslaved Africans, with African-Americans and whites being held in the same contempt and

whites inslaved as well?... wow

assigned similar tasks. White women not only worked in the fields, but were also flogged by the colonial authorities. Barbara Fields, in her <u>Slavery, Race and Ideology in the United States,</u> notes that indentured servants, although white, could be bought and sold like livestock, kidnapped, stolen, put up as stakes in card games and awarded—even before their arrival in America—to victors in lawsuits. The ruling circles and the resulting laws, at that time, did not distinguish between black and white.

Mulatto children born to a slave father and indentured servant white mother were slaves at birth because the prevailing laws were that children inherited the freedom status of the father. In fact, plantation owners that had few female slaves encouraged sexual relationships between the male slave and white indentured woman because the children from that union were the property of the plantation owner. However the relationships between the white indentured male and slave women were severely discouraged because a child born of that union would be free because the father was free. Even today, U.S. census statistics shows that three to five times more children are born to black fathers and white mothers than black mothers and white fathers.

Racism Created for Political Reasons

Segregation was a deliberate choice of the ruling circles. The salient feature in comprehending this fact is the observation that African-Americans and whites, as Bennett notes, "revolted together." This assumes vital significance when one couples the singular economic significance of slavery to the ruling classes with the continual resistance and revolt of Africans. Herbert Aptheker, the renowned historian, documented nearly 250 instances of revolts against slavery in North America. What also stands out is the frequent aid and, in many cases, participation of poor whites in these events, which were also rebellious because the ruling class also oppressed them. Some examples suffice to illuminate the prevailing state of affairs. In 1663, white servants and black slaves in Gloucester County, Virginia planned to stage a rebellion to win their freedom. Their plans were discovered and many African-Americans and whites were executed.

A famous rebellion known as the Bacon Rebellion occurred in 1676, when Nathaniel Bacon successfully maneuvered and escalated a civil dispute between some Indians and white merchants into a race war. The trouble began in July 1675 with a raid by the Doeg Indians on the plantation of Thomas Mathews, located in the Northern Neck section of Virginia near the Potomac River. Several of the Doegs were killed in the raid, which began in a dispute over the nonpayment of some items Mathews had apparently obtained from the tribe. The situation became critical when, in a retaliatory strike by the colonists, they attacked the wrong Indians, the Susquehanaugs, which caused large-scale Indian raids to begin. To stave off future attacks and to bring the situation under control, Governor Berkeley ordered an investigation into the matter. He set up what was to be a disastrous meeting between the parties, resulting in the murders of several tribal chiefs. Throughout the crisis, Berkeley continually pleaded for restraint from the colonists. Some, including Bacon, refused to listen. Nathaniel Bacon disregarded the Governor's direct orders by seizing some friendly Appomattox Indians for "allegedly" stealing corn. Berkeley reprimanded him, which caused the disgruntled Virginians to wonder which man had taken the right action. It was here the battle lines were about to be drawn. Ultimately, Bacon turned the entire colony against all Indians and vice-versa. The fight, which started out as a civil disagreement, became a war of Indians against whites.

Sixty-six years later, in New York in 1741, poor whites and slaves were accused of conspiracy to incite a revolt. They were arrested, found guilty in court and 35 persons, black and white, were executed. It should be emphasized that while African resistance and revolt, widespread and numerous, was the crucial factor in the struggle to abolish slavery, black people did not stand-alone; either before or after the conscious creation of the color line. This aid—overwhelmingly from the lower socio-economic strata—persisted in the face of concerted efforts by the slaveholders to eliminate anti-slavery opponents and organizations. As Aptheker notes, joining this great struggle were white allies who were mostly indentured servants but were later joined by the 'plain' white man and woman: the artisan and mechanic, the factory worker, the yeoman and small farmer. The poor housewife who formed the bulk of the membership of the Abolitionist societies, despite intimidations, contributed the largest part of the pennies and dollars with which the Abolitionist movement printed and distributed the pamphlets, petitions and papers appealing for justice and condemning oppression.

While the ruling elites were terrified of black revolts, they were thrown into panic by the prospect of continued and widespread joint of white-black rebellion. This would threaten to overthrow the existing order. Edmund Morgan, in American Slavery, American Freedom: *The Ordeal of Colonial Virginia,* notes that in the wake of these uprisings, the plantation owners concluded that "if freemen (whites), with disappointed hopes, should make common cause with slaves of desperate hope, the results might be worse than all the up-rises put together."

Thus, the Anglo-American ruling class, by deliberate policy, drew the color line between freedom and slavery, as Theodore Allen notes in his Class Struggle and the Origin of Racial Slavery: <u>*The Invention of the White Race*</u>, "on race lines: any trace of African ancestry carried the presumption of slavery." Consequently, the Virginia Assembly enacted various measures toward this end, including the slave codes that dictated discipline and punishment. Concurrently, Virginia's ruling class, having proclaimed that all white men were superior to black, went on to offer the white indentured servants a number of benefits previously denied to them. The ruling classes eventually saw the Bacon Rebellion, the ideal of turning one race against the other, as a strategy to keep the poor whites and slaves from continuously joining forces, so they began to create laws to turn them against each other. *Why not join forces? Afraid? Of?*

race class struggle + ...?

A law was passed requiring masters to provide white male servants whose indentured time was up with ten bushels of corn, thirty shillings, and a gun, while women were to get fifteen bushels of corn and forty shillings. Also, the newly freed servants were to get fifty acres of land. Black indentured servants would not receive anything. *Guns = masculinity? Motive?*

CPE

Gradually, a resentment and <u>a race divide</u> became to brew between the once close black and white indentured servants; the construction of racist and white supremacist ideology in North American was a direct and carefully thought-out class response to the problem of African slave and white indentured servants' solidarity. By instituting a system of racial privileges for white workers, it was possible to generate, define and establish the idea of the white race, which then operated as an instrument of social control, even the poorest of former indentured whites were now above the black slave in social status.

More laws were passed that further divided the association of African-Americans and whites. Whites in violation could be sentenced up to one year in jail. Laws were passed to void all marriages between blacks and whites and existing marriages were revoke and considered illegal. Interracial married couples who were already married suddenly became lawbreakers unless they separated or divorced. When interracial couples were caught together, they both would be severely punished by vigilante groups. Unless the white woman said that her husband or lover held her against her will; in which case she was usually brutalized by rape and/or beaten, but her life was spared and she was set free. However, the falsely *accused* black man was lynched. Between 1865 and the 1950s, hundreds of black men were lynched after being accused of raping white women. *Died by lies*

During the 1800s, laws also changed regarding the freedom status of mulatto children. Prior to the changes, the free status of a child born between a white and black couple was the same as the father. Many black men were free men by then and had white wives and lovers (usually former indentured servants) and therefore their mulatto children inherited the right to freedom; however, if a black man was a slave during the birth of his child, his child was born a slave. When the new racist laws prohibited marriage between whites and blacks, for black men and white women, the mulatto rate between such unions dropped greatly; how-ever, white men still legally enjoyed relationships with their black female slaves. Rather than allow all mulatto children freedom under the old law, the law was changed. Under the new law, a mulatto child inherited the freedom status of the mother, which in nearly all cases was a black slave. to gain more slaves

During this era, the third president of the United States, Thomas Jefferson was carrying on a love affair with his beautiful (by all reports) young slave girl named Sally Hemming. Although President Jefferson was married, Hemming had children by Jefferson and these children (the president's children) were also born slaves. This was the type of sexual affair that white women feared most—their man in love with a Negro slave. Since Sally Hemming was said to be beautiful, as many female slaves were, I suppose it was in the best interest of white society, women in particular, to make black females feel ugly. I am not claiming that this phenomenon was a direct result of the Jefferson/Hemming affair, though white women in general had contempt for attractive female slaves in their household. Many slave narratives delineate the cruelty female slaves were sub-jected to at the hands of their mistress.

In March of 1857, the United States Supreme Court, led by Chief Justice Roger B. Taney, declared that all Negroes—slaves as well as freemen—was not and could never become citizens of the United States. The court also declared the 1820 Missouri Compromise unconstitutional, thus permitting slavery in all of the country's territories. The case before the court was that of *Dread Scott v. San-ford*. Dread Scott, a slave who had lived in the free state of Illinois and the free territory of Wisconsin before moving back to the slave state of Missouri, had appealed to the Supreme Court in hopes of being granted his freedom. Taney—a staunch supporter of slavery and intent on protecting southerners from northern aggression—wrote in the court's majority opinion that, because Scott was black, he was not a citizen and therefore had no right to sue. The framers of the Consti-tution, he wrote, believed that Negro "had no rights which the white man was bound to respect; and that the Negro might justly and lawfully be reduced to sla-very for his benefit. He was bought and sold and treated as an ordinary article of merchandise and traffic, whenever profit could be made by it." From this point in history forward, the word was out that *blacks had no rights that whites had to respect,* and that alone set the racial tone in America for the next one hundred years.

Seventy-five years after slavery was abolished, Negroes were still not voting, or living in neither desegregated communities, nor being educated in desegregated schools. The line between superior and inferior was drawn and each race knew which side they were expected to stand.

The accusations of black men raping white women continued which gave whites an unchallenged excuse to lynch black men and rape black women. One of the more catastrophic marks of racist injustice occurred in the Tulsa race riot of 1921. The year saw the burning down of the prosperous Greenwood, Oklahoma neighborhood called Black Wall Street—by the invading white crowd. Around 300 people, mostly Negroes, had died, and hundreds were injured in the incident. Thousands were rendered homeless.

From the evening of May 31 to the afternoon of June 1, 1921, the city witnessed the most civilian killings since the American Civil War. A day earlier, a rumor spread in the white locality of the town that Dick Rowland, a black youth, had assaulted a 17-year-old white girl Sarah Page who worked as a lift operator. As Rowland was arrested, tension began building in the area. Whites were waiting for this opportunity. Angry and jealous whites had pledged that they would either buy them out or burn them out. Black Wall Street had to be destroyed and was burned to the ground. Whites flew their crop duster airplanes over Greenwood and dropped bombs on the homes and businesses.

It was worse than the 1965-Watts riot, the 1967 Detroit riot, the 1992 Los Angeles riot and the 1995 Oklahoma bombing by Timothy McViegh. The killings apart; the riot was aimed at crippling the rising economic power of the blacks. Whites had formerly tried to buy the black business and were turned down—that infuriated many.

The crowd brought down around 1,500 African-American homes, destroyed more than 600 businesses, including 21 restaurants, 30 stores, two movie theatres, a hospital, a bank, libraries, schools and the local post office. In less than two days, the Black Wall Street had turned into volcanic ash. African-Americans' dream of creating their own bourgeoisie had died.

Strange Fruit (song by Billie Holiday in 1939)

Southern trees bear strange fruit,
Blood on the leaves and blood at the root,
Black bodies swinging in the southern breeze,
Strange fruit hanging from the poplar trees.
Pastoral scene of the gallant south,

"Strange Fruit" = men lynched & bodies hanging from the trees like they've growing fruit.

The bulging eyes and the twisted mouth,
Scent of magnolias, sweet and fresh,
Then the sudden smell of burning flesh.
Here is fruit for the crows to pluck,
For the rain to gather, for the wind to suck,
For the sun to rot, for the trees to drop,
Here is a strange and bitter crop.

As Billie Holiday later told the story, a single gesture by a patron at New York's Café Society, in Greenwich Village, changed the history of American music in early 1939, the night when she first sang "Strange Fruit." Café Society was New York's only truly integrated nightclub outside Harlem, a place catering to progressive types with open minds. But Holiday was to recall that even there she was afraid to sing this new song, and regretted it, at least momentarily, when she first did. "There wasn't even a patter of applause when I finished," she later said. "Then a lone person began to clap nervously. Then suddenly everyone was clapping."

The applause grew louder and less tentative as "Strange Fruit" became a nightly ritual for Holiday, then one of her signature songs, at least where it could be safely performed. Audiences have continued to applaud this disturbing ballad, unique in Holiday's oeuvre and in the American popular-song repertoire, as it has left its mark on generations of writers, musicians, and listeners, both black and white. The jazz writer Leonard Feather once called "Strange Fruit" "the first significant protest in words and music, the first unmuted cry against racism." Jazz musicians still speak of it with a mixture of awe and fear—"When Holiday recorded it, it was more than revolutionary," said the drummer Max Roach—and performed it almost gingerly. "Its like rubbing people's noses in their own [feces]," said Mal Waldron, the pianist who accompanied Holiday in her final years. Ray Charles, Nina Simone, and James Brown also protested discrimination against blacks through their artistry. According to the hit movie "Ray" Ray Charles (1930–2004) was banned from performing in Georgia in 1961, following his refusal to play to a white-only audience. He later wrote his hit song "Georgia on My mind." Nina Simone (1933–2003) wrote "Mississippi Goddam!" This was her first song of protest, written after the murders of Medgar Evers in Mississippi (June 1963) and four black schoolchildren in Alabama (September 1963). James Brown (1933–2006) recorded "Say It Loud—I'm Black and I'm Proud" in 1968. It is notable both as one of Brown's signature songs and one of the most popular "black power" anthems of the 1960s. In the song, Brown addresses the prejudice towards blacks in America, and the need for black empowerment. He proclaims that "we done made us a chance to do for ourself/ we're tired of beating our head against the wall/workin' for someone else". From the same era, Brown also recorded "I Don't Want Nobody To Give Me Nothing (Open Up The Door, I'll Get It Myself)", which explored a similar theme.

Torment and lynching were rampant throughout the South for the next thirty-five years until the murder of Emmett Till: Emmett Till's brutal murder mobilized the civil rights movement. In August 1955, a fourteen-year-old black boy whistled at a white woman in a grocery store in Money, Mississippi. Emmett Till, a teen from Chicago, didn't understand that he had broken the unwritten laws of the Jim Crow South, until three days later when two white men dragged him from his bed in the dead of night, beat him brutally, and then shot him in the head. Although his killers were arrested and charged with murder, an all-white, all-male jury acquitted them both. Shortly afterwards, the defendants sold their story, including a detailed account of how they murdered Till, to a journalist. The murder and the trial horrified the nation and the world. Till's death was a spark that helped mobilize the civil rights movement three months after his body was pulled from the Tallahatchie River.

Forty Years Later Whites Still Lie To Persecute Black Men

I would not be surprised if one-day psychologists and sociologists come to the conclusion that part of the reason blacks sly away from their natural image is because of the negative connotations associated with being black. Black men especially are constantly being falsely accused of crimes. These false accusations have caused thousands to be lynched and millions falsely imprisoned. Perhaps, some blacks may conclude that if they look less black perhaps life would be somewhat fairer, which may had contributed to the popularity of hair relaxer and skin whiteners.

Susan Smith, 24-years-old, of Union, South Carolina, was convicted July 22, 1995, of murdering her two sons, 3-year-old Michael Daniel Smith, and 14-month-old Alexander Tyler Smith, and later sentenced to life in prison.

The case gained worldwide attention shortly after it developed, because Smith initially reported to police, on October 25, 1994, that she had been carjacked by an African-American man who drove away with her sons still in the car. Smith made tearful pleas on television for the rescue and return of her children. However, nine days later, following an intensive, heavily publicized investigation and nationwide search, Smith eventually confessed to letting her car roll into nearby John D. Long Lake, drowning her children inside. She will be eligible for parole in 2025, after she has served a minimum of thirty years. Can you imagine the number of black men that would have been snatched off the road and lynched if Susan Smith had made her false accusation fifty years earlier in South Carolina? Just a few years before Smiths' national lie, there was another national lie that could've resulted in the deaths or imprisonment of innocent black men.

Many people across the United States and around the world, to whom she and her two "missing" sons had been the subject of an outpouring of sympathy, felt strongly betrayed. Their reaction to the betrayal was further aggravated by the fact that she had attempted to cast blame, falsely, upon an African-American man, making the case racially sensitive and bringing back memories of a Roxbury, Massachusetts case in 1989. Charles Stuart shot and killed his wife in their vehicle and concealed his guilt by making a false police report that a black man had done it, inflaming racial tensions in the metropolitan Boston area for sometime afterward. The classic suburban nightmare: White yuppie couple Chuck and Carol Stuart were on their way home to suburban Massachusetts from a birthing class at an inner city hospital. A black man, 5'5", 150–165 lbs., with a raspy voice and an ubiquitous black jogging suit with red stripes, abducts the couple, robs them, and forces them to drive back to his "home turf" of Mission Hill. There, with no witnesses, he shoots the pregnant wife in the head and her husband in the stomach, a surprisingly flexible move from the back seat. He then runs off to the sanctity of his crime-ridden, drug-infested neighborhood. The husband's first instinct, of course, is to call 911 on his car phone and give them all the details, ignoring his dying wife next to him. Police and ambulances, after tracking the lost gentleman by the frequency of his car phone, make a triumphant rescue that the television cameras, which had rushed to the scene, captured for the thankful nation.

The country was stunned and outraged by this senseless, random murder of both mother and baby. The familiar call for the reinstatement of the death penalty was heard, and the Boston police, aware that the eyes of the nation were upon them, rose to the occasion by initiating what is affectionately called the "stop-and-search" method: the idea being that if you stop every black man within a ten-mile radius, you are going to find your killer much more quickly. Civil liberties had been suspended and a number of black jogging-suit-clad men were arrested as suspects. One might think that perhaps the easiest, most definitive (and legal) method of identification would have been to show Chuck mug shots

... but he was apparently too weak and then too emotionally exhausted to take part.

On November 15, Willie Bennett, arrested on other charges, emerged as the prime suspect—thanks in part to the fine work of the Boston police who had thrown his 63-year-old mother against the wall and trashed her apartment. On December 28, a rejuvenated [Chuck Stuart picked Willie Bennett as the man who most closely resembled their attacker.] The case was progressing to its inevitable and just conclusion. *↳ you decide a fate based on technicalities? wow*

And then it fell apart. Matthew Stuart, Chuck's brother, identified Chuck as the real killer. Chuck Stuart committed suicide before being apprehended, Willie Bennett was freed, and the whole web of lies was finally exposed. There are many underlining fears in being a black person. Racism plays a large role in parents desiring their children to have light skin and straight hair. Feelings of insecurity about being a dark skinned wooly-haired black person arouse fears of false imprisonment and forms of organized persecution. For blacks to wear natural hair and express a sense of pride has always been considered militant by the white community and a large part of the black community. Many black women and men still associate their natural image as an affront to the establishment and therefore, prefer not to buck the status quo. Black women wearing natural hair are often denied jobs and/or discriminated against on jobs. It is not easy to wear natural hair. A black male wearing dreadlocks becomes an automatic criminal suspect and women wearing deadlocks and natural hair are viewed as outcasts and anti-socials.

Dreadlocks are Ground for Refusal of Public Aid

In November 1994, according to a news website, the United Kingdom's then Tory government passed the Criminal Justice Act, one of the most repressive measures in recent British history. Department of Social Services would allow the government to deny public assistance to anyone with "disheveled hair, such as dreadlocks, clothing and piercing or the appearance of an alternative lifestyle (homosexuals)."

Wearing Dreadlocks Can Get You Arrested

According to the Saturday, July 08, 2006 Times-Picayune Newspaper of Louisiana a sheriff's remarks was called overtly racist. St. Tammany Parish Sheriff Jack Strain's statements about the suspects in a recent quadruple murder near Slidell amount to racial profiling that broadly paints Hurricane Katrina evacuees from New Orleans as "thugs" and "trash," the American Civil Liberties Union said in an open letter to the sheriff. Strain countered that the ACLU is distorting his comments, which he said were intended to warn St. Tammany residents about early signs of post-Katrina "spillover crime" from New Orleans. The dispute centers on a TV interview Strain gave after four people were shot June 27 near Slidell, allegedly in a botched drug deal in which the two suspects were identified as young black men, one with dreadlocks and one with a "chee wee" hairstyle. In the interview broadcasted on WDSU-TV, Strain said, "I don't want to get into calling people names, but if you're going to walk the streets of St. Tammany Parish with dreadlocks and chee wee hairstyles, then you can expect to be getting a visit from a sheriff's deputy." (What is a <u>Chee Wee</u>? Think Cheetos. Implication: dreadlocks, braids, twists, cornrows, and certain other African-American ethnic hairstyles look like the Chee Wees snack.) In essence, Strain is painting people who wear ethnic hairstyles as social outcasts deserving of public scrutiny, and there is plenty of history and research to show this can only lead to danger for the people negatively identified. He is saying it is <u>open season on black people</u> who choose to identify with their heritage by wearing their hair naturally or in hairstyles associated with their ethnicity.

racial profiling (margin annotation)

American Civil Liberties Union ACLU Tells Virginia Beach Bar to Rescind Racially Discriminatory Hair Policy or Face Legal Action

Excerpt from ACLU press release 10/29/06—VIRGINIA BEACH, VA—In a letter to sent Barry Taylor, the owner of Kokoamos Island Bar, Grill and Yacht Club, the American Civil Liberties Union of Virginia demanded that the Virginia Beach nightspot rescind a policy of barring hairstyles worn almost exclusively by African-American patrons.

"It is very troubling that a business open to the public in 2006 would seek to ban hairstyles associated with a particular race, creed, or ethnicity," said ACLU of Virginia Executive Director Kent Willis. "The suggestion that people with different hairstyles should attend different kinds of bars does not square with the values of equal rights reflected in our society, especially when the hairstyles in question are so closely associated with race."

Kokoamos denies entry to anyone wearing braids, twists, cornrows and dreadlocks—all of which are styles traditionally worn by African Americans, the ACLU said. The ACLU argues that the policy violates the federal Civil Rights Act of 1964, which prohibits public accommodations from discriminating on the basis of race.

The ACLU is representing Kim Hines, an African-American woman who was refused entry to the club in August because she wears her hair in dreadlocks.

In another incident, Big Daddy's, a nightclub in Richmond's Shockoe Slip, recently dropped its policy of denying entrance to persons with braids, cornrows or dreadlocks, after clients and civil rights advocates claimed that the policy discriminated against African Americans. *If more people recognized their racist ways, it would be better*

"The owners of Big Daddy's immediately recognized the racist aspects of their policy banning braids, cornrows and dreadlocks, and voluntarily changed their policy," added Willis. "We are hoping that Kokoamos will follow suit."

Racial Contempt Carved in Stone by 1900s

biracial baby = illegal at the time

Strom Thurmond, U.S. Senator from 1954–2003 resident of Mississippi was among of the most racial politicians of all time [fathered a daughter by a black teenage maid who worked in his parent's home] when he was 22-years-old. Thurmond, the longest-serving senator in U.S. history, died in June 2003 at age 100. His illegitimate daughter's story was published by the Washington Post on December 13, 2003. Strom Thrumond's family confirms paternity claim. Essie Mae Washington-Williams, now 78 and a retired schoolteacher in Los Angeles, publicly revealed her relationship to the former segregationist after a lifetime of silence.

"niggers" = trigger

Here're a few of Thurmond's typical racist quotes: *word*

"Our [Mississippi] niggers is better off than most anybody's niggers, why, they got washing machines and some of 'um even got televisions. I can't understand why they complaining."—Strom Thurmond

"I want to tell you that there's not enough troops in the army to force the southern people to break down segregation and admit the Negro race into our theaters, into our swimming pools, into our homes, and into our churches"—Strom Thurmond *sense of ownership... smh*

Upon discovering that Governor William H. Hastie of the Virgin Islands was black after he had invited him to visit Mississippi, he said, "I would not have written him if I knew he was a Negro. Of course, it would have been ridiculous to invite him."

There are hundreds of thousands of similar untold stories about the lust of white men and subservient black females employees, the unjustified lynching of black men, and persecution of free white woman who were typically referred to as Nigger Lovers, which was tantamount to a crime. Social pressure greatly minimized relationships between white women and black men, but secret liaisons continued while the sexual assaults by employers, widespread rapes, and other forms of noncommittal sexual relations with black women by white men went unsanctioned, unpunished, and unchallenged, except by angry bewildered white wives who spewed their venom on the victims who worked in their homes and businesses. I dread to give much thought to the hell that black women must have endured by the white man, white woman, and the black man who were beginning to regard her as less attractive than the allured white woman.

Black hair in the 1800s assimilation in its simplest form occurred when slaves attempted to transform their 'nappy' and 'kinky' 'bad' hair into silky and straight 'good' hair. In the process, these slaves erased the black self in order to comply with the rigid standard of American beauty. Erasure through imitation began, in part, with an inferiority complex. The female slaves' familiarity with white beauty standards may have been a result of the field slaves' distant observation of and the house slaves' more intimate contact with their owners. This familiarity often led to internalized feelings of inferiority about the texture and manageability of their hair. Some slave owners even instructed their house slaves to keep their *hair covered* while in their home.

Although Charlotte Forten-Grimke was not a slave, she did possess an inferiority complex resulting from norms established by white Americans. Grimke "adopted white standards of beauty" and "popular views of black inferiority." These views and standards probably "caused her to think of herself as unattractive" and to "fall in love" with a friend possessing "long, light hair, and beautiful blue eyes," as she would later write. The sense of inferiority expressed by Grimke and many of the female slaves due to exposure to and the reinforcement of white American beauty standards was an impetus for assimilation.

Charlotte Forten was born free in Philadelphia in 1837 into an influential and affluent family. She was the first northern African-American schoolteacher to go south to teach former slaves. A sensitive and genteel young woman, she brought intense idealism and fierce abolitionist zeal to her work. As a black woman, she hoped to find kinship with the freedmen, though her own education set her apart from the former slaves. In 1864, she published Life on the Sea Islands in *The Atlantic Monthly*, which brought her southern experience to the attention of Northern readers.

Forten wrote. "Some black female slaves sought assimilation by replacing the African identity, or 'bad' hair, with 'good' hair. Ironically, the very head scarves that white slave owners commanded house slaves to wear transformed African hair by absorbing perspiration and training hair growth so that the hair looked naturally curly. Slaves perpetuated this transformation with the application of easily available products to their hair. Some used axle grease to slick the hair down so that it was wavy or wrapped the hair with string to make it straight. Others relaxed the hair with a mixture of potatoes, potash, lye, and hot fat or pressed the hair with a hot iron comb and hog lard."

During the middle 1800s, products were developed, packaged, and sold to black women by black-owned businesses and beauty parlors and by white-owned companies advertising chemicals that claimed to straighten hair as well as transform blackness into whiteness. For instance, the advertisement for *Black Skin Remover and Hair Straightener* features a "before drawing" of a black woman's profile: her "forehead slopes forward sharply, her nose is broad and short, her hair is short, curly, and looks uncombed." In the "after drawing," the woman's hair is long and straight and is neatly styled. Her skin is white and her forehead no longer slopes forward as drastically. Her nose has become long and aquiline. In other words, the black person has become white by using a product that results in the absence of African hair and the African identity through complete assimilation.

Although black-owned businesses and beauty parlors advertised, sold, and used products that straightened hair, many of these business people emphasized racial uplift. By the 1850s, African-Americans had formed political coalitions, social organizations, churches and relief societies to socially, politically, and economically advance the black community. By the 1900s, the adoption of white hair styles and the fine texture was no longer merely imitation but instead was a way for African-Americans to combat disenfranchisement and attain citizen rights by employing white American standards within the black community.

Ultimately, whites conquered victories of black people's mind and self-image. In professional boxing, trainers are heard to say, "Kill the body and the head will follow." The same must be true in destroying the emotional wellbeing of an oppressed people. Although the lash of slavery was ancient history and the sting of Jim Crow was in remission, the head could not shake off the deep-seated damage. The mindset has been cast and the hereditary loathing symptoms became solid. Once a person is convinced they are hideous, they look in the mirror and hate their reflection and others who remind them of themselves.

To combat this feeling of racial low self-esteem many black heroic entrepreneurs sought to sooth the pain with the miracle wonders of skin bleaching creams and hair straighteners. Skin bleaching creams to mitigate the darkness and hair straighteners to transform their nappy hair into soft and long locks resembling their oppressor's hair. The complexion of one's skin and the texture of their hair became the standards by which African-Americans began the measure their value. They were rewarded with a quasi resemblance of acceptance into the white society by better domestic and servant work.

The feeling of dark skin and kinky hair inferiority raged relentlessly for over a century and is alive today. One of the crowning leaders in the effort to eradicate this demeaning stereotype is Dr. JoAnne Cornwell, the founder of Sisterlocks. Although millions of African-Americans dismiss the notion that the long-reaching arm of slavery controls them, the evidence is in our perception of beauty. All African-Americans have a common bond that cannot be denied. Our ancestors suffered the same bleak existence and our future generations will bear the same pattern of self-hatred unless we reeducate ourselves. Reeducation requires a commitment to honor ourselves. Sisterlocks and other natural hairstyles are not just about hairstyle but also about lifestyle and attitude.

The hair journey of black folk from the early 1900s to the 1970s was paved with acceptance. The chemical mixtures that African-Americans applied to their head and skin were readily acceptable to whites. The stampede by African-Americans to present themselves acceptable was very lucrative for whites and also to a few African-Americans hair product producers. The early pioneers of the black hair industry both white and black made a fortune off the inferiority complex of African-Americans and the phenomenon has not grown weary. The only difference is African-Americans have been burned out, forced out, or bought out of the multi-billion-dollar ethnic hair products industry. Whites, Asians, and Jews are making money off our roots. We grow the crop and they get the profits. Everybody is getting paid, except the slaves that own the plantation.

Systematic Brainwashing of the Black Child Through Books in School

The most popular racist and derogatory movie to African-Americans made during the early 1900s was *The Birth of a Nation* in 1920. It was the blockbuster of the era. The movie depicted African-Americans bullying and attacking whites and even attempting to rape white women. *The Birth of a Nation* depicts how it would be if blacks were in control. Also depicted in the movie were black legislators debating a bill to legalize interracial marriage—their legs propped on tables, eating chicken, and drinking whiskey. A black man proposes marriage to a mulatto woman. He says, "I will build a black empire and you as my queen shall rule by my side." When she refuses, he binds her and decides on a "forced marriage." While this drama unfolds, blacks continue to attack whites. It looks hopeless until the newly formed Klue Klux Klan arrives to reestablished white rule. *The Birth of a Nation* set the standard for cinematic technical innovation—the imaginative use of crosscutting, lighting, editing, and close-ups. It also set the standard for cinematic anti-black images. All of the major black caricatures were popularized in the movies, including, mammies, sambos, toms, picaninnies, coons, beasts, and tragic mulattoes.

During this period, popular children fairytales and books put white girls on a pedestal and/or damsel in distress such as: *Snow White, Cinderella, Sleeping Beauty, Goldie Locks,* and *Rapunzel.* These fairytales were being told at bedtime to black children by their parents. At the same time, children books that had African-American children as characters were demeaning and/or runaway slaves such as: The Adventures of Tom Sawyer, Huckleberry Finn, Uncle Remus, Uncle Tom's Cabin and Little Black Sambo. Distortions and degrading bootlicking images of the African-American were found in many books deemed children's classics. For example: The Story of Doctor Doolittle, by Hugh Lofting in 1920. The character of Prince Bumpo, an African-American, says to Doctor Doolittle:

If you will turn me white. I can go back to the Sleeping Beauty. I will give you half my kingdom and anything else besides … Nothing else will satisfy me. I must be a white prince.

The negative images continued in books for decades. Another typical example was the classic Mary Poppins, by Pamela Lyndon Travers first published in 1934. In Chapter 6, Mary Poppins travels to the South Pole where she meets two African-American characters, a man and woman. The woman says to Mary Poppins:

Ah bin 'specting you a long time Mar' Poppins … You bring dem chillun dere into my li'l house for a slice of watermelon right now. My but dem's very white babies. You wan' use a lil bit black boot polish on dem.

While African-American children, especially girls, were constantly brainwashed with negative images of themselves they most likely viewed the white female as superior and wanted to be like her as much as possible. This burst the money-gates open wider for an avalanche of skin bleaching creams and hair relaxers. Racism was the launching path to the hair product industry for black folk.

Gallant Attempts of Black Educators

During the early 1900s, Negro children were routinely exposed to negative images in children's books, which parents, librarians, and educators realized were detrimental to both Negroes and white children, and which therefore needed to be removed from library shelves. Educator and civil rights activist Mary McLeod Bethune's concern for children and history led her to argue that *the ideals, character and attitudes of races are born within the minds of children; most prejudices are born with youth and it is our duty to see that the great researches of Negro History are placed in the language and story of the child. Not only the Negro child but also the children of all races should read and know of the achievements, accomplishments and deeds of the Negro.*

It was time to examine carefully the books that were being used to educate children, and for Negro writers to create works that could be more useful and much more truthful. The Associated Publishers, a Negro owned publishing company founded in 1927 and backed by Negro authors, educators, and historical scholars such as Carter G. Woodson (known as the father of black history) and Charles Wesley, began publishing informative books that taught the history and culture of Negroes, but the company and its efforts were not large enough to remove the negative depictions of the Negroes from the minds of many children throughout the United States

Negro children's literature enables the Negro child to feel a sense of value and self-pride, and this literature also helps white children to understand and appreciate the rich culture, history, and tradition of the Negro. As Mary McLeod Bethune stated in an address to the Association for the Study of Negro Life and History, "It is important to give to all children a true picture of the races."

Americans have recognized black history annually since 1926, first as "Negro History Week" and later as "Black History Month." Prior to that time black history had barely begun to be studied—or even documented—when the tradition originated. Although African-Americans have been in America at least as far back as colonial times, it was not until the 20th century that they gained a respectable presence in the history books. We owe the celebration of Black History Month, and more importantly, the study of black history to Dr. Carter G. Woodson.

Unfortunately, by the time Dr. Carter G. Woodson introduced Negroes to Negro History Week, we already had over 300 years of ingrained anti-African messages. Throughout the remainder of the world, I am afraid there will always be an underlining resentment by a segment of African-Americans regarding their African heritage though we will attempt to mask it during Black History Month.

The tear-stained rusty knife that cut the umbilical cord separating Africans in the Motherland left an infectious psychological bacterial in our veins. American slaves slowly began to feel superior to Africans and by the time slaves were free, the separation and psychological superiority of Africans was insurmountable. The desire not to look African may have trumped the desire to look white.

2

Distortion of the Black Woman's Image

First published in March of 1852, <u>Uncle Tom's Cabin</u> immediately broke all sales records of the day. It sold half a million copies by 1857. In the best-selling novel <u>Aunt Chloe</u>, Uncle Tom's wife and the Shelbys' cook, often acts like a jovial simpleton around the Shelbys to mask her more complex feelings while nurturing and protecting of "her" white family, but being less caring toward her own children. She is the prototypical fictional mammy: self-sacrificing, white-identified, fat, asexual, good-humored, a loyal cook, housekeeper with an ever-present rag around her head, and quasi-family member. There were numerous plays and films at the first half of the century that zoomed black women in negative mammy images.

In 1934, the movie "Imitation of Life" told the story of a black maid, Aunt Delilah (played by Louise Beavers) who inherited a pancake recipe. This movie mammy gave the valuable recipe to Miss Bea, her boss. Miss Bea successfully marketed the recipe. She offered Aunt Delilah a *twenty percent* interest in the pancake company.

"You'll have your own car. Your own house," Miss Bea tells Aunt Delilah. Mammy is frightened. "My own house? You gonna send me away, Miss Bea? I can't live with you? Oh, Honey Chile, please don't send me away." Aunt Delilah, though she had lived her entire life in poverty, does not want her own house. "How I gonna take care of you and Miss Jessie (Miss Bea's daughter) if I ain't here … I'se your cook. And I want to stay your cook." Regarding the pancake recipe, Aunt Delilah said, "I gives it to you, Honey. I makes you a present of it." Aunt Delilah worked to keep the white family stable, but her own family disintegrated—her self-hating daughter rejected her then ran away from home to "pass for white." Near the movie's conclusion, Aunt Delilah dies of a broken heart.

"Imitation of Life" was probably the highlight of Louise Beavers' acting career. Almost all of her characters, before and after the Aunt Delilah role, were mammy or mammy-like. She played hopelessly naive maids in Mae West's "She Done Him Wrong" (1933), and Jean Harlow's "Bombshell" (1933). She played loyal servants in "Made for Each Other" (1939), and "Mr. Blandings Builds His Dream House" (1948), and several other movies.

Beavers had a weight problem; it was a constant battle for her to stay *over-weight*. She often wore padding to give her the appearance of a mammy. Also, she had been reared in California, and she had to fabricate a southern accent. Moreover, she detested cooking. She was truly a fictional mammy.

"Imitation of Life" was remade (without the pancake recipe storyline) in 1959. It starred Lana Turner as the white mistress, and Juanita Moore (in an Oscar-nominated Best Supporting Actress performance) as the mammy. I saw this movie as a preteen and even I cried. Apparently, the maid Aunt Delilah and been impregnated by a white man in her early life. The movie did not focus of that trivia matter. Nobody ever mentioned the term *deadbeat dad*. The term deadbeat dad didn't come into the public vocabulary until black men began to neglect their children in the 60s; however, the white man is the original deadbeat dad with hundreds of thousands mulatto babies that he never even spoke to, but I digress. The movie was a real tearjerker.

Hattie McDaniel was another well-known mammy portrayer. In her early films, for example in "The Gold West" (1932), and "The Story of Temple Drake" (1933), she played unobtrusive, weak mammies. However, her role in "Judge Priest" (1934) signaled the beginning of the sassy, quick-tempered mammies that she popularized. She played the saucy mammy in many movies including, "Music is Magic" (1935), "The Little Colonel" (1935), "Alice Adams" (1935), "Saratoga" (1937), and "The Mad Miss Manton" (1938). In 1939, she played Scarlett O'Hara's sassy but loyal servant in "Gone With the Wind." McDaniel won an Oscar for best supporting actress, the first African-American to win an Academy Award.

Hattie McDaniel was a gifted actress who added depth to the character of mammy; unfortunately, she, like almost all African-Americans from the 1920s through the 1950s, was typecast as servants. African-Americans often criticized her for perpetuating the mammy caricature as they did her male counterpart Lincoln Perry, also known as Stepin Fetchit. Perry played a dim-witted servant in nearly all his movies. (He was also the first African-American male millionaire.) Hattie McDaniel responded this way, "Why should I complain about making seven thousand dollars a week playing a maid? If I didn't, I'd be making seven dollars a week actually being one."

"Beulah" was a television show, popular from 1950 to 1953, in which a mammy nurtures a white suburban family. Hattie McDaniel originated the role for radio; Louise Beavers performed the role on television. The Beulah image resurfaced in the 1980s when Nell Carter, (1949–2003) a talented black singer, played a mammy-like role on the situation comedy "Gimme a Break." She was dark-skinned, overweight, sassy, white-identified, and like Aunt Delilah in "Imitation of Life," minus the rag around her head, content to live in her white employer's home and nurture the white family. The handkerchief tied around the head was the common denominator in every mammy.

We Wear the Mask

Paul Laurence Dunbar (1872–1906)

We wear the mask that grins and lies,
It hides our cheeks and shades our eyes,
This debt we pay to human guile;
With torn and bleeding hearts we smile,
And mouth with myriad subtleties.

Why should the world be over-wise,
In counting all our tears and sighs?
Nay, let them only see us, while
We wear the mask.

We smile, but, O great Christ, our cries
To thee from tortured souls arise.
We sing, but oh the clay is vile
Beneath our feet, and long the mile;
But let the world dream otherwise,
We wear the mask!

"It is a peculiar sensation, this double-consciousness, this sense of always looking at one's self through the eyes of others, of measuring one's soul by the tape of a world that looks on in amused contempt and pity. One ever feels his two-ness,—an American, a Negro; two souls, two thoughts, two unreconciled strivings; two warring ideals in one dark body, whose dogged strength alone keeps it from being torn asunder."

—W.E.B. DuBois
The Souls of Black Folk

"There is in this world no such force as the force of a person determined to rise. The human soul cannot be permanently chained."

—W.E.B. DuBois
The Souls of Black Folk

"Each night, without fail, she prayed for blue eyes."

—Toni Morrison, *The Bluest Eye*

A Dream Deferred

by Langston Hughes 1902–1967

What happens to a dream deferred?
Does it dry up
like a raisin in the sun?
Or fester like a sore—
And then run?
Does it stink like rotten meat?
Or crust and sugar over—
like a syrupy sweet?
Maybe it just sags
like a heavy load.
Or does it explode?

The lead line from the 1951 poem by Langston Hughes asks the question, *"What Happens to a Dream Deferred?"* The ideology of the poem helped propel the civil rights movement of the 1950s and 60s in the United States. The subliminal message has never died. In fact, the experience of a dream deferred was around before Langston Hughes put pen to paper. The beginning of the black hair industry lifted the lowered heads of black women with euphoria, but the hair relaxers later festered like a sore. Millions ran away from the fruit of their roots. Any remnants of African identity dried up like a raisin in the sun, stunk like rotten meat, and the slightest reminder sagged like a heavy load. Will my dream be pacified, defused or does it explode?

Black Actresses with White Features Had a Stereotypical Presence in Movies

There is a rich history in American film. There is one group of people that were many times overlooked for their great contributions to American film: the black actresses. Unfortunately, as in most things in the past, they did not have the same opportunities as mainstream Hollywood whites actresses. They were only allowed to be coons, tragic mulattos, mammies, and the servants. They were never allowed to be the leading lady. There are many aspects that surround these black actresses. Obviously, skin-tone was a factor because all of the black actresses who were considered beautiful shared the same characteristics: light skin, long dark hair, and European features.

The black actress has ventured through many eras of film. Slowly, she has gone from the servant to the mammy to the sexy vixen. Though dark skinned actresses longed for light skin and long straight hair, the ones born with such mulatto features were cast but carried a different burden, often referred to as tragic mulatto roles. In modern film, she seems to have more chances to play more respectable roles than in the past. From Nina Mae McKinney and Beah Richards prior to the 1960s (both dark) to Sanaa Lathan and Halle Berry after the 1990s (both light), Hollywood has had many changing faces of the black actress.

In the past, black actresses were only cast in demeaning roles. The mammy role is similar to the comic coon, but is a female and very independent. She is usually "big, fat, and cantankerous". The mammy leads her man, but always uses comedy to relieve the pain. She always knows that her place is in the kitchen. The tragic mulatto role was heavily portrayed. This person always brought about her own destruction. This person was usually a fair skinned mulatto who was usually trying to pass to white. The films portrayed this person as likeable because of her white blood. They wanted the audience to pity this person and believe that life would have been better for her, and she would be happier if she were not a "victim of divided racial inheritance".

The three top grossing black actresses Dorothy Dandridge, Lena Horne, and Fredi Washington found work but they usually played the roles of the tragic mulatto. Sometimes, the tragic mulatto was also a seductress. She was always very beautiful. The seductress usually turned the hero's life upside down. She usually had a plan for the submission of her male victim. She is always in control at all times. In some films, the black actress would be portrayed as the sex object. As the sex object, she would be used and abused without reason by both white and black men. This was shown in 1965—black actress Thelma Oliver revealed her breasts in the serious film, "The Pawnbroker." Many movies historians feel that she was used to further give black women a whorish image. Another role that black actresses were often cast to is the docile damsel. This woman is subservient to the man, and her life is surrounded by what he wants. She has a strong sense of loyalty, and there is quite a lack of independence.

Nina Mae McKinney (1912–1967) was the first recognized black actress on the silver screen. She won the role of Chick in "Hallelujah" when she was 17. She had the role of a seductress and a sex object. She was so beautiful and sensational that MGM signed her to a five-year contract. Unfortunately, "Hallelujah" did not bring the success she expected. Five years after "Hallelujah," she was virtually forgotten in America.

Nina Mae McKinney was film's first black screen princess, but she was also the first victim. She set the standard of the seductress for other great traffic mulatto actresses. She also learned the same lesson that they would ultimately learn; there are no leading roles for black actresses.

Fredericka ("Fredi") Washington (1903–1994) began her career in show business in 1921. She started off as an entertainer in nightclubs with her sister Isabelle. They became legendary beauties in the Harlem society. After her sister married Adam Clayton Powell, Jr., she got more heavily into acting rather than entertaining. In 1928, she performed in three movies: "Black and Tan Fantasy" (1930), "Emperor Jones" (1933), and "Drum in the Night" (1933). She married in 1933, and then in 1934, she received her most famous role as Peola, the daughter of mammy, in yet another remake of "Imitation of Life" (1934). Washington's looks were perfect for this role because she had long dark hair, fair skin, and green eyes. The media would say that she was French or Italian. Washington's unique looks were a blessing and a curse. She was beautiful and fair, but she could only play the tragic mulatto who was unhappy. It was very difficult to cast her as anything else because she could literally pass for white. She learned the same lesson that Nina Mae McKinney had learned before there is no leading role for a black actress. However, mulatto women were not victims of hair relaxers and skin lightening creams. Dark-skinned black women envied them and black men adored them, which made everyone victims of a manipulated mindset. The light skins were deceived into thinking they were superior to the dark skins and the dark skins were deceived in thinking they were inferior. As a result the principles of the Bacon Rebellion succeeded in getting and keeping slaves, former slaves, and descendants of slaves separated.

Without doubt, one of the entertainment world's legends is Lena Horne. She was definitely the most popular Negro actress in the 1940's. Lena Horne was born in Brooklyn, New York in 1917. She entered show business at age 16 when she became a chorus girl at Harlem's Cotton Club. She dropped out of school and supported her family. By age 20, she was married and had a daughter. She went to Hollywood, and became the first black actress to sign a term contract with a film studio. In her contract with MGM, it stated that she would not do any stereotypical roles. Many people thought that she was Latin American or that the film studio was trying to pass her as white. Lena's first big musical was "Thousands Cheer" (1943). She said, "They didn't make me into a maid, but they didn't make me into anything else either." Many of her scenes in movies were cut out in the South. Lena's roles were mainly sex objects, but "she always proved herself too much the lady to be believable as a slut". Two of her most famous films were "Cabin in the Sky" and "Stormy Weather."

In 1956, Lena was fed up with her "guest" roles in movies, and left for 13 years. During that time, she focused on her music, and produced the highest selling album by any female artist in RCA Victor's history. In 1981, she opened her one-woman show on Broadway called Lena Horne: *The Lady and Her Music*. The show received a special Tony award. She is a generous and gracious woman who has devoted much of her time to helping others. Lena later founded her own cosmetic company called Lena Horne Cosmetics. She is still thought of as the black-leading lady of the war era. Lena Horne was so adored by black men that their craze for white women started shifting to a relentless lust for light skinned women. It was their subconscious quasi-way of saying I love black women not white women.

Black men saw the straight long hair of mulatto women the same as the hair of white women. She had her eyes, and her skin, plus she was safe to be with. It was a subtler, harder to discern form of self-rejection. Even today, dark skinned women lament that black men want light women. The unfortunate component in this scenario is nobody chooses a substitute if the real thing is available. Would you prefer to have a real *gold* ring or a near-gold ring? However, a *near-gold* ring is better than an *almost-near-gold* ring. I would prefer to live in 10-bedroom mansion; however, I am content in a three-bedroom house, but in a storm—a one-room log cabin would do.

Ed Bradley (1941–2006) of "60 Minutes" interviewed singer Lena Horne in December 1981. Bradley created an intimate portrait of the singer. Bradley asked

Horne, "Tell me about the way black women were treated in the early days in your career?" Horne took a gulf and choked up and remained silence for a few seconds as she thought about the question. The camera zoomed in on her face, as she seemed to recall events of her past. Bradley asked compassionately, "Is it hard to talk about?" Horne mustered a smile with tears now dripping one at a time from her eyes and said softly in her sultry yet raspy voice, "Sometimes it is, it really is." Bradley gracefully took the interview in another direction.

In 1910, Max Factor Cosmetic Company created the first makeup formulated especially for film. The light skinned, straight haired African-American starlets played a fundamental role in the furthering the inferior image of their darker sisters, which made ethnic hair and skin products sales soar. The major cosmetic companies were an essential part of the movie scene because every actor and actress required makeup. I can only imagine that their marketing department realized that blacks knew that they could never obtain true whiteness, but at least could try to get the image of the light skinned movie stars.

In 1919, Mary Pickford, a popular white blonde actress, co-founded United Artists with Charles Chaplin, Douglas Fairbanks. In 1937, Pickford founded Mary Pickford Cosmetics. Mary sold her shares in United Artists in 1956. The fact that the movie industry and the cosmetic industry have been in partnership for decades is no coincidence. The movie and cosmetic industry sets the American beauty standards.

Fifty-one years later, the partnership between the movie industry and the cosmetic industry continues. In the 2005, the brothers Bob and Harvey Weinstein, who have been responsible for producing some of the most successful box office hits for Miramax, have signed a two-year marketing and product placement deal with L'Oreal Paris, the world's largest beauty brand. The partnership, trumpeted by the Weinsteins as the first ever between a motion picture company and a major cosmetics brand, confirms that L'Oreal Paris hair and cosmetic products will be used in all Weinsteins films. As part of the partnership, L'Oreal will be the official exclusive beauty sponsor for all of the Weinstein Company and Dimension Films premieres in the US over the next two years, beginning in January 2006.

The strategic alliance will also include promotional support and the co-hosting of special events such as Weinstein Company parties at the Golden Globes and Academy Awards. In addition, L'Oreal's expert makeup and hair teams will support all promotion of Weinstein Company films. Surely in the films of the future we can expect to see every black actress on the screen using L'Oreal products. I wonder if we'll begin to see smiling black women using hair relaxers in the movies. I know one thing that we'll never see in the movies, and that's a sister comfortable with her natural hair and beauty denouncing hair relaxers and hair weaves, unless she's a militant and wanted by the FBI.

Dorothy Dandridge (1922–1965) was born in Cleveland, Ohio. Her mother was an actress, Ruby Dandridge. Dorothy has been performing all of her life. As children Dorothy and her sister toured the United States as *The Wonder Kids*. By the 1940's Dorothy Dandridge had started her own career in Hollywood. She was beautiful with her long silky hair, light skin, and sharp features, and she possessed the combined attributes of her predecessors. She set many important standards in Hollywood. She was the first black actress to receive a nomination for an Academy Award for best actress for her performance in "Carmen Jones" (1954). She was also the first black actress to be romantically involved with a white man on screen in "Island in the Sun"

Dandridge always made headlines with her interracial relationships. She seemed bold and daring, but ironically, she was portraying the tragic mulatto in her own life as well as in the movies. Dorothy's last important film was "Porgy and Bess" in 1959 with Sidney Poitier. Dandridge refused to play Bess as a whore, and her performance won her a Foreign Press Golden Globe award nomination. In the late 1950's, Dorothy married Jack Dennison, a white restaurateur. She later divorced him and declared bankruptcy. She drifted to alcohol and pills. Dorothy Dandridge died from an overdosed on anti-depression pills. It seems that eventually ... she may have been forced to live out a screen image that destroyed her. The tragic mulatto story came to life.

Diahann Carroll was born Carol Diann Johnson in the Bronx, New York in 1935. When she was ten years old, she won the Metropolitan Opera scholarship for studies at New York's high school of Music and Art. She attended New York University, but soon she was appearing in movies. In 1954, she appeared in both "House of Flowers" and "Carmen Jones." In 1961, she was cast in "No Strings" as a high fashion model. She won a Tony award for that role. Carroll is also a light skinned woman and the first African-American woman to star in her own TV series—*Julia* 1968. Carroll also owns her own cosmetic company.

Halle Berry born in 1968 used to pray she would be "cured" of being black. The stunning actress dreamed of finding a pill to turn her skin white when she was a child, according to Britian's Sun Newspaper. Berry, in 2001, became the first black woman to win an Academy Award for best actress for her performance was in "Monster's Ball"—a movie that depicted the actress nude in sex scenes, is quoted as saying: "Being a black woman, I've struggled with that my whole life—feeling that if I changed, my life would be better." She added, "Although such things [Academy Award] do wonders for my confidence, I'm never able to take them seriously. If they really knew me, they'd realize that I'm far from secure about my looks." Berry is one of the most popular celebrity models for ethnic cosmetics.

Popularity can sway the way cosmetic companies do business. Today, Queen Latifah, though not dark skinned, but a little heavy, is the fresh face of Cover Girl Cosmetics, replacing Christie Brinkley, a white blonde. Queen Latifah said, "I stand behind companies I believe in, and I get involved in projects where I know I can make a positive impact," in an interview with Heather Staible. During the same interview Queen Latifah also stated that with her as the new face of Cover Girl it inspires women of color along with highlighting natural beauty. Noteworthy, in the mid-70s, former dancer, and actress Lola Falana was the first black woman to model for a line of cosmetics that was not targeted solely to blacks, in the successful Faberge *Tigress* perfume ads.

I have seldom seen popular dark skinned celebrities do cosmetic commercials; however, cosmetics company *Flirt* has signed a deal with tennis pro Serena Williams under which she will become the company's new Guest Creator, a position offered to celebrities giving them input into new product lines. Williams says she is a beauty junkie. "Now I am able to create makeup that works with what is in style. Creating cosmetics allows me to be glamorous and adventurous plus show off my flirtatious side, a fun contrast to my life." Serena is young, beautiful, dark skinned and although she is often under a long blondish weave, I think that she represents tennis well; however, a dark woman with laniferous [wool-like] hair is much more representative of an African woman than a dark skinned woman with long straight blonde hair. Serena also has deals with Close-up toothpaste, and Venus Williams, her older sister, shares an Avon Cosmetics deal.

I doubt that we will see a truly natural haired celebrity doing a cosmetic commercial anytime soon, although it would be refreshing. (Oops! This insert was added one month later: I just saw a Dove Soap television commercial with a beautiful dark skin sister with dreadlocks; however, soap is a neutral product that promotes cleanliness not beauty, plus she was no celebrity. Everybody uses soap. Be not deceived, there are many of black female celebrities that represent themselves as natural beauties who are not natural, at least not their hair, such as Beyonce, Tyra Banks, Ashanti, Janet Jackson, Queen Latifah, Venus and Serena Williams and many others that help keep alive the white standards of beauty. Nearly all of them wear extensions, hairpieces, and/or hair relaxes, and yet advertises natural beauty. Every one of them will stand tall, holding an artificial beauty product in the hands, and proclaim their blackness. This seems to be a fraud perpetrated against black women. Most women do not realize that the cosmetic companies themselves are telling them that it is more beautiful to be natural. Natural is a common word in most beauty ads because <u>Natural</u> is truly the beautiful 'N' word. The chemical products on the market may enhance their artificial or superficial beauty but not natural beauty; that is an oxymoron.

Perhaps someday an enterprising lawyer will file a class action suit for false advertising against the cosmetic companies that employs black celebrities with hair extensions, wigs, hair relaxer, and other deceptive products, and present them to the public as natural beauties or natural products. Millions of black women are beguiled to think that these products promote rather than diminish their natural beauty. The cosmetic companies should be forced to stop telling African-American women that they are only beautiful naturally if disguised and covered in cosmetic accessories, namely false and/or chemically enhanced. They should be forced to stop using the word natural and beauty in the same sentence.

An Internet search will reveal that cosmetic companies are sued all the time for false advertising, yet no one, to my knowledge, has challenged the natural beauty claims targeted at black women with the use of black celebrities that are so blatantly false. No other product on the market can get away with advertising something as natural when it knowing is not. The cosmetic companies should be no exception; however, there must be a loophole of protection for them.

MY FAIR FRIEND DEBRA

by Eileen Carole

My fair friend Debra
Takes her color seriously
Challenged daily by a shade she didn't choose
And a face she must present to a darker audience
To gain entry to the inner cultural society
That often prejudices it's very own

My fair friend Debra
Feels a color deeper than its actual hue
Feels the ethnicity that others doubt
Questions the why that separates her
From a sisterhood, a brotherhood
Of people melanin-blessed
Retreating within to an unaccepted space

My fair friend Debra must get beyond
That place and take the task
Move on the mission; teach the lesson
Endure while educating
So that color
As well as shade
Is not an issue

Women of Color and Beauty Pageants and What Oprah Has to Do With It

During the 1960s, Ebony Magazine kept the readers informed about beautiful black women who were breaking barriers in the world of beauty pageants. In 1960, Corrine Huff, Miss Ohio, was a finalist in the Miss USA competition, which qualified her for the Miss Universe Pageant. Miss Haiti 1962 becomes the first black woman to make the semifinals at the Miss Universe Pageant. Dorothy L. Johnson, Miss Idaho 1964, was one of 15 runners-up in the Miss USA competition. Also participating that year was a contestant from Nigeria and three Black women from the Caribbean. The world begins to see the beauty of black women. By the way, Jennifer Jackson was the first African-American Playboy Magazine's playmate of the month in the March 1965 issue.

For centuries America's beauty standards were anti-black; therefore in 1968 the First Miss Black America Pageant is held in Atlantic City as a protest against the absence of black women in the Miss America Pageant, which began in 1921. Rules barring non-whites finally changed, and the first black contestant to make it to Atlantic City was Cheryl Brown, Miss Iowa in 1970. Although she failed to make the semifinals, her achievement paved the way for the selection of the first black Miss America fourteen years later

In 1977 "Miss Universe Crown is Won by First Black" a major racial breakthrough, as Janelle Commissiong of Trinidad-Tobago. The historic moment is televised live by satellite from the Dominican Republic. When Janelle was announced as the new Miss Universe, Trinidad and Tobago went wild. It was another Carnival in the streets, and Trinidadian television aired repeats of the pageant for days. The 24 year-old Caribbean dark-skinned women, daughter of a Trinidadian father and a Venezuelan mother declared that she "believed her election would contribute to erasing racial barriers." Proud of her victory, she noted, "Beauty belongs to all people; it has no racial or geographic boundaries."

In1980, Lenola Sullivan, Miss Arkansas, is the first African-American woman to make the top five at the Miss America Pageant. She also wins the swimsuit competition.

To date at least three black women have won the coveted Miss America title beginning with Vanessa Williams in 1984; however, she later resigned when nude pictures of her taken years earlier created a huge scandal. She was replaced by runner-up, Suzette Charles, another black woman. Although these beauty queens were black they had white features.

1984—For the first time, a Eurasian woman of Philippine and Irish parentage named Mai Shanley wins the Miss USA title. Also in 1984, Oprah Winfrey (who, by the way, at 18 years old, won the Miss Black Tennessee pageant and competed in the Miss Black America pageant in 1971) moved from Baltimore to Chicago to host WLS-TV's morning talk show, AM Chicago, which became the number one talk show just one month after she began. In less than a year, the show expanded to one hour and was renamed The Oprah Winfrey Show. What was so amazing is the fact that Oprah was the exact opposite of the black beauty queens. She was an overweight dark skinned black woman with a large frizzy Afro hairdo.

1985—Another racial breakthrough 1985 became the year of the Latina beauties. Laura Martinez Herring, a naturalized Mexican-American, is named Miss USA, making her the first Hispanic to win a major U.S. pageant title. Deborah Carthy-Deu, Miss Puerto Rico, wins the Miss Universe title the same year.

In 1986, by coincidence the same year that Halle Berry *actress and award winner* was first runner-up at Miss USA *and 5th Runner-up at Miss World,* The Oprah Winfrey Show entered national syndication and the whole world saw a big, dark, kinky haired, unashamed black woman for the first time, and loved her. Oprah was nobody's mammy. She helped me realize that white America had set black women free. They were not bound by stereotypical images except psychologically.

All through history the majority of whites stood back-to-back with African-Americans in their racial battles. We had a bigger problem—we had to overcome the racist attitudes launched at each other. Sure, I realized that there would always be some white bigots but the law and the decent majority was on our side. Here was an intelligent black woman; couldn't sing or dance; didn't act or tell jokes; didn't sleep her away into prominence and was not married to a white man, yet, she was fast becoming the one number TV host in the world.

In 1990 the second black woman to actually win the Miss America title was Debbye Turner. Miss Turner also had white features. Carol Gist, Miss Michigan-USA, becomes the first African-American woman to win the Miss USA title also in 1990, which meant that black women held both the Miss USA and Miss America titles in the same year). Also in 1990, Playboy Magazine named 22 year-old Renee Tenison, an African-American, Playmate of the Year. Tenison was the first African-American so honored, if you equate getting naked for a magazine with honor. These six beautiful women contributed greatly to the positive image of black women worldwide.

In 1991 Marjorie Judith Vincent won the Miss America title, and she was the first winner with African features, dark skin, and a full figure. I believe Oprah opened the door and public acceptance of dark skinned full-figured women.

Also in 1991, Dr. Deborah Williams, a psychologist and mother of one, becomes the first African-American woman to win a national pageant for married women.

1993—For the 2nd time in pageant history, black women hold the Miss USA and Miss America titles simultaneously: Kenya Moore, Miss USA 1993.

In 1994 Kimberly Aiken, Miss America 1994 (selected in September 1993).

In 1995—Chelsi Smith, Miss USA, becomes the first bi-racial American to be named Miss Universe during the first Miss Universe Pageant held in Africa. Her father is black and her mother is white.

In 2001, Nigeria's Agbani Darego became the first black woman from Africa to be crowned Miss World. When Darego proclaimed in her acceptance speech, "Black is beautiful."

There! I have just named a bus load of black women who were recognized as world class beauties; some light, some dark, some with straight hair, some with coarse hair, some mixed and others full African—so there! Black is beautiful with or without chemical help.

Outer Limits

Sometime in the 1980s, I saw a rerun of a 1960s "Outer Limits" television episode that I shall never forget. It had a deep message about accepting yourself. If you ever saw an Outer Limits show, you probably remember how weird the show can get. In this particular episode a woman had been in a horrible crash of some kind. The show started with the woman on the operating table for her second plastic surgery. I could see the backs and hands of the medical staff but not their faces. The conversation in the operating room between the doctors and nurses implied that this young victim was deformed for life unless this second surgery was successful. Nurses were passing instruments to the doctors and swabbing their brow. The clock on the wall could be seen as the minutes ticked into hours.

After five or six hours in surgery they were finished. The young woman was wheeled into the recovery room where her bandages would be removed the next day.

The following day, the medical team went to the patient's room. One of the doctors slowly cut away the bandage from her face. When he had finished, one of the nurses looked at the woman and swiftly left the room in tears. The remaining medical team looked defeated. The young woman saw their hopeless expressions and knew that the operation was a failure; however, she reached for a handheld mirror.

The TV viewers saw her reflection as she held the mirror near her face. This young woman was beautiful by the standards of average human beings; however, for the first time the medical staff faces were seen. Each of them resembled pigs. The young woman, however, looked like a Hollywood scarlet; nonetheless, she broke down and wailed because she wanted to look like everyone else.

As it turned out, they lived on another planet where everyone had the face of a pig. The young woman was the only survivor after a space ship crash months ago on this weird planet. She was doomed to live there but with her looks she was an outcast; however on earth she would have be consider beauty by white American standards.

The Ugly Duckling

Remember the children's fairytale The Ugly Duckling by Hans Christian Andersen? A mother duck hatches her eggs and, while most of her ducklings are normal, one is gray, too large, and too clumsy to fit in among the others. Though she tries to accept him, the entire barnyard realizes that he simply does not belong and after a period of harassment he leaves (or is driven away) to fend for himself. He wanders for the entire summer and fall, for no one will take him in, and he nearly freezes to death in an icy pond. Though a human rescues him, he cannot live in captivity, and he goes back to the wild.

By the end of winter he is miraculously still alive. He comes to a pond in a park or garden, where beautiful white swans are swimming. He is drawn to their beauty, though he has no reason to think that they will treat him better than anyone else has. He approaches with fear but determination. To his surprise, the beautiful creatures welcome and accept him; gazing at his reflection, he sees that he too is a swan. The children declare that he is the most beautiful swan of them all, yet he isn't proud for a good heart is never proud. Because of all that he suffered he now appreciates his happiness so much more. The moral concept of the

"Ugly Duckling" is that beauty is subjective. In the proper setting all can be perceived as beautiful and in the wrong setting all can be perceived as ugly. The most valuable trait a person can possess is inner beauty—it will be with you in all settings. When African-Americans, who comprise 13% of the United States, compare their facial features, skin hue, and hair texture with the remaining 87 % of the United States they have a choice to make. They can either celebrate their god-given uniqueness or strive to assimilate the American standard of beauty.

Beauty standards are perceived according to cultural norms. For example, the cultural norms and beauty standards of the Masai in Africa are different from that of the Eskimos in Alaska. Black Americans, perhaps more than anyone else, carry a heavier psychological burden. The mental damage from centuries of bombardment with Euro-American standards of beauty has had tremendous impact on how we view ourselves within what is essentially an alien country. During chattel slavery (and afterwards), we were brainwashed into thinking that anything African was substandard, or inferior.

When I was a Teen, I Thought Like a Teen

When I was a teenager in the 60s, I was a juvenile delinquent and was sent to a youth detention camp for one year. The experience was educational because it was the first time in my life that I lived among other races. The boys there were in three groups, which were black, white, and Latino. We lived in a large dormitory that housed at least 500 boys. Each inmate had his own single bed and locker. The dorm looked like military barracks that I had seen in the movies. Inside of the lockers on the doors, the guys taped photos of models from magazines. As I walked through the dorm, I noticed that most of the pin-up girls were white, usually cutouts from men magazines. Guys would trade photos and sometimes even get into fights over the magazine clippings.

Most of us black guys did not put any white model's picture on their lockers. Not that we did not admire white girls in bikinis but it was a matter of principle. The pictures on our lockers were of personal girlfriends and family. Then one day my mother brought me a Jet Magazine with her usually picnic lunch.

Back at my bunk, I flipped casually through the magazine and noticed the centerfold pin-up girl, wow! I immediately removed the photo and made space for her inside my locker door. I wrote my mother and asked her to bring the current Jet whenever she visited, which was three or four times per month. Soon my locker was filled with beautiful black models. The other black guys began asking their visitors to bring Jet Magazines also. The slogan 'black is beautiful' was personified in the form of the centerfold girls, who were the epitome of black and beautiful womanhood. I preferred the darker models on my locker to the ones that could pass for white because, from my experience, most light-skinned girls were off limits to dark skinned guys. I did not realize at the time that they were victims too. However, after Angela Davis and Kathleen Cleaver, two "high-yellow" black women in the Black Power Movement, appeared in Jet Magazine wearing huge Afros with their fists raised high, I realized that all light skinned females were not stuck-up and began putting light skinned models on my locker as well.

Some of the models in Jet Magazine wore natural hair, Afros, and Afro wigs, some wore straight or curly, short or long wigs, others had perms or press and curl hairdos. I remember one model that was bald but that didn't matter to me or the other guys, in fact, her picture sold to a *white boy* for three cigarettes when the going price was one cigarette. A beautiful black woman was a beautiful black woman and none of us gave a hoot about her hairstyle, as long as she had on a bikini—everything was everything.

The beauty of a woman is her exemplification of her native country. An Asian looks most beautiful when she appears as a proud Asian woman in every aspect. Every country has its cultural dress and customs. If an Asian woman appeared in a Miss Universe Contest speaking Spanish and wearing a sombrero and poncho, she would embarrass the Asians and also insult the Mexicans, and be ridiculed by the public.

When we, as men, begin to appreciate our women's natural beauty they will blossom into their natural beauty. African-American women should aspire to be the woman God created them to be. There is no greater freedom and empowerment than a healthy potion of self-love. God commands us to love our neighbor as we do ourselves, but if we have been acculturated not to love ourselves—then we have some work to do. Before you can give anyone a rose, you must have a rose. If all you have is bitterness then that's all you can give. If all you have is admiration for the American standard of beauty that is all you can pass along to others.

On a personal level, I feel the true beauty of a woman is self-confidence. Physical beauty is often overrated. I am not impressed by a person's innate physical attributes because they make no contribution to their attractiveness or unattractiveness. For example, a man did not contribute to his stature just as a woman did not contribute to her natural breasts size. Too many people fall in love with physical features rather than character. Natural height and natural breasts are genetic, not a condition to which the man or woman contributed, and therefore, deserve no extra credit or undue criticism.

A common source of insecurity in most black women is their hair and/or complexion. Whether they are flattered or offended, either side of the fence makes them invisible and their true essence is missed. Everybody wants to be judged—but favorably. Nobody resents being called beautiful, which is a judgment but nobody wants to be judged unfavorably. The way to overcome such insecurities is to never become flattered or offended for features beyond your control because you had nothing to do with it.

A person born rich deserves less recognition than a person born poor, but became rich through honest work because his success was within his control. Some physical features and characteristics are fair to judge. For instance, body weight is within personal control. Our dental hygiene, grooming and health habits, altruism, intelligence, manners, sense of humor, solvency, religious and political beliefs, level of loyalty, commitment, accountability, responsibility, reliability, honesty, hobbies, priorities, education, quality of friends, and morals are within our control. All of these things serve to contribute to a person's overall beauty but are often overlooked. Qualities such as skin tone, hair texture, hair length, eye-color, facial features, and derriere is genetically induced.

When people hang medals on genetics, rather than character, the individual behind the birthright is overlooked. That is one of the reasons some attractive people often feel uncertain if people would really like them if they really knew them, the inner person nobody sees. Some people use their good looks to get away with being ugly.

All types get divorced, lied to, cheated on, use drugs to cope and even commit suicide. Light and dark skin women are subject to abuse, loneliness, and low self-esteem. God gave people the right not to appreciate you; let them exercise their right, but He didn't give you the right not to appreciate yourself.

How would you pick your friends and lovers if you were blind? What human qualities would attract you to a person, if you were blind? Would it be the color of their hair, eyes, or skin? Or would it be something greater? The next time you are drooling over the physical attributes of a person, close your eyes and take a good look.

AUNT JEMIMA IMAGE and How it Served to Demean Black Women

In1889, the Aunt Jemima Pancake Mix was born in St. Joseph, Missouri after Chris L. Rutt, a newspaperman, and Charles G. Underwood bought the Pearl Milling Company. Searching for a novel product to survive in a highly competitive business, the two men hit on the original idea of developing and packaging pre-mixed, self-rising pancake flour. Rutt attended a vaudeville minstrel show where he heard a catchy tune called "Aunt Jemima" sung by a black-faced performer, clad in apron and bandana headband. Soon after, the whole town was humming the song, and Rutt immediately decided that Aunt Jemima was the name for his pancake mix, which was the birth of the name Aunt Jemima being synonymous with pancakes. Short on capital, Rutt and Underwood went broke and sold the formula to the R.T. Davis Milling Company in 1890. Davis decided to try a new idea and began looking for a Negro woman to employ as a living trademark for his new product. He found Nancy Green in Chicago, Illinois. She was 59 at the time and worked in the home of a judge. Nancy Green was born a slave in Montgomery County, Kentucky in 1834. Her given name was Nancy Green, but the world knew her as "Aunt Jemima." Although the famous Aunt Jemima recipe was not hers, she became the advertising world's first living trademark. She was attractive, friendly, a good storyteller, and an excellent cook. Her ability to project her warm and appealing personality made her the ideal Aunt Jemima.

There is a book entitled Slave in a Box: The Strange Career of Aunt Jemima, by M. M. Manring. (Charlottesville and London: University Press of Virginia, 1998.) Slave in a Box begins with a provocative title that sets the tone for an investigation of the popular image of Aunt Jemima. The title serves as a metaphor to describe how white male advertisers have capitalized on American racism and sexism.

M. M. Manring's study of Aunt Jemima shows how the popular image emerged from the "mammy" of Southern plantation life and took on a variety of qualities ascribed by novelists ranging from Mark Twain to James Baldwin and by historians ranging from Carter G. Woodson to Darlene Clark Hine. Aunt Jemima became the mirror of the racial class, and gender beliefs of writers and consumers. Aunt Jemima, the fat, rugged, unmarried, asexual servant served as the opposite of the delicate, pure, ultra-feminine southern white woman of the Old South.

As the American food industry moved into premixed, mass produced, packaged commodities, Aunt Jemima became the legal trademark for the first ready-mix pancake flour, which was originally sold in paper bags with Aunt Jemima's name the product label. Later when the pancake mix became available in boxes an artist rendition of Aunt Jemima appeared on the box and also the paper bag.

In 1893, the Davis Milling executives boldly decided to risk their entire future with an all-out promotion at the gigantic World's Fair in Chicago. They constructed the world's largest flour barrel. "Aunt Jemima," in the person of Nancy Green, demonstrated the pancake mix. She kept up lively conversation with the crowd while making and serving thousands of pancakes. She was such a sensation that special details of policemen had to be assigned to keep the crowds moving at the Aunt Jemima exhibition booth.

Davis received over 50,000 orders from merchants all over America and foreign countries. Fair officials awarded Nancy Green a medal and certificate for her showmanship and proclaimed her the "Pancake Queen." Davis signed her to a lifetime contract, and she traveled on promotional tours all over the country. Because of Nancy Green's fame, her arrival was usually announced on giant billboards. The Davis Company prospered, and by 1910, the name of "Aunt Jemima" was known in all 48 states and had attained such popularity that many people tried to infringe on the trademark rights.

Until the emergence of Aunt Jemima Pancake Mix, the bulk of flour sales were made in the winter. After the success of the Nancy Green promotion, flour sales were up yearlong and pancakes were no longer considered exclusively for breakfast. The Davis Company later ran into money problems and had to sell, but Nancy Green maintained her job until a car on the streets of Chicago's Southside killed her on September 24, 1923. In 1925, the Quaker Oats Company of Chicago purchased the Aunt Jemima Mills. The image of "Aunt Jemima" remained on the packages.

Throughout history, labels have been pinned on black women. But there are four that have truly demeaned them: Mammy, Aunt Jemima, Sapphire and Jezebel. They all have individual qualities yet they equate to the same unattractive equation.

Sapphire was mainly the joke of plays and music shows. She was fairly smaller than Mammy and Aunt Jemima. She was a loud mouth sassy woman, usually belittling her husband. She was set up to make her husband look inferior, therefore setting bad standards for the black family.

The most unique stereotype was the character Jezebel because she was slim and half-white. She was always the seducer of a white man. Jezebel was light enough to get him, but not white enough to keep him. She was seen as a pretty but loose woman, always focused on sexual encounters with white men.

Mammy was a figure created in minstrel shows. She was the dark skinned, obese, and a jubilant worker for the master of her plantation, or after the Emancipation Proclamation, her employer. She was always protective of the white family for which she cared. They were her first priority; her ultimate joy was pleasing them. She was seen happy with a constant obnoxious grin. And most of all, she was viewed being content with her enslavement and oppression.

These images of black women were carried throughout America for over one hundred years. Whites in small communities, who had never seen black people before, received their first and long-lasting impression of black women through the mammy character. She was in movies, on labels, made into magnets and figurines. She was even internalized by the children who watched cartoons. Mammy was the first of the four characters to star in cartoons, but not the last.

The next role of the black woman was Aunt Jemima. Aunt Jemima had the same qualities as Mammy, but her main focus was cooking. She would cook the food, wash the dishes and talk to the little white children at the same time. The white children, although they adored their Aunt Jemima, were superior to her intellectually because Aunt Jemima was illiterate. Aunt Jemima became so popular they extended her image beyond the pancake box and onto the syrup bottle.

In the late eighties or early nineties the Quaker Oats Company liberated the image of Aunt Jemima to a slimmer, black woman without the bandana. She now adorns pearl earrings, lipstick and a press and curl hairdo.

The Liberation of Aunt Jemima

by Richard O. Jones

Times certainly has brought about a change
And to a few it might seem strange
Black women are soaring with ambition
No more barefoot, pregnant, and in the kitchen

And she's not slaving like an ox
Have you seen her new image on the pancake box?
Ha, purse full of credit cards; fancy car
And the girl ain't even a movie star

Not long along I was on the bus

Eating fried chicken from the colonel
Reading a girlie magazine and full of lust
Sitting next to a sister reading a Wall Street Journal

I said, "Pardon me baby, where are you on your way
I would like to know your name, if that's okay
Your perfume I surely adore
I believe we've met somewhere before"

She says in a dignified voice, "I'm on my way downtown to City Hall
I must chair a council meeting and that's not all
Then I'm flying off to the United Nations
To advise on a classified situation

"I'm sorry but I fail to remember you
Were you ever in Zaire, Sudan, or Istanbul?
Or perhaps it was Rome, England, or by chance
It was Chad, Morocco, or Paris, France

"You see, I'm multi-lingual, and I travel a lot
And the universe is my melting pot
But once a month, I take this bus
Just my way of staying in touch

"Nefertiti is my name
And universal peace is my game
I attended Benedict College in South Carolina
And earned my Bachelor's degree
Then I went to Fisk and received my Master's,
In Nashville, Tennessee

"At Howard University in Washington, D.C.
That's where I earned my Ph.D.
I have offices in Dallas, Chicago, and Mexicana
A penthouse in New York and a home in Atlanta

"I play a harp and pilot a jet
Now tell me brother, where do you *think we met?*"

I rung the bell, got up and left
Aunt Jemima done got beside herself.

3

Black Hair-Care Pioneers and How Black Women Got Involved

Before the Civil War, not all black people spent their lives picking cotton on a plantation down South. The black-owned barbershops of this era provided a haven for the pampered white elite, offering public baths, spa, and beauty treatment, as well as barbering and hairdressings services. Noted historian Juliet E. Walker, author of <u>The History of Black Business in America</u>, found that black barbers dominated the antebellum barbering industry because "they invested their profits in providing state-of-the-art services in elegant shops for their white clients." Before the Civil War, it was the black male barbers who were setting the trends in the hair-care and bath services field. According to the book <u>Hair Story</u>, authored by Ayana D. Byrd and Lori L. Tharps, "the most fashionable coiffeur" in the city of New York in the early 1800s was a former slave named Pierre Toussant. After buying his freedom and tending to the cosmetic needs of some of the finest French families in the city, he became one of the country's first black philanthropists, donating much of his money to the Catholic Church. There was actually a time when black men made big money off the roots of white people.

John B. Vashon, a black Pittsburgh barber, opened the first public city bathhouse west of the Alleghenies in 1820. Frank Parrish, a black barber and bathhouse owner, prospered for twenty years by offering his [white only] male and female clients "the luxury of the falling spray and the coolness of the flood" at his Nashville bathhouse, where he sold specialty items like "fancy soaps, perfumes, cigars, and tobacco."

Lewis Woodson, another Pittsburg barber and minister, partnered with John Vashon to co-found Wiberforce University, the first all-black university. William W. Watson, a Cincinnati barber and a former slave, had an estimated worth of $30,000 in the mid-1800s ($30,000 in the mid-1800s is probably like saying

$3,000,000 today). Watson used his earning to free his siblings and mother from slavery and to contribute large sums to black churches and abolitionist causes.

John Stanley, a mulatto, opened a barbershop and became extremely wealthy. Stanley, however, owned sixty-four slaves in which his wife and children were among them. Eventually, Stanley emancipated nearly two-dozen of his slaves, including his family. Sadly, these barbers were unable and unwilling to open their services up to black clientele for fear that their white clientele would defect.

In his 1818 Sketches of America, British writer Henry Fearon wrote, "he could scarcely conceal his amazement at the fact that any black hairdresser who wished to retain his white clientele could not service a perfectly respectable-looking black man."

Throughout America, during the early 1800s, black barbers were among the social elite in the black race. Barbershops were often family run and provided financial security for future generations. Eventually, around the 1820s, free black women began to make inroads as hair professionals, due in part to the increase in racial hostility felt around the country toward black men by whites.

In the final decades before the Civil War, black men were increasingly being maligned as violent and sexually aggressive by Southern Confederates looking for reasons to justify the enslavement of the Negro Race. Because of this collective character assassination, black men were forbidden to perform so intimate a task as styling a white woman's hair. Black barbers loss half their business when they loss their white female clientele. White women were accustomed to being pampered by African-Americans and did not want to let go of their southern tradition entirely. Free black women, therefore, were the next likely provider of such a service. They were pleased for the opportunity but troubled by the circumstances. White women in the South, especially around New Orleans, needed their hair done daily because of the southern climate; therefore black hairdressers were in demand.

ELIZA POTTER, hairdresser
Born 1820–Unknown

A young woman named Eliza Potter is the first black hairdresser to set-up shop outside of her home in New Orleans, and perhaps in America, Potter capitalized on the dire situation of the black male barbers. For eleven years, Potter styled the hair of her rich white clientele. She didn't risk servicing black women, at least not in her highfaluting shop; however, on her own time, she trained plantation slaves to do the same. Within the plantation system, slaves who knew how to barber and style white hair were elevated in the slave hierarchy to just below butlers, maids, and cooks but far above the field slave. Some of the slaves and free women trained by Eliza Potter set up hair care operations and began making hair ointments, tonics, and salves, from a mixture of plants, herbs, and natural oils, that were similar to the products made in Africa. A small number of free black women turned their homes into beauty parlors for other black women, styling hair as well as selling their homemade hair goods. Eliza Potter authored a book in 1859 entitled, <u>A Hairdresser's Experience in High Life</u>. The following is an excerpt from her book:

"I was brought up in New York, and went out, at an early age, to earn my living in the service of people by clipping hair. For some years, this occupation was agreeable to me; but at length I wearied of it, and being at liberty to choose my own path, I decided to gratify my long-cherished desire to see the world. Before I settled in Cincinnati, my travels took me to France, where I had the privilege of taking lessons in the art of combing from one of the best hairdressers in Paris. This skill has served me well as I have made a name for myself combing the brides, belles, and beautiful ladies of Cincinnati. In 1859, I published a sketch of my experiences in those walks of life where faith has led me, <u>A Hairdresser's Experience in High Life</u>.

"Fugitive slaves flock to Cincinnati because they know there are many African-Americans and abolitionists here who are willing to help them escape bondage. Some merely pass through as they make their way to Canada; others elect to stay in the city so they can remain in contact with family members who still live in the South. They periodically enlist the services of black boatmen, who work on riverboats and often travel into slave territory, as messengers. Although my people are free in Cincinnati, it is impossible to avoid the long shadow cast by slavery. Slave catchers prowl the streets of the city in search of runaways. Businessmen and planters from the South often bring slaves with them when they visit the city.

"I was once approached by a slave in Kentucky who asked me if I knew of a spot on this wide earth where he could be free. I frankly told him all I knew was Canada. He later escaped and for this conversation I was arrested as accessory to the deed … I was removed to Louisville where I was, for three months, a prisoner. After a trial in which I declared that I recognized no crime in what I had done, I was acquitted and permitted to go free ever afterward in both free and slave states.

"Hairdressing is generally very trying; but I have always had the good luck, with a few exceptions, to work for the higher classes. I have worked for several years from eight in the morning till six in the evening, and, on ball-nights, as late as eleven, and given satisfaction to all my ladies, with the exception of a few meddlesome persons, who were jealous because some one else looked better than they did; for I find in these days people are more troubled about their looks than they were when I commenced hairdressing.

"While my success is extraordinary, there are others of my race who have done equally as well for themselves. Alfred Thompson is a tailor who has a thriving business here in the city, and Robert Gordon is a successful coal merchant who has amassed a fortune with his business. Henry Boyd manufactures a superior article of bedspreads for which he holds a patent, and many of Cincinnati's prominent citizens patronize his establishment. I am fortunate-my avocation has afforded me the opportunity to move freely about a world many free Negroes can only dream of."

ANNIE TURNBO MALONE

Entrepreneur, Philanthropist 1869–1957

Annie Minerva Turnbo was born 1869 in Metropolis, Illinois. As a young woman, only one generation away from slavery, she discovered that there were few cosmetic products available for black women. Women of her time used products such as goose fat, oil and other harsh products to achieve the looks they wanted. Through her interest in chemistry, Turnbo set about experimenting with concoctions of her own. She developed a line of products and by 1900 was soon selling them door-to-door as well as in local stores. She also invented and patented in 1900 a pressing comb to straighten hair—a device still in use today. In 1902 she moved to St. Louis, Missouri. Turnbo also used what are now standard business practices—press releases, advertisements, and use of women who were hired to both sell the products and lend personal testimony to their efficacy.

One of these women was Madame C.J Walker who would become known as America's first African-American Millionaire—although many historical sources have credited Malone as being this country's first black female millionaire. Turnbo founded Poro College, the first school for teaching and studying black cosmetology in the U.S. The college trained women as agents for Poro Products and by 1926 claimed to have graduated some 75,000 agents located throughout the world, including the Caribbean.

Annie Turnbo's fortune was made with the development of non-damaging hair straighten products, hair growers, conditioners, and scalp balms. Under the name "Poro" she built not only a financial empire. After becoming extremely wealthy, she met a handsome smooth-talking young man named Alan Malone, who became her husband in 1914. During the 1920s, Annie Turnbo-Malone was reported to have been worth fourteen million dollars. In 1922, Malone provided a financial gift to the St. Louis Colored Orphans Home for the construction of a new building.

In 1927, Alan Malone filed for divorce and demanded half the Poro fortune. After a long, bitter, and very public battle that nearly caused Annie Malone to lose her businesses, Mr. Malone settled out-of-court for $200,000.

At one time she was reported to have been supporting two full-time students in every black land-grant college in the nation. Malone employed over 175 persons in her business. She also established a finance company, which offered home mortgages and loans for businesses. In 1946, the orphan home was renamed the Annie Malone Children's Home in her honor. Malone became a generous philanthropist donating large funds to different causes. She died in 1957 at 88 years old of a stroke in Chicago's Provident Hospital.

SARAH BREEDLOVE (MADAME C. J. WALKER) 1867–1919

Born to recently freed slaves in 1867, Louisiana native Sarah Breedlove Walker transcended poverty, illiteracy, and prejudice to become one of the most important businesswomen in America. Orphaned and widowed by the age of twenty, Breedlove left the uneasy Reconstruction environment of the Deep South to join her brothers in St. Louis, Missouri, where she worked for years as a washerwoman to support her daughter, Lelia. It was a step up from sharecropping, but at $1.50 a day, it was not very far. Breedlove would ultimately be inspired by the message of Booker T. Washington, whose autobiography Up From Slavery, which was a 1901 best-seller. Washington called for African-Americans to lift themselves up by developing skills, working hard, and emphasizing good character.

Breedlove found her future in beauty products. She learned valuable lessons at the elbow of a black role model, Annie Turnbo Malone, who sold her shampoos and hair-pressing irons to crowds in St. Louis for the 1904 World's Fair. Malone hired Breedlove as a commission agent and sent the former washerwoman to Denver, Colorado in July 1905. Soon, Breedlove had split from Malone and began making her own pomades and shampoos. In Denver, she met Charles J. Walker who would become her second husband, her first husband Moses McWilliams had died. Charles J. Walker, an ad man, encouraged her to use the grand name "Madame C. J. Walker" and helped her create compelling advertisements. Walker's innovations led to grand financial success.

By 1910, Walker had moved the Madame C. J. Walker Manufacturing Company to the railroad hub of Indianapolis, Indiana. Advertising and marketing became the keys to her success. One of the largest employers of African-American women, she carefully screened, groomed, and trained a 3,000-person strong sales force that was motivated by working on commission. In addition to door-to-door sales, Walker sold via mail order, and personally demonstrated her products in churches, schools, and other gathering places. She took lessons in public speaking and penmanship, and cultivated a striking persona in fine clothing and a chauffeur-driven electric carriage.

Walker eagerly embraced philanthropy, contributing to African-American orphanages, old-age homes, schools, colleges, and a new civil rights organization, the NAACP. Walker became one of the best-known women in America. Upon her death in 1919, her business went to her daughter. Though she sold popular products, created job opportunities for thousands, and generously shared her wealth, Walker's greatest accomplishment may have been her inspirational story, which made her a lasting role model for future generations.

Regardless of who was the first black female millionaire, Walker or Malone, or which one discovered *Wonderful Hair Grower*, a product which both claimed ownership, the fact remains that prior to their entrance into the market of black hair-care the manufacturers were overwhelmingly owned and controlled by white men; each woman practiced the principle of "Root Profit"—making emotional or financial profit from the roots of your pain.

MAJJORIE STEWART JOYNER
Born: 1896–Died: 1994

Marjorie Stewart Joyner was born in Virginia's Blue Ridge Mountains. She came to Chicago as a child, studying cosmetology as a teenager. Marjorie Stewart Joyner, one of the first sales representatives for the Madame C. J. Walker Company, advertising strategies are the subject of Noliwe Rooks' delightful 1996 book, Hair Raising.

Marjorie Stewart was the granddaughter of a slave. Stewart's mother left the South and moved to the North where she became a maid. She sent for her daughter Marjorie after she had settled. As a teenage girl, Marjorie Stewart married Robert Joyner who became a doctor of podiatry. Early in her career as a beautician, Marjorie Stewart Joyner worked in a beauty parlor where she was trained to style white women's hair. She tried to impress her mother-in-law by providing her with free hair care; however, the elder Mrs. Joyner was not impressed. She told Marjorie that she knew nothing about styling black women's hair. Her mother-in-law recommended the Marjorie enroll in one of Madame C. J. Walker Schools. Walker owned a chain of hair salons and beauty schools. Marjorie soon discovered that tight, kinky hair needed special treatment, which led to her first invention.

In 1926, she invented the first permanent hair-waving machine and became one of the first black women to receive a patent. Marjorie S. Joyner assigned the patent to the Madame C. J. Walker Manufacturing Company. The device was used in the entire chain of Walker Beauty Salons and schools. In 1929, Joyner invented a Scalp Protector to make the curling process more comfortable. The patent was also assigned to the Walker Company. Joyner was later selected for the board of directors of the Walker Company. In true rags-to-riches fashion, Joyner worked her way up through the ranks, promoting hair care products and demonstrating techniques in hair straightening and styling throughout America. She went on to become the vice president of the national chain of 200 Walker Beauty Colleges.

In the 1940s, Joyner founded the United Beauty School Owners and Teachers Association. After achieving success as an inventor and businesswoman, Joyner returned to school to earn her own doctorate degree. Eventually, she earned a Ph.D. in the humanities.

Joyner worked closely with Mary McLeod Bethune and Eleanor Roosevelt, raising funds for black colleges. For over 50 years, she chaired the Bud Billiken Parade, the largest African-American parade in the United States. She is often called the "Grand Dame of Black Beauty Culture" and the "Godmother of Bethune-Cookman College."

Well-traveled and with seemingly boundless energy, she became a respected civic leader both within and outside the African-American community, using her position in the beauty culture, influence with powerful women, and wealth to advance the welfare of African-American women.

SARAH SPENCER WASHINGTON

Born 1889–Died 1953

"Madame Washington" as she was widely known, was a millionaire black businesswoman and founder of Apex News and Hair Company of Atlantic City. In 1913, she started a hairdressing business in Atlantic City, operating a salon, teaching students and developing hair products. In 1919, she founded the Apex Company, maintaining a lab in Atlantic City as well as an office in New York City. Eventually her beauty colleges were located in twelve states and abroad. Sarah Spencer Washington was born 22 years after Madame C. J. Walker and 20 years after Annie Malone. I infer that they were well acquainted; three black female millionaires in the same business during the same era, perhaps they were friends. Ms. Washington has been called one of the most important business executives in the black community.

Hair Plantation

by Richard O. Jones

Girls gather 'round and listen close
You won't be poor for long
God gave you two sources of strength
A brain and a determined backbone

Don't work all day in cotton fields
Until you're old and dead
Work on your own plantation
There's a crop growing from your head

Every woman has a hair plantation
Go out and work the field
Let's lift the head of the Negro woman
So she can see her true appeal

Dr. JoAnne Jenkins-Cornwell

Born 1948–

Dr. JoAnne Cornwell is of the baby boomer generation. This generation has made a huge impact on the world today. Dr. Cornwell's grandparents migrated to Detroit from the South with their families during the 1930s. This can be said of millions of African Americans who currently live in our nation's Northern cities. The Great Migration increased Detroit's black population from under 6,000 in 1910 to 120,000 in 1930. African-Americans who believed they were heading to a promised land found a northern bigotry every bit as pervasive and virulent as what they thought they had left behind in the Deep South. Recruiters of the new car factories with promises of high wages toured the South convincing whites and African-Americans to head north. They arrived in such numbers that it was impossible to house them all. Southern whites brought their own traditional prejudices with them as both races migrated northward. The influx of newcomers strained not only housing, transportation, and education, but recreational facilities as well. The residents of Detroit endured long lines everywhere, including bus stops, grocery stores, and even at newsstands where they hoped for the chance to be first answering classified ads offering rooms for rent.

Even though the city enjoyed full employment, it suffered the many discomforts of wartime rationing during the 1940s. Child-care programs were nonexistent, with grandma the only hope—provided she was not already working at a defense plant. Times were tough for all. For the black community times were even tougher. African-Americans were excluded from all public housing in Detroit except the Brewster Projects. Many lived in homes without indoor plumbing, yet they paid rent two to three times higher than families in white districts. African-Americans were also confronted with discrimination in a segregated military, public accommodations, and unfair treatment by police. A serious race riot rocked the city in 1943, sending thousands of whites into the suburbs

In spite of the upheavals, mid-century Detroit became a cutting-edge place in many ways. For instance, Master W. Fard Muhammad founded the 'Nation of Islam' in Detroit in 1930. Among the disciplines the Nation of Islam insisted upon was that African-Americans not use hair relaxers, hair straighteners, or other chemicals on the hair. The Nation of Islam taught its followers that this was a white man trick to demean them. However, most men and women, in Detroit and elsewhere, chose their chemicalized hair over joining the Nation of Islam or adopting its teachings. African-Americans in Detroit during this era found plentiful jobs in the auto and other industries, and a large black working class soon developed, creating an important cultural community.

JoAnne Jenkins (later to become JoAnne Cornwell) was born during the period after World War II when Detroit, like the rest of the nation, was slowly and painfully transforming into a multicultural Democracy. The 1960s saw the birth of the black-owned Motown Record Corporation, which gave the black community pride and encouragement and propelled many leading black performers to stardom. JoAnne who was a student at Mumford High School during the early 60s was proud to be a resident of the city that was the birthplace of the greatest musical hits in America. At the same time cultural and social upheavals such as sit-ins and a second major race riot in 1967 were brought about by the need for black citizens to challenge social inequities. At times, these events threatened to turn the city into a domestic battleground.

Fortunately for JoAnne, she grew up in a household where women were skilled in doing hair. Both her mother and grandmother had been salon operators. Her grandaunt had been trained in the Madame C. J. Walker system. The hairdressing business had become a core economic activity for black women and there were more than 3,000 black-owned beauty salons nation-wide. JoAnne's passion for hair care was apparent at age four. I think of the images of Tiger Woods at four years old playing golf, Raven-Symone on the Cosby Show at four years old, and four year old Shirley Temple tap dancing with Bill Bojangles Robinson, but it is hard for me to imagine a four year old doing hair. However, when JoAnne was four, she produced her first braided hairstyle in her own abundant, very kinky natural hair. From that point on, she just had to do it herself. "I thought I knew what I was doing, and no one could meet up to my high, 4-year-old standards!" says JoAnne.

By the time she was in college, in Irvine, California, JoAnne had become the person many relied upon to do their perms, hot comb treatments, braiding, cornrows, Afros, and anything else that had to do with hair care. Although she was a natural talent on other people's head, JoAnne fought a personal war on the battlefield of her own head. JoAnne explains in detail how she fought this hair war as she relives her experiences in her first book entitled <u>That Hair Thing and the Sisterlocks Approach</u>. Upcoming is a chapter from <u>That Hair Thing</u> where you are given an up close and personal view of the conception, gestation, and birth of Sisterlocks.

"So, How Did You Come Up With This Idea Anyway?" (From <u>That Hair Thing</u> by Dr. JoAnne Cornwell—published in 1997)

Those who know me as an academic are usually surprised to learn that I also do hair. In fact, some would say I lead a double life. The academic by day, I'm lecturing, teaching, meeting and talking with colleagues and community folks. It's a full and gratifying existence all of its own, to be sure! By night, off come the suit and pumps, and on go the Tee-shirt and tennis, and the Sisterlocks lady is behind someone's chair, locking and sharing real-people talk, or in front of a computer trying to figure out how to make a business out of a lofty vision. Or, I'm working up a presentation for a beauty college or talking to someone long distance about how to keep those locks from unraveling at the ends.

I've always been a believer in developing transferable skills, and I can truly say that I practice what I preach. What I have lived and learned as the Sisterlocks lady has served me very well in keeping an activist edge on my academic work, which in turn has helped me tremendously in developing Sisterlocks, both as a philosophy and as a business.

In any case, no matter what role I might be carrying out at any given moment, the same hair follows me day and night, and speaks volumes about who I really am. When I stand before a university committee, I am still a sister from Detroit with tight, African-textured locks, When I walk into a community function where alas, my sisters are still seriously grappling with chemical dependency, my hair is a loving, if not so subtle call for us all to look deeply into our reflections in the mirror each day for our true image. My profession does not alter who I am, and I do not alter what I look like. In all of this, I have always found the simple fact that our hair will always bring us back to our bottom line extremely intriguing. It has been both a blessing and a curse for our women as we have tried in many different ways to make our mark in this country.

When people learn that I teach about Africa, they often ask if the Sisterlocks concept came to me as a result of knowledge I picked up about hair practices. It would be great if I could claim to have re-activated a lost African adornment tradition, but this was not the case. In fact, in most of the African cultures I know about, hair-locking techniques are not generally practiced. When people wear locks, they tend to be associated with specific religious cults. Though women traditionally wear a host of short and medium natural styles, these are usually twisted, wrapped, plaited or sculpted into artistic shapes. For longer styles, before the advent of the foreign hair extension industry, added extensions made of natural fibers were used. Although I cannot claim to have been called by an African deity to carry out this good work for our women, I can assert that there is something deeply spiritual about what I do. The type of spirituality I experience through sharing Sisterlocks with others is not connected to any specific belief system or religion. Nonetheless, it often pervades my interactions with clients in an almost tangible way. Most often, these are people—both male and female—who are in the process of embracing their sense of self in a way that they never have done before. They are beginning to look deep inside for answers to long-held, unanswered questions. They are becoming courageous enough to love themselves, sometimes after a lifetime of feeling under-valued. They are becoming strong enough to be self-critical, and learning how to live in a manner more true to their nature.

I often say Sisterlocks is not about a hairdo. It is about a way of life, and a process of redefining oneself on a very deep and spiritual level. There is tremendous power in that redefinition. Those who take that step are ready to take on the last frontier of self-love and self-acceptance. They are soul searching and finding ways to heal themselves. This is a movement that is gaining momentum, and will soon be unstoppable.

There is no way, ten or fifteen years ago, that I could have imagined myself ever owning a natural hair care business that would play a vital role in ending what I call the 'aesthetic crisis' our women have been steeped in for several generations. As I reflect on the aspects of my life that finally synthesized around the Sisterlocks idea, I realize that there were several factors at work. For example, I have always been obsessed with my hair. Now, I realize that it is not unusual for young girls to become more conscious of their appearance as they gain a keener awareness of the people and attitudes around them, but I think you will grant me that four years old is a little early to launch a hair styling career. I mean, nobody could do my hair right but me. By that age, I could already braid (or so I thought), and the only thing I lacked was the authority to dismiss the adults around me who insisted on messing with my creations. The biggest offenders were my mother and grandmother, salon owners and beauticians, who of course thought they knew what they were doing!

I grew up in beauty salons, and quite frankly, I disliked them intensely! I almost never got what I wanted in a hairdo there, and I almost never saw anything on the other ladies' heads as they left the salon that I would have wanted. However, in these places where 'necessary evils' were carried out, I did learn many of the important skills of the trade. I can remember my grandmother teaching me the 'right way' to wield a curling iron, for example, and how to finger wave. I was still a preteen at the time. I learned the fine points of hot combing too, but this was done by trial and error on my sisters, mom, and myself at home. (ouch!)

By the time I was a young adult, I had taught myself every new chemical technique out. I became the resident beautician wherever I went. When I went off to college, I took my trade with me. My late night beauty parlor activities have saved many a black coed from embarrassment in those days when you would die before letting them know that you had to straighten your hair to get it like theirs. Sisters came to me when the humidity had gotten to their dos, when their roots were causing their hair to break off, or when they simply wanted me to snatch up that kitchen. Oh, I could tame me some Mother Nature!

By the time I was in my late 20s, like many African—American women, I was sick to death of relying on all of the magic tricks that seemed to be required of me in order to make myself acceptable to both others and myself. I knew that locks were an alternative, but I had never seen any done in a way that suited me. Most of the women I saw looked as if their locks were wearing THEM rather than the other way around. I never seriously considered locks for myself until I began seeing professional women at conferences year after year. Each time I saw them, their locks would look more stunning. This was the period I call my "wanna-be" stage. I loved the way the locks looked on these other women but I, as yet, lacked the courage to try locks on my own hair. Mind you I had worn a short natural for many years, but like most women, I could only relate to my natural hair when it was short and manageable. During this entire period, braids were becoming more popular, and more commonly seen on women from all walks of life. I am sure that this, combined with my admiration of locks on other women, gave me the courage to decide to try locks for myself.

The decision was made! But it took me two more years to get up the courage to try them. Even then, I chose to start growing my natural locks under the cover of extensions. About every two months I would undo and retighten the extensions, and in the process, monitor the growth of what I believed to be my pre-locked natural hair. When I had let my hair grow for about eight months, I started gradually eliminating the extensions, which I had made very small. At that point, I began experimenting with ways of keeping my natural locks very small and avoiding the common problems of bunching and breakage.

Believe me, I met with a lot of setbacks here. The main problem was that I discovered my hair had not really locked while in braids (twists, actually). Yes, it had matted in spots, but the tight structure of the extension hair had kept my own hairs' natural interlocking process from taking over. On the positive side, going through this process of growing my natural hair under the cover of extensions was making me feel very much at home with it. I worked diligently over the next year or so to come up with a way to make my full, very expressive mid-length natural hair with relaxed ends, more style-able.

Finally, I had taken all of the extensions out and (kind of) had the look I wanted. The next problem I faced was that each time I went into the shower to wash my hair it just bunched up like mad. I would end up spending hours stretching and twisting my locks back out. I had to keep them wet during this process, because if they dried out in that state I never would have been able to pull or rip the lumps out. At one point, I resorted to washing my hair on rollers to keep the locks smooth and controlled during the washing process. I would roll my hair up, shampoo it, unroll each roller and thoroughly towel dry the section, then re-roll it. After three long tormenting hours I was ready to sit under a dryer for another hour—minimum. Needless to say I had to find a better way, or cut the doggone mess off.

I was going through a lot of intense feelings about my hair during that phrase. On my good days I was determined to see this experiment through and not give up on my natural hair. On my bad days I was constantly fighting back the urge to give in to that old lie about our hair being not exactly real hair at all, but whether some kind of curse that made us not as good as everybody else. I knew I had to detach myself from my feelings about my hair in order to be able to analyze and solve the issues logically. I tried imagining myself to be a Martian with no emotional attachment whatsoever to the meaning my hair held for me—meaning that made me so self-conscious I couldn't even think. Maybe the solution would come then.

This detachment thing was very hard for me though, because my hair was not just some malleable neutral material that could be made to conform to my will. It spoke to me of my past, my family, my culture, and all of the things I had never resolved in my life. Thank goodness I'm so stubborn! I kept at it. Soon I realized that my type of hair wasn't to be combed, it was not designed that way. Any coily-structured material will respond better to hand shaping, twisting and weaving procedures than it will to those that seek to flatten it out. I finally settled on the weaving idea, but I just couldn't come up with anything that topped the braid. I knew I still wasn't thinking about the problem in quite the right way.

I can remember the day I successfully locked on to the necessary mindset. (Pun intended.) I was watching someone's hands. They were gesturing about how to weave the strands of a rope and I remembered that multi-strand weaving is not always done from the base to the tip, but also in some cases from the tip to the base. I must have latched on to a memory of some of the weaving gadgets we played with as kids. Not just knitting and crocheting, but all manner of thimble and loom shaped contraptions seem to have fallen into our hands. With these toys I looped yarn into many an article that defied description, but that my mother always loved.

Working with these toys successfully instilled in me a tactile understanding of many weaving principles. Connecting with this understanding provided the final key to the problem I was grappling with how to create tiny braid-like structures in hair that, unlike braids, would not have to be taken out as the hair grew. Working from the tip to the roots would accomplish this.

I had my concept down, and I was ready to try it on myself. Now, I have to describe to you the condition of my hair at this time. I had relaxed ends that melded into quite lumpy but still relatively small locked sections of hair that, as you got closer to the root area, exploded into loose, natural tufts of hair. I'm telling you, I was going on faith. I carefully 'locked' this loose area in each section of hair. Compared to today's Sisterlocks standards, my technique was really crude, but when I'd finished, that section of each lock looked more uniform than the rest. However, I knew that the real test would come when I washed my hair.

I went a couple of days before that fateful shampooing. I knew I would be risking having to start from scratch again, and I wanted to enjoy my hair a little first. I was more than a bit nervous when I finally stepped into the shower to shampoo my hair. I'm sure I washed it very gently, but honestly, I don't remember anything about the experience. What I do remember is getting out of the shower and going straight to the mirror to check on whether my new technique had survived its maiden voyage. I couldn't believe it. My locks looked exactly the way they looked when I'd gotten into the shower. No more lumpier than before, and they hadn't shrunk up or blown out. They were just sitting there.... I don't know how much time passed before I could react to what I was seeing. It couldn't be this simple!

It was almost embarrassing. What I had done all of a sudden seemed so obvious, so logical that I couldn't believe it had not been thought of before. I remained in this incredulous state for quite some time—days, I think. I kept inspecting my locks for signs that their integrity was degrading, but nothing! They just stayed neat. My state of near-disbelief gradually turned into elation. I was almost afraid to give over to what I was truly feeling. It seemed too big for me. Those around me began to notice my hair more. I began to experience what women today who get Sisterlocks routinely experience. I couldn't be out in public without being stopped with questions, compliments, and strange people staring at, or actually wanting to touch my hair. They all had the same questions: "Are they just little braids?" "How do you do that?" "Can you take them out?" "Is that really your hair?" and so on and on. Many women with braids tell me they get these reactions too, but the fact that this was my NATURAL

HAIR was a difficult concept for most women to process. I began to 'complain,' [about the attention] but I loved the attention my hair was getting. It was the kind of confirmation I needed for my belief that I was really on to something with this technique.

More than any other reactions, those of African-American women really gripped me. To borrow a phrase from Zora Neale Hurston, it was like something fell off the shelf inside them when they saw my hair. I knew that look. I understood it deeply. I had felt what they were feeling a million times. It is a combination of fear and longing that is so strong it will instantly set you off your center. I got so that I could pretty well judge a black woman's mindset by the length of time she stared at my hair. Some women recovered quickly from the force of their feelings, especially if they weren't ready to face what the spectacle of my hair brought up inside them. These women tended to look for something to negate the power of what they felt by asking things like, "What if your want to go back to your own hair?" I took this to mean relaxed hair. I even had women unconsciously refer to their hair in its relaxed state as "normal."

Most black women wouldn't say anything at all, but simply couldn't take their eyes off my hair. I could feel their stares if they were sitting out of my gaze; however, if they could be seen, they would try to sneak peeks as best they could, and if we were talking face to face, they would really be talking to my hair, not focusing on my person. These were usually the women who had gone at least part way down the road to accepting their own natural hair. They were like the "wanna-be" I used to be. Then there were the women who were comfortable commenting on, or complimenting my look. These were the women who had worn, were wearing, or would soon wear a natural look themselves.

The men were looking too, and talking! Overall, they were less inhibited than the women, and would actually volunteer compliments about my hair—something I'd never experienced before. Virtually all of the reactions I got confirmed how much power this 'hair thing' holds for us as a people. This was especially true for our women who, practically without exception, reacted to my hair were echoed in the faces of the women I encountered over that first year of Sisterlocks. That is how I came to the feeling that I had been given a calling. Receiving a calling is a strange and wonderful thing. I'm not sure exactly how to talk about it, because it is not something that happens the same way to everyone. For me, it has been like being in a state of abandon, but without the recklessness you would normally expect. I feel very calm, but at the same time I feel absolutely fearless in taking on whatever challenges come my way. There is no place in my mind for the thought that the Sisterlocks vision will not be *realized. Nothing I can imagine feels too great to face, and I know with absolute certainty that the outcome will be positive. What a high!*

Obviously, with this new perspective, my sense of purpose changed. Though I loved the uniqueness of my hair, I realized that this was not just something for me alone. In the beginning I would play-complain to my companion, who was often with me in public to witness the reactions my hair received from other women. "I should carry brochures!" I would lament to him after having to answer the same questions over and over again. I went from saying this jokingly to taking it seriously, and without knowing much at all about business, I knew I had to start one.

Mind you, these feelings came to me before I had done anyone else's hair at all! Fortunately, not too long thereafter, my sister, Carol, announced she wanted her hair like mine. Unfortunately for Carol though, I didn't have the slightest idea what I was doing. I had assumed that I could simply do what I had done on my own hair, but since she had a different texture, nothing was coming out like I had planned. It was on my sister's hair that I learned the importance of things like choosing the right locking sizes; parting appropriately; varying the locking pattern to the specific texture and density of the hair. When I think about it today, I can't believe she trusted me with her magnificent head of hair. She had an extremely well cared for relaxer that was shoulder length. She had a beautician she loved and who kept her hair healthy and well manicured. What gave her the courage to become my guinea pig, I will never understand. I'm sure that my 'learning curve' cost her about a year of hair growth, but she hung in there with me.

Because of Carol and my five or six next 'victims,' the Sisterlocks approach evolved from a technique to a full-blown hair care system. I couldn't believe it, but each new head I did was different in some way, and none of them was like mine. I felt like screaming, "Could I please just get a sister with a head full of tight, kinky hair!" But, no-oo! I got hair that was extremely soft and thin, hair with an extremely deep coil to it, hair that was excessively stiff, you name it! Each time, I had to adjust my approach to meet the challenges posed by that particular hair type.

I gave away a lot of free time in those days, redoing locks, undoing bunching and matting, splitting or combining locks, working with those hairlines, but I was learning the whole time. One thing I learned was that an understanding of the full range of our hair types was a necessary prerequisite for doing Sisterlocks, and this became part of the standard approach to teaching the system to others. I also developed techniques *for dealing with the specific problems I had to work through. For example, I soon real-ized that I needed tools for locking the hair neatly to the scalp. I first tried a crocheting hook, which was the right concept, but the wrong shape. Not only does it tug unneces-sarily at the scalp, it is cumbersome and slows the operator down. I've heard that some enterprising sister has even come up with a weed-wacker-looking implement that yanks the hair through the open spaces to create the locks. Not good for creating uni-form locks, Also not good for the tender-headed or those with fragile hair types. If somebody comes at you with one of these instruments of torture, beware! They proba-bly don't have the skill level or the proper training needed to give you a professional job with good long-term results. The tools I designed reflect what I learned from years of problem solving. They take into consideration both locking efficiency and customer comfort.*

After working through these kinds of problems, I thought I was ready for the big leagues, and from a technical standpoint, I was. But I was not ready for the attitudes and questionable practices I discovered to be the norm once I stepped out into the pro-fessional arena of natural hair care. I went gaily tripping into East and West Coast salons, both traditional ones and those for natural hair care. I wanted to showcase my system and learn what the professional reactions might be. At the time I was literally ready to lie this in the lap of someone within the industry who could take it to the next level. Well, I discovered that nobody wanted it. The traditional salons generally saw it as a threat to their business. I was actually told this to my face in a San Francisco establishment. The natural hair salons were more generous in their acceptance of the idea, except for a few lock extremists who continue to view Sisterlocks as imitation, "instant locks," as one beautifully locked, but vehement sister put it.

Over all through, the established natural salons didn't seem the least bit interested at first in making Sisterlocks a part of their trade. This confused me a lot before I understood the economics of salon management as it is taught from the cosmetologist's perspective. Simply stated, salons have difficulty making profit on lengthy procedures. This goes for the natural salons as well. They may be 'down' with the sisters, but when it is all said and done, they use basically the same customer service criteria to meet their overhead as traditional salons. This means that they have to select their services based on whether or not these will generate a predetermined profit margin.

My little adventure taught me that I would simply have to do everything myself: Establish a training program; create a demand for Sisterlocks by getting it 'out there' and seen; educate the public about what to expect from the system and from the prac-

titioner claiming to do Sisterlocks; establish some legal protection against those who would try to steal or misrepresent the idea, or downgrade the quality of the system.

This last point has really been important because I've discovered that not everyone in the industry puts quality first and does business with integrity. For example, I have had established salons give out all kinds of misinformation about what Sisterlocks are and what they will do, instead of referring questions to the company, or finding out for themselves about the system. I want readers of this work to know that Sisterlocks does not do business in this way. When someone calls the home office with questions about braided extensions, they are referred to braiding professionals who are known to have a good reputation. If someone wants cosmetology services—hair coloring for example—they are referred to a reputable salon.

I also learned that some people who claim to want to bring professionalism to the natural hair care industry resent having to go through the kind of serious training that Sisterlocks involves. They want to look over someone's shoulder and 'get it' in ten minutes, so that they can go out and start making money for themselves. Don't they know that our women deserve more than to be subjected to practitioners with just a superficial knowledge of any system?

There are also scores of people—among them, the very women for whom the Sisterlocks is intended—who are just waiting to steal (can you believe it?) the Sisterlocks system, despite the fact that it is trademarked, and offer a BRAND X version that they think will bring them more money. "You can't trademark a hair system" they spit. They don't see that the trademark approach is for the protection of the CUSTOMER! It is not meant as a challenge to others within the industry. It is meant to help professionalize it. I have had people with an ounce of training try to hang up their shingle as Cerified Sisterlocks professionals. I have had people with two ounces of training go out and set up copycat training programs of their own. What discourages me is that our women have come to expect so little in the way of quality hair care, that pseudo-professionals can get away with this kind of deceit. Unfortunately for those who fall for their scams, they usually get inferior quality and empty promises, but rarely lower prices.

Have these experiences discouraged me? Not in the least. As I move through the world, I am daily reminded of the power of this vision that is unfolding. The experience I relate here have made me all the more determined to stand behind my structured, professional approach that puts the needs of our women first. Our women deserve the assurance of high standards and an approach that is a celebration of our *sisterhood. This will always be the driving force behind the Sisterlocks idea. Count on it!*

4

Cosmetics and Hair Care Products

Chicago residents participated in the rise of the cosmetics industry during the twentieth century not only as consumers but also as producers and distributors. As they spent more time and money on personal grooming and so-called beauty products, the area's women—and men to a lesser extent—participated in a development that was going on throughout much of the United States and the industrialized world. Chicago played a more distinctive role in the development of the cosmetics and hair care industries through the leadership of several of the area's business firms in this economic sector. At the same time, Chicago entrepreneurs built one of the most important industry sub-sectors: hair care products and cosmetics designed for consumers of African descent. Chicago firms led the development, manufacture, and marketing of cosmetics and hair care products for African-Americans for much of the twentieth century

In 1927, Gerald Gidwitz and Louis Stein started a cosmetics manufacturing company in Chicago. During the years following World War II, Stein named the company Helene Curtis, combining the names of his wife and son, and the company expanded with the success of products such as "Suave," one of the first modern shampoos. By the 1950s, Helene Curtis was also selling hairspray and deodorant and it had branches around the world. Meanwhile, a competitor arrived from California. In 1955, Leonard and Bernice Lavin moved the Alberto-Culver Company from Los Angeles (where it had started as a supplier of hair care products to the film industry) to Chicago. By 1960, the company was moving into a new headquarters and manufacturing facility in nearby Melrose Park. Like Helene Curtis, Alberto-Culver prospered by selling branded lines of products such as shampoo and deodorant—items that, although they were virtually unknown before the twentieth century, many consumers now regarded as indispensable.

During the 1910s and 1920s, the Kashmir Chemical Company of Claude A. Barnett, a graduate of the Tuskegee Institute, manufactured specialty hair care products. In 1935, S. B. Fuller established the Fuller Products Company, a cosmetics company, on the city's South Side. Fuller, the first African-American member of the National Association of Manufacturers, led the company through an expansion that peaked in the 1950s. By that time, an army of 5,000 salesmen sold nearly $20 million a year worth of various Fuller Products cosmetics—to European Americans as well as African-Americans. Fuller proved that African-American people could go outside their race and make mega-bucks; however, you cannot be held back by a lack of confidence. Regardless of whether you reach the masses like Fuller or focus on your own race like Madame C. J. Walker, the common denominator is to have a well-trained and motivated sales force that branches out beyond your resident city and state. Remember Eliza Potter is the first black hairdresser to set-up shop outside of her home in New Orleans. She went out and trained slaves to become hairdressers. She became very wealthy and traveled all over the world.

One of Fuller's employees, George Johnson, left the company in 1954 to start his own business. Along with Chicago barber Orville Nelson, Johnson created the company that would soon become the most important of all manufacturers of African-American hair care products: the Johnson Products Company. Johnson Products leaders in the hair care sector was challenged by Chicago's own Soft Sheen Products Inc., a company established in the 1960s by Edward Gardner that found success with brands such as "Care-Free Curl." The company's "Ultra Wave" hair straightener proved popular, as did its "Ultra Sheen" and "Afro Sheen" lines, and by the end of the 1960s annual sales were over $10 million. During the 1970s, as sales expanded even further, Johnson Products ranked as the largest African-American—owned manufacturing company in the nation. Johnson Products was not the only Chicago company engaged in the manufacturing of beauty products for African-American consumers. The Johnson Publishing Company, creator of *Ebony Magazine*, entered the cosmetics business in the 1970s.

Chicago's status as a center of the hair care and cosmetics industry declined during the last years of the twentieth century. Johnson Products encountered declining profits and market share by the mid-1970s, when large cosmetics companies such as Revlon and Avon began to target African-American consumers. 1993, the company left local hands when it was sold to the Ivax Corporation, a large company based in Miami. Soft Sheen, which had about 400 employees in the Chicago area and $100 million in annual sales by the mid-1990s, was sold in

1998 to French company L'Oreal. Helene Curtis, which had grown into a billion-dollar company by the early 1990s, experienced declining growth after the 1980s and was bought in 1996 by Unilever, the huge British-Dutch corporation. Of the several Chicago companies that had been so prominent in the industry since the 1950s, only Alberto-Culver—with about $2 billion in annual sales and 16,000 employees worldwide—was still based in Chicago at the end of the century.

"Never be afraid to sit awhile and think."

       —Lorraine Hansberry (1930–1965), playwright and painter.

Cosmetics and Your Health from www.womenshealth.gov navigation

What are cosmetics? How are they different from over-the-counter (OTC) drugs?

Cosmetics are put on the body to:

- cleanse it

- make it beautiful

- make it attractive

- change its appearance or the way it looks

Cosmetic products include:

- skin creams

- lotions

- perfumes

- lipsticks

- fingernail polishes

- eye and face makeup products

- permanent waves

- hair dyes

- toothpastes

- deodorants

Unlike drugs, which are used to treat or prevent disease in the body, cosmetics do not change or affect the body's structure or functions.

What's in cosmetics?

Fragrances and preservatives are the main ingredients in cosmetics. Fragrances are the most common cause of skin problems. More than 5,000 different kinds are used in products. Products marked "fragrance-free" or "without perfume" means that no fragrances have been added to make the product smell good. Preservatives in cosmetics are the second most common cause of skin problems. They prevent bacteria and fungus from growing in the product and protect products from damage caused by air or light. But preservatives can also cause the skin to become irritated and infected. Some examples of preservatives are:

- paraben

- imidazolidinyl urea

- Quaternium-15

- DMDM hydantoin

- phenoxyethanol

- formaldehyde

The ingredients below cannot be used, or their use is limited, in cosmetics. They may cause cancer or other serious health problems.

- bithionol

- mercury compounds

- vinyl chloride

- halogenated salicyanilides

- zirconium complexes in aerosol sprays

- chloroform

- methylene chloride

- chlorofluorocarbon propellants

- hexachlorophene

Puppet on a Chain

By Richard O. Jones

I own the tree—he owns the lumber
No time to pause, to rest, or slumber
Carved from wood—like you do a fence
Taught to respond to trifling wench

Chains attached to my hands and head
More chains on my feet and legs
Iron brace tight around my neck
Just a reminder to stay in check

A vile white man my puppeteer
He bought me from an auctioneer
After years of being tugged along
I walked behind him on my own

His trifling wench did like he said
Though the floor was warmer than his bed
But he promised if I continued obey
My chains would be cut someday

One night he died while he slept
In his Will a promise kept
He cut my chains legally

At last, you hear, I was free!

But the new cold world I met at dawn
Gave privilege to wenches white and blonde
So I saved my money and bought blonde hair
The Koreans get rich but I don't care

Black folks say I'm still on a chain
My white puppeteer is in my brain
What they say might make some sense
Cause I still feel like his trifling wench

I own the tree—he owns the lumber
Someday God will call my number
But before I go—I must be me
My only hope to be free

Cornrows Goes To The Movies

Cornrows are a traditional style of hair grooming of African origin where the hair is tightly braided very close to the scalp using an underhand upward motion to produce a continuous raised row. This technique is somewhat similar to that used to produce a French braid, which is braided using an overhand or inward motion, resulting in a flat braid. Cornrows can be formed, as the name implies, in simple straight lines or in complicated geometric or curvilinear designs. Often favored for their easy maintenance, cornrows can be left in for weeks at a time simply by carefully washing the hair using a stocking cap or hair net and then regularly oiling the scalp and hair. Cornrow hairstyles are often adorned with beads or cowry shells, in the African tradition. Depending on the region of the world, cornrows can be worn by either men or women.

Common in West Africa, cornrows survived for centuries as a style of hair in the United States among African slaves and their progeny primarily in the American South. In 1963, when most African-American women were loathe to be seen in public with unstraightened hair, popular African-American actress Cicely Tyson drew immediate notice when she sported cornrows on the popular network television series "East Side, West Side." The style gained popularity in the U.S. in the late 1960s and 1970s as part of the Black Pride Movement, when the trend was away from straightening hair to wearing "natural" hairstyles. Afros, strands of hair twisted into tight coils or wound with twine, and the wearing of geles (colorful, often elaborately wrapped head cloths) became other common-place African styles adopted by African-American women.

In the wake of the Black Pride Movement, hundreds of beauty shops and salons sprang up across the U.S. delivering services exclusively, or as part of a range of options, to African-Americans that prefer natural (unstraightened) hair-styles.

Many salons specialize in hair wrapping, braiding techniques, and executing styles which can be not only exceedingly time-consuming, but expensive. The tradeoff for the clients in the cost, time, and money expended is that a well-exe-cuted braided style could last a month or more without restyling if properly groomed and cared for and if executed on the naturally coarse, tightly coiled hair typically possessed by people of indigenous African descent. Such hair holds cornrows better over time than the hair of other ethnic groups because it gener-ally has more tensile strength and tends to be less oily, which means it requires less frequent washing; to some extent, that fact alone renders naturally coarse hair superior.

Cornrows also enjoyed some popularity among whites after blonde actress Bo Derek wore beaded cornrows in the popular Blake Edwards movie, "10," in 1979. The white actress was mistakenly credited with the popularity of cornrows in the black community. Bo Derek got the credit for two reasons: her movie was widely seen around the world, and she was a white woman with a black woman's hairstyle.

Cornrows Goes To Court

Renee Rogers, an African-American employee at American Airlines, wore corn-rows to work. American Airlines had a grooming policy that prevented employees from wearing an all-braided hairstyle. When American sought to enforce this pol-icy against Rogers, she filed suit, alleging race discrimination. In 1981, a federal district court rejected her argument. It first observed that cornrows were not dis-tinctively associated with African-Americans, noting that Rogers had only adopted the hairstyle after it "had been popularized by a white actress in the film '10.'" As if recognizing the unpersuasiveness of what we might call the Bo Derek defense, the court further alleged that because hairstyle, unlike skin color, was a mutable characteristic, discrimination on the basis of grooming was not discrimi-nation on the basis of race. Renee Rogers lost her case.

Musician, songwriter Stevie Wonder was also instrumental in the popularization of cornrows and braids among black men during the 60s, whereas ballad and soul singer Roberta Flack helped popularize the Afro in the 60s and braids in the 70s among women.

Over the years, cornrows, braids, and Afros have been the subject of several disputes in the American workplace. Some employers, usually whites, have deemed them unsuitable for the office and have banned them. African-American employees and civil rights groups have countered that such attitudes evidence racial and cultural bias; however, there have been African-Americans who protested other African-Americans about their dreadlocks, and twistlocks.

Chemically treated Hair Leads to TV Judge Getting Fired

(Excerpted from TMZ.com) Judge Mablean Ephriam, who from 1999–2006 presided over the syndicated television show 'Divorce Court," says that she was given her walking papers from the show, in part because FOX would not cut her slack when it came to styling her hair. "When will FOX and the rest of America accept our cultural differences as African Americans and embrace us with all of our different hairstyles, hair textures, hair color?" she asked in a press conference statement.

FOX says that it was not all about hair but the judge was asking for a lot more money than the network was willing to shell out. However, Judge Ephriam replied, "The most unacceptable demand to me was when FOX said, 'There will be no changes in the current hairstyle to avoid time consuming issues regarding her hair.'" She believes FOX's position could violate Federal law, calling it "a racial and ethnic issue."

Ephriam rhetorically asks why her hair was suddenly an issue: "Because of my ethnicity—African American, Black, Negro, whatever term you prefer to use." Ephriam adds that she wore a wig last season after **losing a substantial amount of hair because of a chemical process gone bad**. She feels that FOX wanted her to continue wearing a wig to save time in taping the show.

The former TV judge said there was another issue—she did not want to tape as many as eight cases a day because "divorce is a very emotional issue." She was also upset that FOX would no longer pay for the show's holiday luncheon. Lynn Toler, an ex-Ohio judge, replaces Mablean Ephriam. Toler is also African American.

The Natural Look—I Hoped It Was Here to Stay—Dr. JoAnne Cornwell

The Natural hairstyle that began as a symbol of protest was a big fashion trend and JoAnne Cornwell sported hers as a crown of glory. A not-so-small segment of white girls in metropolitan cities throughout the United States during the 60s and early 70s boldly wore kinky natural wigs and/or had their hair frizzed. These young women were frequently seen alone or escorted by black men in clubs, restaurants, and other public places everywhere. The sight became so offensive to black women who began to cry out in black women magazines that white women were trying to be black and stealing their men, again. The proof of black uniqueness was becoming apparent, but few African-Americans acted on the social impact. Whites were now covering their own heads and covering it with kinky hair. It was a switch blacks resented rather than celebrated. It was time to make money off their roots, for a change. We should have embraced them and fibbed about how soulful they looked and gave them a high-five. Instead, we whined and spewed insults, which ran them back to their superior posture. The opportunity was there to declare their blackness but instead most African-Americans continued to display their loyalty to hair relaxers and perms.

Some of the largest department stores carried natural wigs and they were becoming an increasing popular item at "in" boutiques, which featured them in shades ranging from black to platinum blonde. Bold stylists, always eager for something new, were experimenting with combinations of straight hair and kinky ponytails or topknots. Even in the nuclei of America's black ghettos, where women customarily have "grown their own," natural wigs held a place of honor beside the more common and concealing straight hairpieces.

National magazines that serve as arbiters of style were exploring the adaptation of natural hairstyles to the white market. Even "Women's Wear Daily" a bible of the trade, regarded this trend and declared: "A feeling of inferiority has been replaced by pride. "Quoting a black girl on the street in Los Angeles, the publication noted, "Suddenly it has become fashionable to be black," adding, "but black girls are perceptive enough to understand that fashion exploits everything ... now it's the Afro hairdo. Now everybody wants to be a soul sister. Where would black people's self-esteem be today if Madame C.J. Walker had invented the Afro comb and Soft Sheen instead of the hot comb and hair relaxers?"

"... I want to say to every Negro woman present, don't sit down and wait for the opportunities to come ... Get up and make them!"

—Madame C.J. Walker
National Business League meeting, 1913

In the midst of writing this book, on October 5, 2006, I took a break and turned on television. Oprah happened to be on and her subject was "Great Women Growing Older." Among her several guests was the beautiful black actress Diahann Carroll, 71, and three well-known white women on stage and on a roll-in clip Oprah interviewed the white actress Susan Sarandon 60, via satellite. Their attitude about life and aging was the subject not their looks; however, I could not help but notice their hair. Diahann Carroll wore a well-groomed reddish brown tinted or dyed press and curled hairstyle or wig and Susan Sarandon wore dreadlocks. That's right, dreadlocks! Since I happened to be writing on the subject at the time, I was floored. White women in the 1960s were wearing natural wigs and white women in 2006 are wearing dreadlocks. Yet many black women fail to recognize their natural beauty. The mental damage of slavery and the early 1900s remains a formidable foe, and the mammy images haunts black women to this day. In my opinion, it is not that dreadlocks are beautiful; it is the woman beneath the dreadlocks who is beautiful. I don't even think dreadlocks were created as a beautification style but created or so-named *dreadlocks* by the Rastafarian movement as an expression of <u>dread</u> or grief for oppression and as a proud heritage and worship to God. I admit, it takes a confident woman to wear dreads; they are not for emotional babies. Just as squeezing into a tight dress does not make a woman skinny, neither does hiding beneath straight hair, wigs, perms, dreads, or Sisterlocks make her beautiful. Beauty is an inside job. And to that end, many blacks that wear hairweaves, and/or hair relaxers are indeed beautiful and self-confident. It's the ones that are in African denial that I have a problem with.

Oprah mentioned nothing about anyone's hairstyle because that was not the focus of the show but each guest spoke about being free and enjoying life at her age. Diahann Carroll said something to the affect of facelifts and dying her hair was a necessity to her feeling good about herself. Diahann Carroll's statement was not surprising; however, I was shocked to hear her say that she never *really* thought of herself as being a black. It was not until she starred in "Julia" in 1968 that she became so overtly conscious of her color because of the public response. I thought about what she had just said and realized that I had not seen her in any roles where she was discriminated against because of her race. In fact, I then remembered that she was married four times and three of her husbands were white, also she was engaged to another white man named David Frost who was a British TV personality. Perhaps she did not feel the wrath of a black woman because powerful white friends and lovers shielded her. However, I understood Diahann Carroll and wished that the hand of God would erase her innate shame. But she was born in 1935. My God! 1935! She was born in the worst of times, in the midst of Jim Crow, in the midst a demeaning black literature in the schools and harmful images in the movies. Although she was smiling with Oprah, it was unlikely that she was smiling inside, beneath the plastic surgeries, heavy makeup, and superficial tresses. She came up during a time when any black person that was marginally accepted by white society happily rushed in and shook the ghetto dust from their feet. I thought, "Wow, out of all that money spent on plastic surgery, it seems like she could've set some aside for a good black psychologist—Oprah why didn't you tell her about Dr. Robin Smith?" I thought.

My thoughts zipped to the black female celebrities who often wore natural hair, dreadlocks, or braids; author and professor Alice Walker; playwright Ntozake Shange; actress, comic, director Whoopie Goldberg; author, professor, and Nobel Prize in literature recipient Toni Morrison; singer India Arie, musician/singer Tracie Chapman; professor, poet, and author Nikki Giovanni, I suspect they all have battled with America's image of beauty; according to a 2006 recording, India Arie certainly have.

In a May 2006 musical release called "Testimony" by India Arie there's a song entitled, *I Am Not My Hair*. But the scientific fact is that we are our hair more than we realize. Your hair has your DNA and your DNA is uniquely yours. A single strand of your hair will distinguish you from anybody else on earth. Though I doubt that India Arie is confused. Her message in *I'm Not My Hair* seems to be, don't judge me by my hair. Don't look at my hair and think you know me. Don't inspire me to mask who I am in order for you to accept me. Don't be enchanted by my fake wigs, extensions, braids or any artificial allure; neither be repelled nor drawn to me by my skin and miss the beautiful person underneath.

The lyrics of *I'm Not My Hair* speak to the frustration black females go through, apparently, a journey in which India Arie is familiar. In the final lyrics she encourages females to be themselves. The following is an excerpt of the song:

Little girl with the press and curls
Age 8 I got a jeri curl
13 and I got a relaxer
I was the source of so much laughter

15 when it all broke off
18 when I went all natural
February 2002
I went on and did what I had to do

(Chorus)
I am not my hair
I am not this skin
I am not your expectations (no)
I am not my hair
I am not this skin
I am the soul that lives within

Good hair means curls and waves.
Bad hair means you look like a slave
At the turn of the century
Its time for us to redefine who we be

Mary J. Blige is another black female singer waging a melodious protest concerning the burden of black women in relationships, on the job, and in competition with white women. In her 2006 song and video called *Take Me As I Am* she exposes poignant scenarios. In the video she is portrayed as four women; a waitress with a lazy man that stays home while she works; an exclusive who is sexually harassed on the job; a model that is replaced for a photo shoot by a white model with long blonde hair; and a meek date with a man that tells her what to and what not to eat and openly flirts with another woman with lighter skin.

By the end of the video, she stands up against each of her emotional stresses except the white woman, which she obliviously felt that she could not compete. The model commits suicide in the bathroom after leaving a message on the wall that read, "Take me as I am."

Below is an excerpt of the lyrics played throughout the video:

She's been down and out
She's been wrote about
She's been talked about, constantly
She's been up and down
She's been pushed around
But they held her down, NYC

She has no regrets
She accepts the past
All these things they
helped make to make she
She's been lost and found
And she's still around
There's a reason for everything

[Chorus:]
So take me as I am,
or have nothing at all.
Just take me as I am,
or have nothing at all.

[Verse 2:]
Now she's older now
Yes, she's wiser now
Can't disguise her now
She don't need
No one tellin her
What to do and say
No one tellin her
Who to be
She's on solid ground
She's been lost and found
Now, she answers to G-O-D
And she's confident
This is not the end
Ask me how I know
Cause she is me.

   In the video *Take Me As I Am* the cosmetic world was the death of the model. Maybe that was not the overt message of Mary J. Blige but with her corpse on the bathroom floor, it certainly was the deeper message. The words *take me as I am* translates to mean, accept me naturally, the way I was born, the way I was intended to be. And in the end of the lyrics, she drops the pretense, acquires confidence and answers to G-O-D.

In an *Upscale Magazine* article, Angie Ravenel, stylist and owner of Angie's Hair Studio in North Charleston, South Carolina, says, "Nowadays, wigs are more like a hat or scarf. It's all about using it to achieve your desired look at any given time with great convenience. There're many brands to choose from," she continued, "Especially Yours, Naomi Sims, Beverly Johnson, [Diahann Carroll] and Star Jones' Lines, plus Lords & Cliff, and Motown Tress make wigs [all black owned companies]." There is also a major cosmetic company that is black owned called Barbara Walden Cosmetics. Actress turned beauty mogul, Barbara Walden was the forerunner in designing the first cosmetic line for the African-American woman.

In my opinion, false hair is the *Big Mama* of identity denial for black women because they create a façade as a lifestyle. Unlike the press and curl or relaxer where your own hair is still a part of your identity, hairweaves are a total masquerade. I have heard it said that the greatest compliment you can give anyone is to imitate them. If that is true then black women are giving other women the greatest compliment ever, which in part might explain the attraction to other races of women by black men, they have been endorsed as superior by black women in hairweaves.

An excerpt from Maya Angelou's autobiography I Know Why the Caged Bird Sings captures the internalized pain and anger that many African-Americans experienced. Angelou writes of growing up in the 1930s: "Wouldn't they be surprised when one day I woke up out of my black ugly dream, and my real hair, which was long and blonde, would take the place of the kinky mass that mama wouldn't let me straighten? Because I was really White and because a cruel fairy stepmother, who was understandably jealous of my beauty, had turned me into a too-big Negro girl, with nappy hair, broad feet and a space between her teeth that would hold a number-two pencil."

During the eighties, songstress Anita Baker sashayed memorably through the video of her song *Sweet Love*. Clad in a simple black dress, she exuded a sultry womanliness that could teach the barely dressed singers of today a lesson in being a classy black female performer. In an interview back then, Ms. Baker was asked if she had a message for black women. She did have a message; one which she thought could be controversial, but which she was convinced needed to be said. Baker wanted black women to take pride in their natural hair. According to her, if you had hair down to your waist, great—and if you did not, that was wonderful too. She was expressing concern at black womanhood's obsession with long European-looking hair—nearly always bought in a shop.

By the nineties, hordes of black celebrities wore multi-hued and multi-layered wigs. Added to sew-on, glue-on hairweaves of every texture imaginable—natural hair became as elusive as a fugitive in disguise.

One can understand some black women wearing wigs for the same reasons that some white women do, because they are losing or have lost their hair. One can even make allowances for wigs being worn for variety. But there's something psychologically impaired about young women with full heads of hair that will never be seen dead with their natural hair or those who will never admit that the fake hair on their head is exactly that? It is these attitudes that have created the multi-billion dollar fake hair industry.

It is a given that there are cheap and expensive hair extensions; therefore, not all hair extensions compliment the purchaser especially the coal black ones on an older and wrinkled faces. Young women with extensions have robbed men of the chance to know them and accept them. It is better to be rejected for the real you than be accepted in disguise. I understand that the popular culture quasi-embrace them as a manipulated damsel, but I would rather see them proudly stand independently and be ridiculed than be applauded as a puppet.

Music stars are among the most visible black women on earth, and they have not helped. Golden-voiced Whitney Houston sprung upon the scene in 1985 with short natural hair and looked more like a beautiful African Princess on the album cover than a singing star. Her first album was a major success; however, Clive Davis, the Jewish founder of Arista Records and architect of Houston's stardom, was reportedly unhappy with the look. He felt it was too ethnic to be sold to white America. On her next album she appeared with straightened hair, and then came the blonde weaves. Her natural hair was last seen peeking from beneath a wig in 1986. Perhaps it was the loss of her African identity that led to her fall from grace for a couple years between 2000 and 2006 and into drugs and drug rehab. Makeup and hairweave did not fill the void. Cosmetic surgery, fame, money and popularity are not the key to inner peace—maybe the key to happiness but not inner peace. Too many women think that if they get more compliments they'll feel good about themselves. Apparently that is not the answer because the long list of pretty girls on drugs and abusing their sexuality would stretch from wherever you are to the next two states. It may be a coincidence, but the facts are that drugs and emotional breakdowns less often ruin women who are not obsessed with the American standard of beauty.

Janet Jackson and her sister LaToya, bless their lascivious hearts, have no reservations whatsoever about provocative wardrobe, baring their breasts and/or posing nude, but their natural hair seems to have a chronic case of modesty and prefers being covered up by human hair from the head of a Calcutta indigent.

Lauryn Hill. Her statement is powerful! This beautiful gifted singer came out—boldly ethnic—with *The Fugees*. And with her groundbreaking solo debut, *The Miseducation of Lauryn Hill*, she inspired a whole new generation of black women and female artists. Lauryn is contemptuous of hairweaves and sang on one track, *Doo Wop (That Thing)*: *Look how you be in hairweaves like Europeans.* She is not a prisoner of Americas' standard of beauty, although there have been reported sightings of her in straight, bobbed wigs. However, in my opinion, variety is a healthy thing and does not make one obsessed just as an occasional drink of alcohol does not make one an alcoholic.

South African singer, Miriam Makeba, was one of those who embodied the spirit of Black Power during the 60s and was admired by African-Americans for refusing to straighten her hair. I mean she actually refused executives from her record label. Most performers don't possess that kind of confidence. "I see other black women imitate my style, which is no style at all, but just letting your hair be itself," she once said in an interview, which she concluded with, "Black is still beautiful."

I often heard people say that they *wouldn't be caught dead* doing this or that, or *wouldn't be caught dead* wearing this or that. There was a woman at my former church who often said, "I wouldn't be caught dead without Jesus." We knew each other for about eight years before she died of cancer at seventy-six years old. The church was packed for her funeral; people came from several states to pay their last respects. During the funeral service her family treated the church to a slideshow stroll down memory lane with the late Sister Hattie Franklin (not her real name). The Franklin family had hired a professional video company to piece together dozens of her old photos and many recent photos and present a slideshow. The photos dated back more than fifty years.

In college Sister Franklin played the flute and had long sandy hair. In a wedding photo Sister Franklin fed her husband cake and had long red hair. In a surprise photo she was caught off guard changing her daughter's diaper. By reflex, she covered her short black uncombed hair with both forearms, leaving the baby dangerously at the edge of the bed. At her fortieth high school reunion she wore a long black gown and danced in a pink wig. As I continued to watch the slideshow, it became oblivious that Sister Franklin had always been a snappy dresser and loved wigs of different colors. Even during the time I knew her, she always dressed well in lace gloves, and wore a blonde or sandy wig and greenish contact lens, which I thought were her real eyes until one fell out in church service when she got a little too *happy*. Sister Franklin was a plain woman with a dark complexion who wore beautiful hats and perfectly applied light makeup, which made her face look two shades lighter although her neck betrayed her.

As she lay in the casket in her blonde wig, heavily powered face, closed eyes, I imaged that she wore her green contacts. The thought that she had been a fugitive from her own features all her life and now in death reminded me of the movie *Imitation of Life*. I began to sop silently. It was sad to witness a 76-years-old black woman go to her grave who had never exposed her natural features and who, according to the slideshow, had internally declared the she *wouldn't be caught dead* without her wig. I thought of the scripture in Hosea 4:6 "My people perish from lack of knowledge." Sister Franklin's spirit was dead long before her body. It was through Sister Franklin that I discovered that there are black women so ashamed of their natural hair that God cannot appear to them except in the form of artificial hair.

In 1998, Ruth Sherman, a white teacher in a predominantly black public school in Brooklyn assigned the children's book Nappy Hair by African-American author Carolivia Herron to her third-grade class. This well-intentioned attempt to encourage self-esteem among young black girls by celebrating "natural" hair backfired when a black parent complained that the images of kinky hair in the book were derogatory and offensive and did not make *her* daughter feel good about herself. I suppose images of wigs and hairweaves would have been better; anyway, a heated discussion ensued among parents and teachers, with some arguing that the assignment was empowering (in the spirit of "black is beautiful") while others felt it was patronizing and racist (why is a white teacher teaching black children about self-love anyway?). (Maybe because she detected self-hate and low self-esteem in the classroom.) The incident eventually reached the pages of *The New York Times*, where columnist Clyde Haberman denounced the debate as "an ignorant cry of racism (that) makes all knees jerk." Dismayed at the angry reactions from parents, the teacher asked to be reassigned to another school.

5

Beauty Obsessions and the Vanity Merchant

Universally, humans have chased the latest image of beauty as long as they have chased the foundation of youth. The pursuit of youth and beauty is as infinite as God himself; however, God does not change. In the beauty industry, the items for sale are; breasts and hair implants, tummy tucks, lip enlargements, skin creams, hair dye, wrinkle removers, hip enlargements, liposuction, cosmetic surgery of every type including vaginal beautification called labiaplasty. Then of course, there is the health spa, the weight loss centers, and the piercing, waxing, and tattoo parlors. Becoming a vanity merchant is a sure path to wealth. Several current 2007 television vanity shows are; *America's Next Top Model* (girls vie for a modeling contract); *The Biggest Losers* (obese people compete in weight loss); *Extreme Makeover* (people who consider themselves extremely unattractive get an extreme makeover); Nip and Tuck (a close-up view of the professional and personal lives of plastic surgeons). There are hundred of subliminal messages on billboards, radio, TV, and in society at large that makes the public, female public especially, subconsciously insecure, and therefore never completely satisfied with their appearance, which translates into big money for the vanity merchants. There are thousands of cosmetic surgery nightmares reported every year; many lawyers specialize in suing plastic surgeons and beauty salon owners that severely damage those desperately seeking beauty.

The standard of beauty is forever changing. The pale face was the norm for centuries. Centuries ago a pale face was the desired look because it defined your place in society. It was recognized that those who worked in the fields had tanned and rugged skin. They were the lower working classes and not to be associated with by the upper refined class, who had pale white skin. Those with pale skin were the ones who had enough money that they did not need to work. And to achieve that look, women *and* men used a powder made of hydroxide, carbonate, and lead oxide. Unfortunately, there was a price to pay for looking "proper"—lead poisoning. During the Victorian era, the hat was one of the most important fashion accessories in a lady's wardrobe. It was an indicator of her social class, her fashion sense and even hinted at the generousness her husband or her father. A hat was an indicator that she was a lady-a woman that attended a church service without a hat would be brandied an eccentric at best and a floozy or commoner at the worst; however, the main purpose of the lady's hat, and it's often accompanying veils, gloves and parasols, was to protect the skin from the sun and other environmental elements that might cause freckling or tanning. Victorian women valued a white complexion, the paler, the better, so much so that women would go to great lengths to attain the 'ideal" skin tone-even ingesting such materials as talcum powder and/or arsenic (which occasionally cause death) to achieve a fashionable pallor. That is why an alternative was sought. And they found it, in the 19th century—a facial powder made of zinc oxide. And it is still used today.

As the cosmetic industry moved into Hollywood in the 20th century, the white face look was gradually replaced by the tanned look. And that became the source of a whole new line of cosmetic products—artificial tanners. In 1929, there were ads running for tanning liquid and powder. If you couldn't get a tan naturally, then you could still have bronze skin with tanning aids.

Fat was revered as a sign of health, wealth, and being scrawny was viewed as a symbol of a struggling life. Once upon a time, poor people were depressively thin and rich people were proudly fat. During the Great Depression in 1929, emaciated people were seen standing in soup lines, while fat rich people continued to eat in diners. The point was made during testimony on the genetics of body weight in the fall of 2003 when members of Congress were treated to slides of President William Howard Taft, Socrates and King Henry VIII—all fat prosperous men. Only the rich had access to enough food to gain large amounts of weight during most of human history. Women sought pale fat men as their lovers, husbands, and fathers of their future children because they were likely to be the most educated and prosperous.

The Venus of Willendorf, an ancient carving unearthed in 1908, depicts a robust woman's body with large hips, full breasts and a fleshy belly. Recognize that Venus in Roman mythology was the goddess of love and beauty. To be pale and fat was a symbol of higher class—not beauty. Today being pale fat man does not get you a glass of cool water from a woman.

People change. Trends and fashions change. There was a time when single mothers would fabricate a story that their child's father was dead or in the military because of the stigma of single motherhood. However, today women flaunt their single motherhood like a badge of honor. At least a dozen times a week either on a television, radio, or newspaper advertisement or TV commercial, a female is being introduced as a single mother and they always show a sense of pride about their station in life. Nothing is worth hiding or covering except their natural image.

Times change. We now bus our own trays and dishes in many restaurants and think nothing of it. We pump our own gas at gas stations and think nothing of it. The time has come for African-Americans to change their attitude about their self-image. Women changed from dresses and skirts to pants in the workplace. Many women resisted, but today practically most women wear pants, even to church and think nothing of it. Tattoos were a curse to behold. Only pirates, sailors, prisoners, and motorcycle gang-members sported tattoos. Today professors, teachers, and the girls in the choir are proud tattoo bearers, though the name tattoo is often softened to the euphuism of "body art." Even lipstick, though it has been around for thousands of years, has had its day on the hot seat. In Ancient Egypt, Cleopatra had beetles crushed up so that she could use them to color her lips deep red. Yet it is only in the last century or so that the popularity of lipstick really exploded, thanks to the worldwide influence of Hollywood movies. It used to be much more associated with sinners, prostitutes and other outcasts in society, such as women who were trying to lure and tempt men. During the witch trials of the 18th century, some women were even accused of being witches because they had supposedly used lipstick to fool men into thinking they were attractive and marrying them.

Still, to the average woman today, lipstick feels like an essential of life. Many say they feel naked without it and refer to applying lipstick and makeup as putting on their face. Things change. Our ethnic pride is beginning to bob its beautiful head, again. Let us not make it merely a trend, this time.

Black women, in particular, have an aura so unique that it remains in the vanity merchants' best interest to down play it because, unlike the beauty of other women, the uniqueness of black women cannot be duplicated. The innate charm of black women has never gone unnoticed. For instance, if you hear someone say of a Caucasian that she has the butt of a black woman, you most likely imagine that the Caucasian woman has a nice round full butt. On the other hand, if you hear someone say of a black woman that she has a butt like a Caucasian woman or Asian woman, you think flat butt. Of course, that is not always true, but that is what everyone has instilled in his or her psychic. When we hear fair skin; we think light skin. When we hear good hair; we think long and silky. Another myth. Black people think other people's hair is good and theirs is bad because of its uniqueness; however, black people's hair protects them from hypothermia in freezing cold. Ask yourself this question: If you were going out in the snow, would you whether wear a laniferous [wool-like] hat or thin silk hat?

One of the indisputable reasons that blonde hair is so revered is because of its uniqueness; it is the most rare color of hair. Most countries produce dark haired people. Finland, Norway, Dutch, Sweden and a few other Scandinavian countries produce the most natural blondes. The tresses of black people are more rare than the Scandinavians, and the most beautiful with proper treatment. I do not mean hairweaves, perms, and press and curls; but the dreads, naturals, twist, Sisterlocks, and all other non-chemical treated styles. Uniqueness is beautiful. Black people's dark skin is also unique. It gives them added protection from skin cancer whereas light skin or pale skin is much more susceptible. So how is it that our skin is inferior? Our skin definitely attracts bigotry, but it is not inferior.

One person's low self-esteem is another person's retirement fund. Black people became a mental slave through humiliation yet we were not the only ones. Foot Bindery enslaved Chinese women for centuries; however, I am not going to go into the full history of foot binding in China and the Far East except to say that for over a thousand years, beginning in the tenth century (around 940 A.D.) women were mentally conditioned to want their feet bound until the 1940s. This was to keep their feet from growing beyond a size four. Large feet were considered extremely unattractive; therefore, young girls feet were heavily bound and the big toe was curled under the foot. Asian girls grew up to be women with deformed feet. Even today, podiatrists report that many elderly Asian women's feet are damaged beyond recovery. Special shoes had to be made for the crippled feet. Somebody made a lot of money off crippled Asian feet although that was not the original purpose. It is estimated that over 3 billion women suffered this cruel atrocity before it was outlawed. Three billion women, that is about half of earths' population today. Black people must not allow the public to make them feel like they are the only ones obsessed with vanity. Women, in general, are often more vulnerable and the first targets of psychological ploys that makes them ashamed of their appearance, which ultimately fattens the pockets of big companies; however, men have recently joined the line with dollars in hand to buy off their insecurities, especially in the area of male enhancement pills and gadgets.

Competition For Jobs Spark Height Craze In China

Competition for jobs and marriage partners have sparked a national height craze in China that has people lining up to be surgically stretched or to purchase torture rack-like stretching machines, according to a Local KCAL9 News report November 20, 2006.

In recent months, advertisements on Chinese television are regularly promoting "stretching machines," which look like benches reminiscent of the medieval torture rack.

Users are supposed to strap themselves in by head and foot and turn a crank to extend the bench beneath them. A voice-over on one of the TV advertisements claims that the "body stretch and exercise machine" can stretch human cartilage and "boost young people's height." Also, a private hospital in Beijing has become famous for its height-extending practice, which puts patients out of action for six months or more. Supposedly, the procedure can extend the length of your bones by more than "fifteen percent," according to Dr Xia Hetao, a doctor who performs the surgery. Xia uses an adaptation of a method originally developed in Russia more than a century ago. Xia breaks his patient's legs, then attaches metal pins to the separated bones, which are held in place by metal frames around the patient's legs.

The patient then has to twist a knob daily to gradually drag the ends of broken bone apart gradually, encouraging new bone to grow to bridge the gap as the fracture heals resulting in longer bones and a taller person, according to the report. Xia insists that his procedure has a high rate of success. However, he said that there are other operators in China who botch the job. As leg-lengthening becomes more popular, Xia is calling for official regulation of the practice.

China's Ministry of Health says it is very concerned about the trend. One of Xia's patients, Wang Junhong, traveled thousands of miles from southern China to get her legs lengthened in Beijing. She said she knows of doctors that offer the surgery near where she lives, but she does not trust them to get it right. Competition for work and business success in China can pressure job seekers to take drastic action to increase their height.

Job advertisements often prominently list height requirements for potential candidates.

The average Chinese woman is about 5 feet 2 inches tall and the average man about 5 feet 6 inches, according to the report. It is probable that these new beauty standards in China was adopted from American beauty standards where the average height for an American white woman is 5'5" and the average American white male is 5'10".

Ironically, Yao Ming (born in 1980 in Shanghai, China) a professional basketball player drafted in 2002 by the Houston Rockets is considered one of the premiere centers in the National Basketball Association. At 7'6" Yao is currently the tallest player in the NBA and is regarded as the most dominant player to come out of China. Isn't it incongruous the average or norm is considered flawed or inferior, but the abnormally tall or deformed is praised and celebrated?

Another example of torture for beauty can be traced back to the corset. The corset, which was made of iron and quite heavy, was used as a medieval outer garment to correct poor posture in women, which was contrary to the feminine standard of beauty during 1700 A. D. As centuries passed, the corset, which weighed from 15 to 30 pounds switched from iron to fabric, was wore inside the clothing to restrict the waistline. The 16th century ladies in waiting (unmarried and in pursue of a husband) were instructed to cinch their waists to a size no bigger than thirteen to eighteen inches around. Even given the difference in average body size of a woman in modern times, thirteen inches would have been extreme. These corsets often required the aid of strong slave women to squeeze their tearful white mistress into the garment for appearance sake. The corset was fashionable from 1908–1960s, but enjoyed its greatest popularity in 1920s. Its demise began with the thigh-length dresses of the 1930s.

The corset formed the basis of fine clothing but the use of fabric decreased with society's economical growth, rendering the corset obsolete. The final disappearance of the corset in the 1960s was due to the increased use of panty hoses, which do not require the use of a suspender belt.

In the 1950s, girdles were what women wanted most. Doctors today warn women about wearing tight and restrictive clothing because it creates back pain and can cause intestinal damage. Garment companies profited millions of dollars annually. It is highly unlikely they were unaware of the discomfort and muscular-skeletal such clothing created.

Women with normal sized breasts want larger breasts, while women with natural oversized breasts physically suffer. I imagine that few Hollywood stars and aspiring stars are ever encouraged to have their oversized breasts reduced. The world loves a freak show; however, women and teenage girls with very large pendulous breasts may experience a variety of medical problems caused by the excessive weight from back and neck pain and skin irritation to skeletal deformities and breathing problems. Bra straps may leave indentations in their shoulders. Moreover, unusually large breasts can make a woman or a teenage girl feel extremely self-conscious. Nevertheless, millions of females opt to endure the negative effects in exchange for disingenuous admiration and need to feel admired.

Breasts reduction, technically known as reduction mammaplasty, is designed for such women. The procedure removes fat, glandular tissue, and skin from the breasts, making them smaller, lighter, and firmer. It can also reduce the size of the areola, the darker skin surrounding the nipple. The goal is to give the woman smaller better-shaped breasts in proportion with the rest of her body.

African-American women, according to the American Society of Plastic Surgeons, most commonly requested procedures in the order of popularity are nose reshaping, liposuction and breasts reduction. The most requested in the order of popularity among Hispanic and White women is breast augmentation, liposuction, and tummy tucks; however, among Asians women are nose reshaping, eyelid surgery, and breast augmentation. It seems that women, other than African-Americans, seldom request breasts reduction surgery even if their breasts are disproportionately large; however, nose reshaping is a premium.

Even the wise are deceived by beauty

In the Book of Ecclesiastes King Solomon learns that all is vanity under the sun. He learns this lesson through seeking vain things. Solomon discovered the vanity of those things in which men and women commonly look to for happiness, including beauty and sex. Remember, Solomon is the King of Jerusalem, the wisest and wealthiest man in the Bible. Yet he sought happiness in ways that proved not to be a trait of godly wisdom. Solomon had 700 wives and 300 concubines. How wise is that? Being misled by his ego, he put one thousand lovers in his household.

Solomon later wrote in Ecclesiastes all is vanity under the sun. He sought the most beautiful women only to eventually realize that all of God's creations are beautiful. Even the wisest man in the Bible was deceived by the vanity of the world. However, to his credit, he ultimately saw the error of his judgment. This is apparent in his writings of the Book of Ecclesiastes. Solomon let us know that there is beauty in everything that God has made; although, the finite wisdom of man tries to distinguish what is beauty and what is not. Then the foolishness of man tampers with God's works in pursuit of perfection. Ecclesiastes 3:11 *He hath made everything beautiful in his time; also he hath set the world in their heart, so that no man can find out the work that God maketh from the beginning to the end. 3:14 I know that whatever God doeth, it shall be for ever; there is nothing to be added to it, nor anything to be taken from it; and God doeth [it], that [men] should fear before him.* 5:10 *He that loveth silver shall not be satisfied with silver, nor he that loveth abundance with increase: this is also vanity.* Solomon is also attributed with writing most of Proverbs, which is mostly about wisdom. Proverbs 31 speaks about a virtuous woman but the only reference about beauty is in 31: 30—*Favour is deceitful, and beauty is vain; but a woman that fearth the Lord, she shall be praised.*

It is amazing the way the human mind works. You can treat a nation of people as slaves for so long that even when they are liberated they will continue slave behavior. Take women for example, they have been treated as mere sex objects in harems since the beginning of time in all parts of the world (the Holy Bible confirms that). Now despite of the milestones made during women's liberation movement, women desperately position themselves to be sex objects. Consider the phenomenon of Playboy Magazine (a major player in the pornography industry) and the ever-increasing hordes of females clamoring to be Playboy bunnies; the thousands of females selling their souls to male rap artists for an opportunity to be in sex objects rap videos, the numerous pornography actresses under the direction of male directors and producers, and the prostitutes under the sadistic authority of pimps. According to mental health studies, most of these females have unresolved psychological issues, as do most females obsessed with cosmetic beauty, which often stems from their environmental childhood influences. The males involved with the creation and promotion of female sex objects, as King Solomon, are fulfilling their fantasies, egos, and passive/aggressive misogynistic impulses.

Female sex objects are fifty-one times more likely to meet violent end

According to Wikipedia national studies for 2004 reports that female sex workers are at risk of violent crime as well as possibly at higher risk of occupational mortality than any other group of women ever studied. For example, the homicide rate for female sex workers, which includes exotic dancers, nude models, porn actresses, and of course prostitutes was estimated to be 204 per 100,000 (Potterat et al, 2004), which is several times higher than that for the next riskiest occupations in the United States during a similar period (4 per 100,000 for female liquor store workers) (Castillo *et al.*, 1994). However, there are substantial differences in rates of victimization between street prostitutes and indoor prostitutes who work as escorts, call girls, or in brothels and massage parlors (Weitzer 2000, 2005). Perpetrators include violent clients, pimps, and corrupt law-enforcement officers. Prostitutes (particularly those engaging in street prostitution) are often the targets of serial killers, who may consider them easy targets, or use the religious and social stigma associated with prostitutes as justification for their murder.

In my opinion, male opportunists who inspire or encourage women to indulge in any of the aforementioned professions are passive/aggressive misogynists. It has been my observation that women who find themselves being sex objects have several things in common such as: a pathological need to be accepted, a history of drug abuse, a history of child molestation, personal insecurities, and/or have been drawn in by their superficial outer beauty.

$$ The Multi-billion Dollar Vanity Business $$

The first two great women of Hollywood movie stars were Lillian Gish and Mary Pickford. Although Pickford typically portrayed spunky and rebellion girls and Gish portrayed sweet girls, both always portrayed sexually innocent girls. To do so, both kept their hair long, usually blonde curls for years after other fashionable women twirled their hair in a ball on top of their head called a bob. Pickford did not cut her blonde locks until her late thirties, Gish not until her early forties.

In 1921, a unique American tradition began as a promotional gimmick when Atlantic City hotelmen decide to stage a flashy fall festival, or "pageant" to entice summer tourists to stay in town past Labor Day. The fall festival included a "National Beauty Tournament" on the beach to select "the most beautiful bathing beauty in America." Local newsman, Herb Test, added the crowning touch when he exclaimed, "Let's call her 'Miss America!'" Eastern newspaper editors were invited to run photo contests to pick winners to represent their communities at the new pageant. Eight contestants competed for the first Miss America title. Margaret Gorman, who represented the nation's capital as Miss Washington D.C., won first Miss America title. The sixteen-year-old schoolgirl was a dead ringer for reigning matinee superstar, Mary Pickford, which officially, in the minds of white American validates Margaret Gorman, *Miss America*, as the standard of American Beauty.

In 1933, in the classic movie, "King Kong" the giant ape takes a shine to the beautiful Fay Wray, who dyed her hair blonde in order to get the role. The causative factor in his capture and his demise is his fatal attraction to a blonde white woman. A male actor says in the last words of the film, "Oh, no, it wasn't the airplanes. It was beauty that killed the beast." These lessons did not go unnoticed; female moviegoers interviewed by researchers between 1920 and 1933 admitted readily that they modeled themselves after their favorites stars rather than popular political, business, or educational figures. Consequently, females with brunette, or red hair felt less attractive since the top female movies stars and the first Miss America were blonde. Consequently, blonde hair dye became the best seller and has not let-up. Hollywood lengthened the image with its unrelenting lineup of blonde starlets, such as: Mae West, Brigette Bardot, Diane Shore, Jean Harlow, Marlene Dietrich, Joan Blondell, Grace Kelly, Zsa Zsa Gabor, Ingrid Bergman, Gwyneth Platrow, Charo, Britney Spears, Paris Hilton, Ginger Rogers, Marilyn Monroe, Farrah Fawcet, Debbie Reynolds, Sandra Dee, Madonna, Pamela Anderson and hundreds more, including Barbie, the world's most popular toy doll.

The list of famous *fake* blondes could go on forever because, according to Miss Clairol, the number one selling hair dye company, only 1 out of 20 women are born blonde but 1 out of 3 women are living as a blonde. By the way, the popular believe that blondes are dumb is a logical deduction. Though there's no scientific proof that natural blondes are any dumber that anybody else but the mere fact that more women dye their hair blonde than any other color equate to more blondes. There're millions of African-American, Hispanic, and Asian women with dyed blonde hair even though blonde hair is not even a natural trait in their genes. Add that to the hundreds of millions of white women with fake blonde hair. The fact that so many women dye their hair blonde in hopes of utopia is enough to perpetuate the negative stigma.

In the book Rapunzel's Daughter by Rose Weitz, 2004, in *The History of Women's Hair* chapter she said, "Hair colors never seen in Africa have grown in popularity. For some reason, more black women feel free to dye their hair lighter colors—an inherently more damaging process than dyeing hair dark colors, since to dye hair a light color it must first be chemically stripped of its natural color. Between 1995 and 1998, retail sales of hair-color products for black women rose 8.3 percent, three times as fast as the overall growth in hair products for black women, with 42 percent of those buying hair color choosing blonde or red shades."

The popularity of blonde hair grew through the movies just like the popularity of cigarettes. While all the good girls were blonde, all the male heroes and tough guys smoked cigarettes. Practically every male star prior to the 1970s smoked on the screen. It was many years before women smoked on the screen because smoking was not a good-girl image; it was a male thing. Men wanted to be like the tough guy in the movies.

Another obsession is muscles, which lead many to illegal steroid use. The trend for males to be muscular has been here since the early days of Charles Atlas and the comic book ads of a skinny boy on the beach, with a girl, getting sand kicked in his face by a muscular bully. Lean boys began to feel inferior about their body, which turned out to be major profit making ideas for the body building industry.

Likewise, the rush to be thin is a major slot machine payoff for the diet pill industry. Women are dying to be thin, and not only white women, but primarily white women. Black and Latin women have escaped this bullet because black and Latin men are attracted to plumb curvaceous bottoms on women while white men apparently perk up for smaller rear ends, which creates a gold mine for the health spas and all-night gyms. Black women trying to be super thin, signals me that they're more interested in white men than black.

"I did a movie with Chris Rock who said, 'I know you want to lose weight because you're supposed to be sexy, but I don't want you to."—Kerry Washington—African-American actress (People Magazine Oct. 2006)

Weight Attitudes Different as Black and White

Human beings, especially females, are very susceptible to popular media and controlled by whatever is trendy in the movies, magazines, and the cosmetic industry. Since the 1970s, one such trend continues to cause the deaths of many white females. This is the craze to be super thin, which was created by the popularity of super model Twiggy. Twiggy was born in north London in 1949. The Daily Express named her "The Face of "66." Twiggy became famous at the age of sixteen, and gained her nickname from her toothpick-thin pubescent figure. She was also known for the high-fashion mod look that she created. White girls rushed from their dining table into the bathroom to regurgitate their food in a desperate craze to be thin.

In 1983, the death of popular singer Karen Carpenter brought national attention to white girls starving themselves to death. Immediately following Karen's death, there was a massive surge in the media regarding the singer and her battle with anorexia. Eating disorders all of a sudden became highly publicized. Magazines and journals began publishing articles, and the TV news had top stories about anorexia and its devastating effects. All of the media coverage on Karen's death encouraged other celebrities to go public with their stories. The death raised the profile of eating disorders in the entertainment community. Jane Fonda and Cherry Boone O'Neill, daughter of singer Pat Boone, admitted to their eating disorders and committed themselves to getting help. Also coming forward with their problems was gymnast and actress Kathy Rigby and actresses Jeannine Turner and Lynn Redgrave. Karen Carpenter's death gave white women quite a scare. In the days and months to follow the tragic incident, there were flurries of frightened phone calls to medical centers from people who had been jolted by the singer's death and wanted help. Psychologically oriented groups had a doubling in attendance following Karen's death. In addition, many people began to launch voluntary support groups for victims of eating disorders.

White adolescents are more occupied with thinness than black adolescents. LSU AgCenter nutritionist Dr. Heli Roy examines this phenomenon found in a Pennington Biomedical Research Center study. Conducted by Dr. Donald Williamson and reported in the "Journal of Eating and Weight Disorders," March 2003, (20 years after the death of Karen Carpenter) the study tested the hypotheses that black adolescents were less concerned with body size than white adolescents and that dieting behavior was related to body size, according to Roy. Williamson found that white adolescents tend to be obsessively concerned about their body size and have more eating disorders than black adolescents. They tend to overestimate their body size and desire to be thinner than do black adolescents. Furthermore, the heavier black adolescents have lower incidences of eating disorders than white adolescents. "There seems to be a cultural standard that drives a desirable body size," Roy points out.

The list of areas in which people become insecure about themselves is extensive. There is the fear of looking older, even though you are indeed an old person. That's another multi-million-dollar business. There is the expense of esoteric oils, crèmes, face-lifts, Botox injections to hide wrinkles. And then there's the shame saddled upon women with small breasts. They are bombarded with messages that claim blondes have more fun, but skinny blondes with big breasts have even more fun. More pressure. Now comes the breasts implants, which not only are unnecessary, but also have caused many women scarring and deformities, just as the hair relaxers and skin bleaches damaged and scarred black people.

Tanning salons, another branch of the American standard of beauty. And what is wrong with having white skin if you call yourself *white*? Why are tanning salons so popular among white folk? First they are calling white the superior race then they are slipping off to become darkened. More manipulation. The following is an excerpt from a October 10, 2006 Mayo Clinic newsletter posted on the Internet:

Are Tanning Beds Safer Than Natural Sunlight?

by Lawrence Gibson, M.D., Mayo Clinic dermatologist

Answer: No. There is no safe tan. Exposure to ultraviolet (UV) radiation—whether from sunlight or tanning beds—damages your skin, increasing your risk of skin cancer and premature skin aging. (People are dying to be dark.)

GOD CAN USE IT FOR GOOD

One of the most undesired human traits in American is being fat. No American wants to be overweight. Fat people are considered unattractive, lazy, and to have less leadership qualities. They are the most discriminated against group in America. It always amazes me when I think of Oprah Winfrey. She entered to public eye not only fat but black, female, and with an Afro. Oprah's fatness changed the exercise habits of America. She encouraged TV viewers worldwide to become more concerned about their health and lose weight. She started a walking program, which got millions walking as a daily routine. She introduces health experts who advise the public on physical and mental health issues. Oprah went on to encourage people to read more. She single-handedly inspired hundreds, perhaps thousands of reading and book clubs in this country. She helped millions of females overcome the emotional trauma of being sexual abused by sharing her own experience of sexual abuse.

When I see Oprah, I often think of 'Sofia' the character she played in her acting debut "The Color Purple" in 1985. Sofia was strong, fierce, and daring to a fault. In fact, it is her refusal to lessen or belittle herself that almost leads to her destruction. As a black American woman reared in the South in the 1930s, she rejects the systematic oppression that engulfed blacks. In that system, a black person had to remain absolutely subservient to whites—economically and socially. In addition, a black woman came under the rule of her husband. A black woman was a virtual prisoner in the system. White men controlled the state, and black men controlled the black households. Sofia had no chance in such a setting. She simply wasn't suited for it by her very nature. Sofia is not tragic as much as she is symbolic of a woman who had the courage to fight against insurmountable odds. Within every black woman lives a Sofia.

Of all the blonde beautiful white females who has hosted their own national TV show in the history of television, Oprah's show has outlasted all of them. Oprah's harshest critics are black people especially the black comics and rappers. No, Oprah is not attractive by American beauty standards but she allowed God to use her and in doing so a lot of good has been bestowed upon the world as she constantly gives large sums of money to charities around the world, including opening an all girl's school in South Africa in January 2007. After the establishment of this school Oprah stated, "This is what I was born to do."

We must learn to make the best of whatever history and physical features we are working with. The things we look at as ugly God may call it beauty because it was intended for a divine propose that's not given to our limited understanding. ECCLES 3:11 *He hath made everything beautiful in its time; also he hath set the world in their heart, so that man findeth not out from the beginning to the end the work that God doeth.* 3:14 *I know that whatever God doeth, it shall be forever; there is nothing to be added to it, nor anything to be taken from it; and God doeth it, that men should fear before him.*

We must make the best of that which is, and must believe it best for the present, and accommodate ourselves to it. He has made everything beautiful in its time (which means for an appointed time). Cold is as becoming in winter as heat in summer; and the night, in its time is a black beauty, as the day, in its time, is a bright beauty. There is a wonderful harmony in the divine Providence and all its disposals, so that events considered in their relations and tendencies, together with the seasons of them, appear very beautiful, to the glory of God and the comfort of those that trust him.

Stevie Wonder, a black man, Tom Sullivan, a white man, and Jose Feliciano, a Latino man, all three, were born blind. However, they have accomplished musical feats far greater than most sighted musicians. Yet, many would call them imperfect and want to fix them. Nobody fully understands the ways of God.

Dr. JoAnne Cornwell, like millions of black people before and after her, felt that she was cursed with unmanageable hair. Most people did not know that black people's kinky hair could grow so long and beautiful without the help of man's chemicals. Dr. Cornwell took the time to discover the blessed hair black people inherited. Scientists, chemists, inventors, the human hair industry, and cosmetic companies were quick to discover methods to assist Gods' creation through hot combs, wigs, extensions, and toxic products. But the natural beauty was there all the time. Cosmetology colleges did not teach the art of natural hair care—they taught beauticians how to press and curl, fry and dye, and to lessen chemical burns to the scalp and neck of black people. Today millions of black people still suffer from low self-esteem because of lack of knowledge about their hair but there are also a growing number that are thankful for their healthy natural hair. Natural health and beauty is not always seen at first glance but that is no reason to resort to a temporary fix.

102 Natural ... The Beautiful 'N' Word

There will come a time that all superficial things will fade and what is left will be the real person. It is essential that every woman meets and falls in love with that inner soul as soon as possible because that is the spirit she will take to the grave and be with for an eternity.

Love Me As I AM

by Richard O. Jones

Please somebody
Take me—fake me
Cut me—gut me
Mold me—roll me
Scrape me—shape me
Silicone me—Honey-tone me
But love me as I am

Nip me—clip me
Slowly dip me—gently flip me
Make this bigger—Make that smaller
What can you do to make me taller?
Everybody admire the shell you made
But I loss my identity in the trade

Make me over—bake me over
Give me new eyes—Give me new thighs
Super size me—minimize me
Weave me—don't leave me
Here's my money—don't deceive me
And love me as I am

I am a strong black woman
And will not compromise
After I get
A thinner nose—straighter toes
Longer mane—smaller frame
Softer skin—made a '10'
Whiter teeth—cuter feet
And somebody to

Love me as I am

The day should come that I wakeup
And love myself
Without your makeup
Without your hair weave and extensions
Without your chemical hair intentions
I don't want green eggs and ham
Only to love me … as I am

American Cancer Society Finds Dark Skin Superior

Inferior hair is 50% of the damming dual that taunts some African-Americans; the other half is inferior skin; however, the American Cancer Society sees it differently. Cancer researchers have identified and reported six separate skin categories for sun induced skin cancer.

TYPE 1 HIGH RISK

- Fair skin and hair and freckles that always burn easily and never tan. [white people with blonde or red hair]

- Usually have a light eye color [blue, green, gray, hazel]

- This category is the first to show signs of aging and should wear a sun block everyday, rain or shine.

TYPE 2 HIGH RISK

- Fair skin that always burns easily and tans minimally [white people]

- Often slightly darker eye and hair color [hair slightly darker than blonde]

- Shows signs of aging quickly

- Should wear a sun block everyday, rain or shine.

TYPE 3 MODERATE RISK

- Fair skin that burns minimally but tans gradually and uniformly

TYPE 4 MODERATE RISK

• Burns minimally, always tans well [darker white people]

• Usually has brown eyes and hair

• Shows signs of aging at a slower rate

• Examples; Italian, Portuguese, Spanish decent.

TYPE 5 LOW RISK

• Rarely burns, tans profusely

• Usually has dark brown eyes and brown or black hair

• Shows signs of aging very slowly [darker people age slower than light people]

• Examples—American Indian, Eastern Indian, <u>light skin tone African-American</u>.

TYPE 6 LOW RISK

• Never burns, deeply pigmented skin [<u>dark African America people</u>]

• Fewer wrinkles and age spots

• Low melanoma cancer occurrence

Although African-Americans were indoctrinated with an inferiority complex, the facts are that nappy haired darker skinned people are less susceptible to skin cancer, which should be perceived as black people being innately blessed. Another comforting feature about black people's nappy or curly hair is that it is easily distinguished from that of dogs, cats, horses, goats, and other four-legged creatures; whereas, a stand of a white person's hair, especially blondes, must undergo microscopic exam to determine whether it's human or beast. Instead of us buying skin lightening cream and hair straighter from whites, it would have made more sense if they bought skin darkening cream and nappy hair enhancement cream from us. Come to think of it, why aren't scientists specializing in healthy natural lotions for whites to become darker? The advertisement could have a pale, homely, feeble, white woman with thin stringy blonde hair and dull blue eyes milking a cow, in the before picture, and a shapely dark beautiful brown eyed woman wearing African hairdo and long glittering evening gown sipping champagne in the after picture. It is all a matter of perception. If the images just described had been circulated for the last 400 years. Today 75% to 80% of white women would be wearing Afro wigs instead of 75% to 80% of black women wearing press and curls and hairweaves. Africa-Americans would own the corporations that earn billions of dollars per year as a direct result of the inferior complex that we inflicted upon whites about their unique God-given beauty.

OBSESSION WITH BEAUTY LEADS TO DESIGNER BABIES

It is an uncommon but not an unheard of situation in African-American beauty salons to see a mother bring her infant daughter, still in diapers, in for a perm or mild hair relaxer. I saw a televised court proceeding on the Judge Hatchet Show, where a licensed beautician was being sued for chemically burning a teenage girl's scalp and neck. The teenage defendant's mother produced pictures and a medical report that substantiated her claim that her daughter had been chemically burnt. The beautician, in her defense, said that the chemical product that she uses is too mild to cause that much damage. She further stated that she has used the same product on babies as young as two-years-old without incident. When I heard that my jaw dropped, as did Judge Hatchet's. Some African-American mothers are indeed obsessed with hair and physical features. These are the type of would-be-mothers that fertility companies are gearing up to service.

Imagine a world where every child was perfect. They need never get ill. They are always happy. They could be bred to be geniuses or those brilliant at music or sports. Some say this is no dream. Soon we will be able to select the genes of our children and have *designer babies*. Until now we have been limited to changing our children's overall looks and demeanor until after they are born. In the future parents are going to be able to select their looks, personality, intellectual, and athletic prowess at the very beginning, at the point of fertilization. Some say that the idea of designer babies is taking technology too far and playing god. Any child with potential handicaps or unattractive features will be denied a chance at life, yet this is where society is headed because of our obsession with physical perfection.

The fact that women who have experienced difficulty in having children can have genetically engineered fertility assistance to greatly enhance their likelihood of a successful childbirth has sparked interest. A friend of mine, whom I will call

Phyllis, kept miscarrying all the time. I interviewed her for this book about her experience:

Phyllis: I loss four babies by miscarriage, it just actually got quite normal, and that was actually how awful it was, it was very hard but ... and it sounds really harsh, but you just kind of get ... it just becomes part of life. I mean I just used to get pregnant, lose it, get pregnant again, lose it again and that was it.

Question: Did you discover why you were having so many miscarriages?

Phyllis: Yes. I underwent tests. The cause of my miscarriages was genetic, the result of a chromosome disorder. That meant most of my embryos didn't have the right combination of genes they needed to grow healthily.

Question: Were you hopeless at that point?

Phyllis: Yes, until my doctor told my husband and me about a technique called pre-implantation genetic diagnosis, or PGD. Using PGD scientists can screen embryos outside the womb, long before they developed into babies. Then they can select just those embryos that carry healthy genes, to ensure the baby is free from genetic abnormalities. He said that some people call it *Designer Babies*.

Question: Have you ever heard the term *Designer Babies*?

Phyllis: "No but Bob (her husband) had read about it and understood it more than I did. Bob (not his real name) The doctor explained it but Bob explained it better at home. They would take a very early embryo and take out a cell and diagnose it. To do PGD the doctors first had to extract eggs from my ovaries and they would be fertilized in the lab with Bob's sperm. The fertilized eggs were allowed to develop into a cluster of cells. Then 48 hours after fertilization, acid was used to etch a hole in the membrane of each embryo and a single cell sucked out. They do their lab work until they find an embryo that's normal. That part took about a week of waiting. Eventually they found cells from two embryos that had healthy genes. They called us and said we've got a couple. The geneticists came down to see us and said there's one that is not, it's not divided so well but the other one brilliant, absolutely brilliant, so we're going to implant, two back in."

Two embryos that did not carry Phyllis' chromosome problem were implanted back into her womb. PGD was developed so parents like Phyllis and Bob could eradicate genetic abnormalities from their family tree, and have healthy children. But some say that in the future it will not just be used to prevent devastating genetic diseases.

According to medical journals, there is little doubt that in the future people are going to want to use this technology for uses that go beyond medicine *but for uses that are cosmetic, for things like eye color and height* and other things that are on the border of medicine like longevity. As the use of PGD expands some experts are worried about just what genetic choices we will make. We might select genes that affect looks or personality more so than for health and only genetically perfect babies will be granted the right of birth. The possibility of abusing PGD to create a perfectly beautiful race draws closer as science discovers more about what our genes do.

The human genome project has already catalogued all 3 billion letters of the human DNA code. And barely a week goes by without scientists claiming to have discovered how yet another gene affects us. Some of these genes are clearly linked to disease. But others seem to have the power to influence our behavior. Some scientists had successfully linked genes to mood. Genes also have been found that are linked to homosexuality, others to alcoholism, risk-taking and even perfect pitch. And if scientists know what genes to look for, it is said they could use PGD to choose a child with brown eyes, or blonde hair. Select a boy or a girl; a child that would be more intelligent, taller, stronger, or more well balanced than its peers. By using PGD we could design a baby with exactly the characteristics we want. A man and a woman that want to have a child will walk into a fertility clinic and the doctors will take 100–200 eggs out of the woman. They will be fertilized with the man's sperm and then they will do a genetic profile on all 200 embryos and choose the embryo that has the combination of genes from the two parents that the parents want to see in their child. That is where they will start.

The Designer Baby business is huge and currently underground to a large extent because governmental regulations prevent the outright practice for the time being. There is currently legislation in debate over stem cell research and human cloning, which fertility clinic investors are watching closely. Once government approves the medical innovations and enacts laws to control its practice and usage, all hell is likely to break loose in the designer baby business. Similar to the medical marijuana use law that was finally passed after years of legal wrangling but now experiences rampant abuse.

Among the troubling aspects of new reproductive technologies is the takeover of reproduction by the marketplace. There are many aspects of the high-tech commoditization of procreation, among which are the fabulous revenues commercial fertility clinics earn from couples' desperate desire for children and the ensuing conflicts between medical ethics and the profit motive; nevertheless, wealthy women and couples have no problem locating medical facilities willing to take their money under the table for the production of designer babies. Many single women and couples travel outside the United States in pursuit of their parental dreams. A quick Internet search will turn up many clandestine opportunities for genetic engineering assistance. In the meantime, single women are openly rushing to sperm banks in droves for their ideal child.

Growing Demand for American Sperm

The popularity of sperm banks is growing. Many single career women who do not have time to nurture a relationship are choosing to have babies without the physical attachment of a male counterpart. These women are said to select their child's physical features like they were picking a new car. There are approximately 150 sperm banks in the United States. From deposit to delivery—discover the process sperm donors and prospective mothers go through to create new life. At the California Cryobank in Los Angeles, one of the largest sperm banks in the country, hopeful parents meet with counselors who help them find donor candidates. Anonymous donors are chosen by characteristics such as eye color, hair color, education level, ethnicity and even personality.

The California Cryobank requires that potential donors have a high sperm count and have a clean medical history. Once a donor has been accepted into the program, he must return two or three times each week for a set period of time in order to make further donations. Technologists then analyze samples, and reject those with any serious genetic flaws, sexually transmitted diseases or less than 20 million sperm.

Acceptable samples are then frozen at -320 degrees and quarantined for six months before being sold. Vials can cost as much as $275 each, and are shipped all over the world in liquid nitrogen, which keeps them frozen for seven days.

Shopping for Sperm Online

The Xytex Corporation sells sperm through their online catalogue. Future parents can browse through donor profiles with complete confidentiality, and it is one of the only companies in the world that allows customers to see exactly what the donors look like both as adults and as children. The donors often make videos introducing themselves, where potential parents get a chance to learn even more about them

"People are very choosy," says an executive of Xytex. "We've had requests for actor Brad Pitt's semen." Celebrities and politicians have used Xytex's services, although Xytex would not name names. And while folks can be very specific in their requests, you can't yet purchase sperm of the stars. However, if you want a donation from a blue-eyed, 6-foot, blond doctor who is Catholic and likes the outdoors, many sperm banks can deliver. That is one-reason U.S. sperm banks have a competitive advantage. The biggest demand is for the semen of white good-looking men. Xytex often provides clients with photos of the donor and the offspring he helped produce, along with detailed biography. The women look at his picture and the picture(s) of the fruit of his handiwork along with his attributes such as IQ, career (often college students), height, hair, eyes, hobbies, favorite book, movie, politics, athlete prowess, size of feet and other body parts, then decide if he is the donor for them.

I discovered that Middle Eastern and Asian sperm is harder to come by, for cultural reasons; therefore, it is quite common for a Japanese couple to travel to the United States for fertility assistance. Single Asian and Middle Eastern women also visit the United States for semen. Approximately 40% select American white male semen as opposed to men of their race.

Xytex provides physical, medical, and social information about a donor to the patient. Donors are described by basic physical traits and medical histories on him and his family. All donors also take a written psychological evaluation requiring about two hours to complete. According to sperm bank insiders, the great attraction for artificial insemination is the ability to select a child's potential good looks, natural hair color and IQ as well as the beauty craze in America and social acceptance of single motherhood.

Sperm Banks: Obsessed With The American Standard of Beauty

With nearly 150 sperm banks in the United States and tens of thousands of donors, it was bound to happen. As reported in the *Journal of Pediatrics*, a sperm donor from Michigan passed on a rare and potentially deadly genetic disorder to five children. Doctors thought it was more than a coincidence when five kids born to four couples in the Detroit area were discovered with a serious disorder. They traced it back to one sperm bank and one man, a young white blond male who stood 6'2" and had blue eyes.

The disorder, called severe congenital neutropenia, affects only one in five million newborns. Those with the disorder lack a certain type of white blood cell, and this leaves them vulnerable to a host of infections and also leukemia. Fortunately, medication, albeit at $200 a day, can keep white blood cell counts high.

For now this seems to be an honest mistake. The donor, known but unnamed in the report, could have been an asymptomatic carrier of the disease. (The only problem is that his whereabouts are unknown; the children are several years old now, and the donor has fathered other children.) The sperm bank, known but unnamed in the report, only screens for about ten of the most common hereditary diseases, such as cystic fibrosis.

Maybe the incident will bring about more rigorous genetic testing. But no one seems to care about the biggest flaw in the system, the heavy concentration on physical appearance.

What is really wrong with sperm donation? Einstein would not have stood a chance. He would have been deemed too short. Genius? Yes. Humanitarian? Yes. Height? What? Under 5'10"? Hit the road, Albert. That's right! Most sperm banks draw the line at 5'10". They weed out the weaklings. Sperm banks cannot be expected to screen for rare genetic disorders when there are so many more pressing concerns to find out about the donor, such as baldness, color of eyes, color and texture of hair, skin complexion, salary history, hobbies and taste in clothing. Sperm banks are obsessed with the American standard of beauty and care far less about health. I know there are fatal fashion mistakes, but I did not think that a lack of fashion savvy was genetic. Nevertheless, sperm is big business, and most sperm banks carry only those donors with characteristics most desirable to their clientele.

A March 2006 *New York Times Magazine* article relayed tales of single women shopping for sperm as if it were online dating. And sperm donation questionnaires viewable on the Internet confirm the ridiculous selection criteria. Some women are looking for donors from wealthy families or with an agreeable list of heroes and aspirations, as if that will somehow magically rub off on their child who will never know the biological father. Some are looking for donors of a specific religion and specific height but overlook deeper emotional needs of a child.

Sperm banks weed out the short and bald and even those potential donors with a grandparent who died young and gives women a choice of good-looking jocks. Sounds innocent enough. But it is not so innocent. Darker skin donors are not as desirable as those with lighter skin, even among African-American clientele. Yet who can blame the parents when the stupid society we live in shuns darker skin (and short stature and bald heads). African-American women chose light skinned and mixed race donors at a much higher rate than donors with strong African features regardless of the educational or intelligence factor. Thousands of black women willing have children by dark skinned men every year but given a choice to select their child's father from an application or computer data of unknown candidates it becomes a difference matter.

Adam Pertman, executive director of the Evan B. Donaldson Adoption Institute and author of <u>Adoption Nation: How the Adoption Revolution is Transforming America</u> Basic Books, 2001, says current trends include more single African-American women adopting children from foster care and more single women adopting a child of a different race or ethnicity but consistently rejecting the darker skinned African-American child. This mindset is not an intentional and conscious racists act but an almost unnoticeable act of colorism. (Colorism is a term used when blacks discriminate against each other based on skin complexion.)

Are You Recognized Without Makeup?

Many women and a few men are unrecognizable without their public mask. Can you imagine the lack of attention Little Richard or Michael Jackson would receive if they cut their long chemical or weaved hair and went bald without a touch of makeup and costumed clothing? I suggest if either man appeared in public looking like an ordinary man they would not be recognized. Performers such as Eddie Murphy, Martin Lawrence, Arsenio Hall, Flip Wilson, Wesley Snipes, James Earl Jones, and hundreds of other black men have performed in feminine makeup but it did not become their lifestyle; however, if it did they wouldn't be recognized without it either. Makeup is a plaything and meant to be removed after the act. In the movie Frankenstein (1931) the actor Boris Karloff had to wear heavy makeup to play the role but he did not live that way, neither did the first Ronald McDonald clown in 1963, who is currently a popular weatherman on NBC named Willard Scott. It is makeup for crying out loud not your daily bread. It would be great if men collectively would let women feel that they are loved as a woman and not a canvas. (However, masculine makeup for men is being developed as I write and I would not be surprised if black men are targeted for the masculine makeup to match their *masculine* earrings.)

Many women are not recognized without their makeup because it has become part of their daily face. When makeup becomes so ingrained in a woman's life that she feels unnatural without it, I think she has been push over the top by the American standard of beauty. When the natural becomes the unnatural in any woman's life she needs to slow down and catch her breath. The cosmetic company stockholders love the fact that women are so gullible.

Dependence on daily facial cosmetics for every occasion creates a false sense of confidence and rather than its use as a cosmetic, used to make you look, and/or smell better, it becomes a drug, when is used to alter your mental state of being.

In other words, if you need cosmetics to feel good about yourself or to cope with the outside world, it has become a drug. As with all drug addictions, the addicted person cannot forego it without suffering agonizing side effects, such as shame, subconscious feelings of being stared at, overly concerned about other peoples' feelings regarding you, and/or the need to explain or apologize for less than a perfectly cosmetic appearance. A woman can discover whether or not she has become cosmetically addicted or dependent by challenging herself to go shopping in a busy public place without any makeup—none—not a pinch, dab or smear. Also leave the wig behind and cover her head with a head-wrap. To make it easier, she should go to an area where she's least likely to see anyone she knows, even if she has to drive an hour out of town. If that test is passed, then she should challenge herself to go to church, work, school, social club, or on a date or anywhere familiar people will be present. If the two aforementioned tests are successfully achieved, the woman taking the tests is not cosmetically addicted and is still in control of her emotional happiness and should not be concerned about her use of makeup. However, if she failed the tests or refused to take it, she probably has a lack of confidence and should work on it rather than succumb to it.

The addiction to cosmetics can be compared to the addiction of alcohol. A moderate drinker is okay; in fact, many doctors recommend a glass of wine or whiskey every night. The key is moderation; however, if a drinker gets to the point that he/she needs a drink to cope with daily routine situations and cannot leave home without a drink then a problem exist. Even in the Holy Bible Jesus' first miracle was turning water into wine. Additionally, women in the Bible used cosmetics and perfumes. Jesus himself was even anointed with perfumes and oils. *Mathew 26 (6) Now when Jesus was in Bethany, in the house of Simon the leper, (7) a woman came to him having an alabaster jar of very expensive ointment, and she poured it on his head as he sat at the table. (8) But when his disciples saw this, they were indignant, saying, "Why this waste. (9) For this ointment might have been sold for much, and given to the poor." (10) However, knowing this, Jesus said to them, "Why do you trouble the woman? Because she has done a good work for me. (11) The poor you will always have with you, but you will not always have me. (12) When she poured this perfume on my body, she did it to prepare me for burial.*

Jesus welcomed the ointments because it made him smell good as he was preparing for the grave (a special occasion) but he did not need it or and relied on it in order to come out in public. Moderation is the key. The cosmetic companies and movie industry keeps the fear of being seen without makeup alive by paying paparazzi to catch a female celebrity in public without her makeup. The normal looking celebrity (unrecognized celebrity) in the market doing her Saturday morning grocery shopping is spattered across the front page of tabloids with the headline—*WHATEVERHERNAME* CAUGHT WITHOUT MAKEUP! Suddenly the normal looking woman in the market, which no one recognized except the paparazzi that followed her from her home, becomes awful looking. The paparazzi earn a good payday for embarrassing another human being for being normal and the cosmetic company sells another ton of makeup. If more celebrity women would purposely, commonly, and often expose the natural face without makeup, not only would the price of makeup go down, the spies with cameras would have to get a real job.

Actress Reveals the Truth of Makeup Illusions

In September 2002, actress/model Jamie Lee Curtis, at 44-years-old, posed, for *More Magazine* in a sports bra and tight spandex briefs that revealed what she looks like when she is not glammed up as a movie star. Curtis says that she has often spent three hours prepping with a team of 13 people making sure she looked just right before a magazine shoot or movie scene. Now she wants to be shown without being [glammed] up. Curtis then asked photographer Andrew Eccles to shoot with her no makeup, no manicure, no professionally done hair, no diamond jewelry or high fashion outfit, in an unforgiving light with a full-body straight-on shot. She says she doesn't have a perfect body.

"I don't have great thighs," she tells *More*. "I have very big breasts and a soft, fatty little tummy. And I've got back fat. People assume I'm walking around in little spaghetti-strap dresses. It's the insidious Glam Jamie. And I don't want the unsuspecting 40-year-old women of the world to think that I've got it going on. It's such a fraud. And I'm the one perpetuating it." The word 'makeup' itself means to lie, the whole business of 'makeup' is to play make-believe, and the same is true of wigs and hairpieces.

The myth of the perfect Jamie is something she "actively participated in and, by the way, profited from. She knows that her body, held up as an icon of female perfection in movies such as, well, "Perfect" which was in 1985 when she was 27-years-old and considered a sex symbol, has made some women think that they don't measure up. She knows how that feels—not being good enough. The daughter of two members of Hollywood royalty, Janet Leigh and Tony Curtis, this actress has struggled with feelings of inadequacy all her life. In youth-obsessed Hollywood, where the dearth of good roles for women over 28 is a constant lament, it's a bold move to admit your age at all—let alone to revel in it. But Curtis is seeking something bigger than her next acting job. She wants to feel at peace with her flaws, her genes. "Now, I'm sitting here on my high hill, debunking the very foundation that I sit on. Don't think I'm not afraid of it. I'm not financially independent enough that I don't rely on outside income still. I want to do my part, as I develop the consciousness for it, to stop perpetuating the myth. I'm going to look the way God intends me to look ... with a little help from Manolo Blahnik not the major cosmetic companies," she declares. [Manolo Blahnik a celebrity shoe designer. His shoes are synonymous with high glamour and full-throttle sex appeal and have become as famous as the women who wear them.] She admits she has gone under the knife to improve her looks. "I've had a little plastic surgery. I've had a little lipo. I've had a little Botox. Yes, that's right, I'm a veteran of the nip-and-tuck. And you know what? None of it works—none of it. I've done it all."

Jamie Lee Curtis is not the only white celebrity that is exposing the lies of the beauty industry. In Naomi's Guide to Aging Gratefully, (2006) by Naomi Judd, the *New York Times* bestselling author and country music superstar reveals how to embrace the opportunities that come with age and make one's later years truly golden. The superficial forces of the world even trick you to be ashamed of something as natural and inevitable as aging. To be ashamed of getting old is to be ashamed of not dying young. Anti-aging creams are a big seller. Jobs discriminate against able-bodied workers because of advancing age. This is the product of the movie and cosmetic industry that even rejects its own.

Judd debunks society's myth s about aging. She helps us define ourselves from within, find our *real beauty*, and enjoy the benefits that come with growing older. With fifteen important life choices, she shows how to find freedom and simplicity in the latter half of life. Judd uses the term making "lemonade-out-of-lemons wit and wisdom" (a term that I refer to as Root Profit) as she shows readers to turn their advanced years into their best years.

Judd speaks out against the excessive hairstyles and makeup as a self-esteem booster and encourage women to utilize their *free-no-charge* natural beauty, which will never be encouraged by the cosmetic industry. "The number one cause of mental illness and unhappiness is not knowing who you are. You should look in the mirror of truth and realize and embrace who you are in mind and body and spirit."—*Naomi Judd*

Hairweaves Are for Anybody but <u>Natural</u> is the BEAUTIFUL 'N' Word

Ten years ago, I thought hairweaves were just for black woman. Everybody knew but me, hairweaves are for anyone who is insecure about their hair. My sister-in-law, who has been a beautician for thirty-five years, told me that the race doesn't play a major role in the customers of hairweavers. White, Hispanic, Asian, and African-American women select to have hairweaves. I began to try to detect hair-weaves on women, which was nearly impossible, except on black women. The common denominator remains the same—insecurity. Extremely long straight hair on black women is not natural and everybody knows it. The longer the more unrealistic. My wish is that they someday learn to create attractive hairstyles with what God gave them, no matter how limited. It is hard to cherish a fake any-thing, painting, jewelry, or women. Below is an example of the typical hairweave ad I discovered on the Internet. As you read the ad, notice the buzz words that's targets insecurity:

Let Your Natural Hair Breath & Flow.
You can Look Dynamic.

No Tape, No Glue

'Make-Me-Special' (not real name of business) Hair Weaving Extensions AND get ready for this … Permanent makeup. That's right! Become a natural-looking beauty with a flowing weave and makeup that won't run or smear. Wake up in the morning looking just as good as you did the night before.

Have you ever wished that you could

- Have long beautiful hair?
- Have naturally beautiful eyebrows?
- Have beautiful eyes WITHOUT make-up?
- Have distinctive luscious lips?
- Have a beauty mark?
- Have natural-looking permanent blush?

- Cover up scars?

- Remove freckles?

We do it all and much more! With a New exciting Permanent Make-Up Update

Hair Weaving Consultations

'Make-Me-Special' is the HOTTEST thing in African American Hair Styling today—we give women the 'natural look' hairlines that brush back into ponytails and other versatile styles. Look like the Queen you were meant to be and have power over your men.

'Make-Me-Special' used catchy words like: dynamic, luscious, natural, beautiful/beauty, and exciting. Natural and beautiful and/or beauty was used eight times in this short ad. Such an ad would only attract an insecure woman and 'Make-Me-Special' knows it. This commercial is disingenuous because seldom can an African-American woman become a natural-looking beauty with a hairweave. Either she is beautiful or she is not. A hairweave automatically robs you of your *naturalness*; however, the ad implies that you are not beautiful without long hair, thus, the closest a nappy-headed woman like you can hope to be is a *natural-looking* beauty, not a natural beauty. Natural-looking means to look natural. Why become unnatural to look natural? Even the ad is unwittingly saying that natural is better than the weave and/or makeup. (That's right! Become a natural-looking beauty with a flowing weave and makeup) An ugly woman is not made beautiful by tricks—anymore than a beautiful woman is make ugly by the lack of tricks. The problem is perception. Whose image of beauty are you relying on, your creator's or the one who will call you beautiful only after you pay them? Remember, it was the fake hair and cosmetic industry that convinced you *and the world* that you were ugly without makeup and long hair in the first place.

When a female cancer patient loses her hair from chemotherapy does she become ugly? If she had a man that she caught because she had long <u>natural</u> or <u>fake</u> hair, she will lose him because a relationship built on superficial things, is a superficial relationship. The same thing holds true with your very own natural beautiful legs, if that's the only thing you have going on. If you loss a leg; you will also lose your man and your will to live. Your spirit and your man is not the type that will love you just as much with one leg.

The grand prize in life is love, although, youth, beauty and money have lots of pursuers. Money often creates false friends. Beauty is a fickle perception, and youth has no loyalty; yet, many spend their life chasing these temporal solutions to happiness. When your version of beauty is worn thin by the rising and setting of the sun and your cherished youth has snuck out in the middle of the night, the best that you can hope for is to be loved. If you run a good race and acquire love and friendship you are truly blessed.

Most women are endowed with a good measure of common sense and therefore, indulge in practices that sound sensible, as told to them by other women, such as *you can catch more flies with honey than you can vinegar*. That is the type of logic that causes women to set themselves up to attract *flies*. They often miss out on the type of men that are committed to one woman instead they get a man that *flies* from one woman to the next. When a woman invests much of her time in shopping, to keep up with the latest fashion, and is always in a tizzy about her hair, then she is investing too much time in coating herself with honey to catch flies. Love is seldom attracted by honey—a fling perhaps, but seldom love. The American standard of beauty is all about pouring on the honey, artificial honey at that. Love is attracted by honesty and American women are not taught to be honest—in fact, quite to the contrary. From the feet up, you will find dishonesty in the average American woman. From her toenails to the top of her head and several places in between there is dishonesty.

Women that spend a disproportionate emphasis on her superficial beauty attract superficial men. These types of men fall in love with feminine body parts, but not women. Women who have invested in artificial breasts and women who flaunt naturally large breasts are at risk of attracting breasts-men. What happens to her breasts-man if life presents her with breasts cancer and she gets a mastectomy? Her breasts-man will then be forced to get to know her, the human being for the first time. Perhaps nothing so drastic as cancer will occur but definitely gravity will tap at the door of her body. Superficial men love body parts and endure the woman that comes with their favorites parts.

Physical beauty fades like the scent of flowers in a vase. Men who love young body parts will not endure old body parts. Women that want love throughout their life must not use bait that will vanish with time. False hair and breasts implants are examples of catching men with honey—instead of with the spirit. The libido of a woman (or man) is likely to diminish with aging and/or episodes of depression and/or sickness. Relationships built on sexual attraction will surely suffer when the inevitable cycle of life moves in; however, if one is not a slave to the superficial and temporal embellishments of the physical, a relationship that can endure to the end may develop. Even movie stars for abandoned by the movie and cosmetic industry when the naturalness of life intervenes.

Women mature old more gracefully than men. At a certain level of maturity a woman with commonsense will not be interested in the superficial. She may allow her natural graying and thinning hair to breathe. The interest of the superficial man that she attracted years ago with her superficial hair might waiver towards a younger woman as often demonstrated. More often than not, women that spend much time chasing beauty ends up alone and bewildered, while the less provocative lady down the street has been (sometimes happily, sometimes unhappily) married to the same man fifty years. I have studied this phenomenon, which is the untold story of women obsessed with the American standard of beauty—they grow old alone or with flies that swarm other women. Women should abandon the vanities taught to them before they become set in their ways. Does anyone ever stop to consider that the beautifully made-up, designed, and sculptured people that the movie and cosmetic industry created has a higher divorce rate than the general population? Apparently the longevity of happiness is not all about long hair, big breasts, and dazzling smiles. Some of the most so-called beautiful people (of all races) have been married and divorced multiple times. A few marriages barely make it through the honeymoon.

God offers you beauty in exchange for the ashes of your mind, joy for mourning, and praise for a spirit of heaviness. The Bible says in Isaiah 61: 3—*To appoint unto them that mourn in Zion, to give unto them beauty for ashes, the oil of joy for mourning, the garment of praise for the spirit of heaviness; that they might be called trees of righteousness, the planting of the LORD, that he might be glorified.*

Let the self-hatred ingrained in your culture crash and burn to ashes. Gather those ashes and hand it over to the Lord and He will give you the beauty of self-confidence in exchange. I assure you God's gift of beauty will not be a free cosmetic makeover from L'Oreal or free wigs and hairweaves until Judgment Day.

If would be wonderful if young girls were taught to truly feel good about themselves instead of the American standard of beauty lessons, which is a highly infectious condition.

Your Legacy

What type of ancestor do you want to be? What is the life lesson you choose to leave? You have a choice—we all do. You can pass on the Jim Crow lessons that was passed on to you through the media and perhaps your foremothers and forefathers. You can endorse the idea that your beauty is found only in drastically altering the texture of your hair, the tone of your skin, and/or reconstructing your genetic facial features. Somebody in your family must be the example that challenges this connived anti-black system. Someone must express to the future generation by way of example that beauty begins self-love. The biblical scriptures teach to love others as you do yourself. Without it there is no outside substance that can suffice.

Someone must be the role model for your family, the children—their children. Don't leave it in the hands of the America media and cosmetic industry. They will send the subliminal message, as they told your ancestors—in not so mild of terms, that your natural beauty is ugly, your natural hair is savage, and your only salvation is through an identity makeover. Don't be a carrier of the self-hatred seed.

The condition and set of values that you inherited by your ancestors, if it was not a proud cultural heritage, is not your fault and therefore you should not wallow in submerged grief about your devalued identity. However, it is your responsibility to teach by word and example that the legacy and dignity stolen centuries ago is indeed the cause of so much mental anguish, confusion, unexplained anger, substance abuse, and self-denial among your people today. You are not empowered to give back what was stolen but you are empowered to be a beacon of the future and not to perpetuate the ancestral abomination.

That Gal Latasha

When that gal Latasha was sixteen years old
She worn her T-shirts wet
With no bra underneath
To dazzle the men she met

When that gal Latasha was twenty-one
She wore purple contact lens
She said cat eyes doubled her chances
To make some midnight friends

When that gal Latasha was twenty-eight
She danced nude at the all-night bar
The tips from men was her reward
They treated her like a movie star

By the time Latasha turned thirty-five
She loved her blue hair weave

It matched the blue diamond in her nose
In her world of make-believe

When that gal Latasha was forty-nine
Her man found a gal nineteen
She fought back with all her tricks
Even dyed her blue weave green

Latasha caught her flies with honey
She never had a lick of self-confidence
It finally occurred to her that all a good man wants
Is a natural woman that has good sense

Latasha told she daughter Keneesha
Not to waste her time dangling temporal bait
Keneesha danced at the all-night bar
With orange hair at twenty-eight

6

Changing Times

The 60s and early 70s steam of black pride has long evaporated. Very few African-Americans still wore African clothing in the "Say it Loud, I'm Black and Proud" tradition. By the 80s, the Afro hairdo was merely a relic of Black Power. Cornrows, braids, and dreadlocks sailed through the community as small vessels in the night amidst cosmetic warships armed with tons of human hairs from India. The new wave on the sea of vicissitude was the Jheri Curl. The semi-relaxed curly style was a switch from chemically straightened hair to chemically curled hair. Other than the occasional sores in your head from the chemical treatment, the burning from the application, the itching days after the application, the oily stains on your clothing and furniture from the heavily oil saturated hairdo, everything was cool.

It was the 90s and rap was in. No more "Say It Loud—I'm Black and Proud." The rappers were determined to *keep-it-real*. The men were no longer called brothers in songs but niggas and dawgs (nigga spelled different than nigger was a term of endearment, and dawg spelled different than dog meant friend). Rappers even celebrated and redefined the word 'Pimp'. Transposing it from a man who makes a living extorting gullible and/or enslaved prostitutes to a man of honor and a symbol of *the good life*. Ultimately, a rapper best known by his stage name Nelly commercialized and further glorified the term 'Pimp' with a song and beverage by the name Pimp Juice, which most mature, socially conscious and/or educated black females found offense. Outrage by the black community kept Pimp Juice out of mainstream markets. That was a violation of the Law of Reciprocity, which is similar to karma. You should not selfishly and/or greedily use the root profit principle knowing that to do so will harm or offend the innocent.

Youth crime plagued urban American and the Bloods and Crips street gangs became the nightmare of every African-American mother with a son under 30 years old. Drug dealing and violence was celebrated lyrically. The prison population rose to an all time high with black male and female inmates. Females were no longer the recipients of love songs but were the subjects of derogatory lyrics by rap artists. This new era of young men with the strange new 'talent' were oblivious and or apathetic to the documented historical fact that if it were not for black women banning together in great forces against the lynch laws, black males would have been lynched in much greater numbers for a longer length of time. Now these strange entertainers were calling black females bitches and hoes—in music. No other race resorted to this 'keeping it real' tactic of making money.

What is 'keeping it real'? Is the message regardless of all the good that the black community tries to do it is in vain and beneath it all lies the truth, which is blacks are nothing but niggas, hoes, dawgs, and bitches? The racist whites went on terror hiatus because African-Americans had become their own worst nightmare. Hardly a day went by throughout the United States that a black mother was not seen on the TV news crying over the senseless death of her male or female (usually teenage male) child. The make an ugly era even uglier, young African-Americans loved the gangster rap music, which blatantly and effectually lead many youth to crime. Their spirit of youth was slowly and quietly lowed into a state of oblivion. The rap artists were fast becoming icons and dubious role models. African-Americans were no longer claiming to be 'Black and Proud' but 'Thugs' instead. Females began to proclaim that they preferred thugs. Boys began to act up more, on a quest to prove that they were thugs. They slowly lowered their pants until the waistline of the trousers were below their buttocks as seen on Rap Videos.

During this era, I became convinced that no matter how idiotic a behavior, if it is seen on TV often enough it becomes the status quo among the immature and those with a flawed self-image. It was riveting to observe so many modern day black males act like developmentally retarded boys. White men referred to black men as boys less than 25 years earlier and it was considered belittling. In 1968, black garage men picketed for equal employment rights in Memphis and carried signs proclaiming I AM A MAN. Now, black adult males are dancing and singing about being thugs.

Lovelorn females endorsed the behavior of the immature males; yet, the males withheld their support of black females and failed to appreciate their natural beauty. The fact is that both genders suffer from insecurities. Society toys with black males about their masculinity and females about their appearance. When we take a look at what is really going on, we began to see traps all around us. Look at the ridiculousness of black males as their pants sag like a baby's soiled diaper. This act is rooted in a misguided effort to demonstrate manhood, coupled by the need for attention. If they were not made to feel so inadequate in the first place they would not feel compelled to act so menacing.

The need for attention drives outrageous behavior and subculture fashion for most insecure people. The sudden attention could serve to uplift a downtrodden spirit as well as foster a sense of superiority. Once they have captured attention, they are flattered, although they pretend indifferent or annoyed. Males wearing earrings once captured attention but has loss its magnetism. There are way too many copy cats and therefore it is no longer a subculture. Yet some males feel obliged to justify their feminine persona. The average black male rationalization is that he is man enough not to be intimidated by wearing earrings—yet some are elementary and middle school students. Furthermore, as a result of our history in America, many black males counteract the feeling of underclass by being materialistic and adorning themselves with "bling-bling" and trinkets.

In every person's life there is insecurity, which can be characterized as a weak link. It is the job of their adversary to discovery that weak link and use it against them. That is the reason sport teams seek to get a copy of their opponents practice tapes so they can discover the weaknesses and decide how to defeat that team. Boxers watch recorded tapes of their next opponent's fights. Governments all over the world send spies to foreign countries to gather intelligence so they can capitalize on the weak link. Once your insecurity is discovered, you are rendered vulnerable. Do you realize that human predators roam like lions seeking out whom they can devour? When a child molester detects insecurity in a child he or she seeks a long-term friendship with that child. One of the surest sign of an insecure girl is her obvious yearning for attention. This is apparent by their tattoos, piercings, make-up, hairstyle, and other superficial accessories.

While I was interviewing criminals for my first book in the early 90s called Tips Against Crime, Written from Prison I learned that child molesters could spot an insecure girl on first sight. Insecure adult women are also easily spotted and swayed. Females who use their cosmetic beauty as their calling card often becomes the sexual puppets of men in every walk of life but especially in the movie, video, modeling, and music industry.

In 1998, in was reported in an investigative report on the pornography industry that over a million females from early teens to late forties aspire to be porn stars. The one thing that most have in common is their mindset that they can make it off sex appeal alone. They soon become a slave to the superficial world of sex appeal. It is easy to understand why so many drop out of high school or college and head for the dim lights of the sex industry.

One such young woman and mother lowered herself to the level of sleeping with dozens of rappers, actors, and movie industry executives. She was passed around like a football on Sunday afternoon; however this victim of the American standard of beauty culture turned the tables on the men who used her like a sex toy and wrote a tell-all book in 2001 called <u>Confessions of a Video Vixen</u> by Karrine Steffan. This is what *Pimp Hop Internet Magazine* writer Leslie C. Alessandro said about her just prior in an interview:

"Once video chick Karrine Steffans speaks out about her life, the celebrities she slept with, the rape that changed her life forever and her book <u>Confessions of a Video Vixen.</u>

Not since Delilah tamed Samson has one woman made so many men run for cover. Not since Monica Lewinsky, has one woman made oral sex the topic of the hood, the media as well as the "ghetto glitterati". To some Karrine Steffans is a traitor. To others she is simply a hoe that was able to have a brief "come up" with some of today's most celebrated artist and superstars. For many, she is despised because unlike most of the girls in Los Angeles who have done the same thing and then some, you know, give "head" as they say, Karrine unlike her "Cali counterparts" was able to parlay serious cash wire transfers, gain the confidence of multi-millionaires as well as parlay a pending movie deal. Oh please forgive me let's not forget the book deal with a prestigious NY publishing house. I don't know about the "other video" girls that have given head to video directors, artist and "back up dancers" but I will say this, they need to line up and take classes from Steffans.

There is more to Steffans than meets the eye. When one looks back at most women who end up disrespecting themselves only to gain favor from men who aren't deemed worthy, you often find a person who has suffered some form of abuse. This is surely the case for Karrine Steffans. There was a time in her life when Karrine's confidence had been broken, not only by the people she loved and cared about, but by those who saw her as nothing more than a pleasurable tool and a means to an end. Fortunately for Karrine, her life turned around and instead of being a "victim" for the rest of her life she took control and became the victor."

In the book Steffans tell of the whorish lifestyle she and many other video girls endure as sex objects in their quest for fame. A sex object is an object to be used for sex—nothing more. Steffan did not fully comprehend that her chosen ambition as a sex object was fulfilled. A woman cannot market herself as an object and later want the respect of a living breathing person. In the Court of Rap Music (where raging testosterone is the judge and jury) an object has no rights, which any man is bound to respect. In the domain of highly sex-charged young men an object is considered as inhuman as blacks were in the Dred Scott Decision of

1857 when the Supreme Court declared that blacks had "no rights" which the white man was bound to respect.

Steffans reportedly walked off the Tyra Banks Show on 11/28/05 after Tyra showed distain to her for exposing the names of the famous hip-hop artists with whom she reportedly slept. Steffans later said in an interview that Tyra Banks herself had slept with many of the same men and many more in her rise to the top and has false breasts and the glorious hair on her head is a very expense blonde hairweave. Tyra responded to the claims by having a breast exam on her national TV show to prove her fleshy endowment was a gift of God. However, her did not address the hair issue perhaps because she has been very open about her hairweave.

In her book, Steffans says that she is now all about truth and honesty and that pretty girls in the video world are treated as nothing but whores. The following is an excerpt of an interview with Karrine Steffans:

Steffans tells the New York Daily News, "Banks insisted I wrote 'Confessions' because I was angry and wanted revenge. She said, 'These are my colleagues. They're people I know well!' Despite what she thinks, she and I are not that different. I have even heard her being referred to as a 'Hollywood Hop,' for the many men in Hollywood who have bedded her and moved on. I was so angry all I could think about was snatching her wig off!"

There is a general resemblance to Banks and Steffans, both light skin, blondish hair, grey or green eyes, small waist, heavy makeup, and large breasts. Steffans now pursues a legitimate acting career but confesses she allowed her looks to lure her into whoredom. She was seldom complimented on her intelligence—but often on her beauty. In my conservative estimate, Steffans is only one out of millions of females who are slaves to superficial beauty. Nonetheless, to her credit, she has allegedly overcome her promiscuity and drug use brought on by low self-esteem, lack of confidence, and obsession with being accepted.

Moreover, none of the light skinned mixed race video girls are respected. In December 2006 issue of *Essence Magazine*, hip-hop artist and singer Kanye West said, "If it wasn't for race mixing, there'd be no video girls. [Me] and most of my friends like mutts a lot. Yeah, in the 'hood they call 'em mutts." A mutt is a cross-bred dog or a dog with an unknown pedigree. That is an awful name to call young black women because of their light skin. Apparently it is easier to mistreat a woman once she is dehumanized. These light skin girls are preferred for videos but are treated as disposable mutts. So where does a dark skinned or light skinned black woman go to receive love and respect if not internally? Apparently, the long hairweaves bring no respect. In their desperate quest to be accepted the only thing most superficial females get is disrespected; even by the men they worship. I suspect that false hair and layers of makeup on dark skin women and *mutts* auditioning for work is the first flashing sign men notice that broadcast their vulnerability.

During slavery the mulatto females were most preferred by white men to abuse. In modern times they are most preferred by black men to abuse. However, during the Jim Crow era most mulatto women preferred to be sexually used by a white man than loved by a black man. The tragic mulatto story is no myth.

To Tyra Banks moral account, (I must show appreciation where appreciation is due) she works indigently to teach naïve young women the pitfalls of the modeling industry; the scams, the financial and sexual conspiracies against them including rape and murder. Tyra often speaks about these horrors on her show. Yet to her chagrin, the aspiring models lured by the false security of their beauty rather than intelligence are the most vulnerable and easiest accessible females around.

In November 2006, Tyra TV show setup a phony modeling scam by renting a hotel suite and using phony photographers and phony makeup artists to see how many females would fall for it. The TV show placed ads in various newspapers for models. A very large number of girls showed. Within a short while all but one of the applicants were talked out of her clothes down to her bare skin. Trya then barges into the room and reveal the scam. Most of girls were so embarrassed that they gathered their clothes and fled in shame without giving Tyra a full interview. Hidden cameras aired to whole thing.

If it is your appearance that is your weakest link—some opportunist will have just the right makeup, wig, sex video opportunity, or bargain nose job. Speaking of nose jobs, Jews are stereotyped with having larger than average noses. This feature is sometimes the basis for anti-Semitic images. After World War II Jews coming to America sought nose jobs so they would not be discriminated against. The nose job became a popular way for Jews to look less Jewish, according to an article in the *Jewish News of Greater Phoenix*. Many people changed their surname so that they can hide their true nationality and/or ethnicity for example: actress Winona Ryder is Jewish, and her birth name is Laura Winona Horowitz; singer Vickie Carr is Hispanic, and her birth name is Florencia Bisenta de Casillas Martinez Cardona. Many people, because of prejudices in society, are compelled to make their ethnicity less obvious though it is a self-loathing thing to do. African-Americans are not alone in trying the cover their identity because of racial and appearance discrimination although their cover-up is harder to ... *cover-up*.

The scriptures in Genesis 3: 7–11 is a good example of what we go through in our insecurities. When God called Adam and Eve they tried to cover their nakedness. They had suddenly become ashamed of who they were and how God created them. The serpent had been talking to Eve and she in turn influenced Adam. So they hid from God because of their nakedness. And God asked, "Who told you that you were naked?" God is asking black people, "Who told you that your hair was bad?" And the black man says, "Your white folks!" And then God ask, "What's that on your head?" And the black woman says, "It's 100% human hair Lord, I bought it from your Koreans. The American standard of beauty promised it would make me naturally beautiful and even YOU would love me more." Then the Lord does a double-take at the black woman and she quickly says, "They're breasts implants Lord. The American standard of beauty …"

Genesis 3

7—Then the eyes of both of them were opened, and they realized that they were naked; so they sewed fig leaves together and made loincloths for themselves.

8—When they heard the sound of the LORD God moving about in the garden at the breezy time of the day, the man and his wife hid themselves from the LORD God among the trees of the garden.

9—The LORD God then called to the man and asked him, "Where are you?"

10—He answered, "I heard you in the garden; but I was afraid, because I was naked, so I hid myself."

11—Then he asked, "Who told you that you were naked?

◆   ◆   ◆

Dr. Cornwell Strives to Make A Different

After earning her doctoral degree from the University of Irvine in 1984, Dr. JoAnne Cornwell became an Associate Professor of Africana Studies and French at San Diego State University. On campus, Dr. Cornwell observed that the majority of African-Americans on campus were female. This revelation disturbed her. Dr. Cornwell sought a method to do something of a positive nature that would attract more males to college. She began to speak-out more at schools, civic groups, churches, and social organizations with a focus on African-American youth. Her message to them was to stay in school and become entrepreneurs in a field in which they enjoyed. Dr. Cornwell knew the problem was bigger than a hundred mentors could eradicate and her lone efforts would barely make a dent but at least it was an effort to reach a few.

Dr. Cornwell became the personal surrogate big sister and mentor to several young black women on and off campus. Sometimes they met at her San Diego home where she braided their hair and also taught them the art of natural hair care. During these didactic sessions the protégés would be informally lectured on self-pride, saving money, and preparing for their future. In an effort to counter a negative self-image in the young people, Dr. Cornwell spoke to them about the pessimistic messages in the music of their generation and how it subliminally becomes a part of their mindset and the way they viewed themselves. She challenged each young woman to begin to see herself differently and expect better out of life.

It is a peculiar sensation, this double-consciousness, this sense of always looking at one's self through the eyes of others.... One ever feels his twoness—an American, a Negro; two souls, two thoughts, two unreconciled strivings; two warrings ideals in one dark body, whose dogged strength alone keeps it from being torn asunder.

—<u>W.E.B. Du Bois</u> (1868–1963) *The Souls of Black Folk (1903)*

Debate Goes to Another Level

In June 1997, California's Department of Consumer Affairs (DCA), posing as state police officers, staged a "sting" operation at a popular braiding salon in Los Angeles, Braids & Dreads by Samantha. An undercover female investigator spent five hours having her hair braided by shop owner Samantha Ryan. After paying her eighty-dollars with four twenties, she excused herself to the bathroom and returned in a DCA jacket while communicating on a walkie-talkie. Four more DCA investigators, two females and two males barged through the front door with one hand on their gun and the other flashing a badge, as later reported by Ryan. They searched her shop and seized appointment books, hair spray, scissors, and clipped hair from the floor as evidence. Ryan was told that if she resisted the search that she would be arrested. The customers present thought that they were witnessing a drug raid but that was not the case. Before leaving the raiders took the names and identities of all the customers including photographs and told the shocked patrons that they were aiding and abetting a crime by patronizing an unlicensed hair operator. The officer that got her hair braided retrieved the four marked twenty-dollar bills from the cash register and photographed them then stuffed them in a brown evidence bag along with the hair spray, scissors, appointment book, and hair clippings. Ryan was given a written citation to appear in court.

Samantha Ryan was cited for braiding hair without a cosmetology license, which carried a stiff fine and/or time in jail. During this era, several states were trying to force braiders to become licensed. In past time this was not a problem but in the late 80s braids became popular and many black women were styling them. City officials were alerted that hundreds of braiders operated out of their homes without licenses and hundreds of thousands of dollars in licensing fees were being deprived from the city. Suddenly a braider sweep across the nation swung into action.

Ryan and other African-style braiders refused to be licensed. They did not feel that the cosmetology laws applied to them because they were not using chemicals on hair while during braids and dreadlocks. The official position on the matter was that the state cosmetology regulations had authority over anyone who earned money by hairstyling.

The 37-year-old single mother of three was fined for the same charge the previous year but this was the first time that she had be raided in such a fashion; however, she was aware that such a thing could happen because a nearby braiding salon had been raided a week prior.

The cosmetology industry was a billion dollar per year revenue and the fact that women were now braiding hair, which was estimated to be worth millions annually, was money the government was not going to let go easy. As long as black women were wearing press and curls, perms, and other relaxed hair treatments, even wigs and hair extensions everything was fine. It is extremely profitable for a great number of people, including local and state government, for black women not to shun their naturalness and embrace the American standard of beauty. The raid was reported by the newspaper to be more of a show of force more than anything else and to intimate the braiders who had filed a lawsuit in protest of the licensing requirements.

Recent legal victories favoring braiders led state boards to step up enforcement of licensing laws and engage in what braiders viewed as undue harassment. In states such as New York, Missouri, Texas, California, Ohio, and South Carolina investigators, often accompanied by police, have threatened to lock up braiders, their customers, and fine the landlord as if he or she was knowing allowing an illegal activity. All of the braiders being charged and threatened were African-American women—some of whom started braiding to make the transition from welfare to work.

Cases such as Samantha's were piling up by the week. Raids were taking place throughout the United States. A young African-American woman in South Carolina named Rita Robinson, owner of Miss Queen Braiding Salon, reported to her attorney that she had being made a scapegoat. Robinson's shop was the only all-braiding salon in the city. The state board issued her a cease and desist order and threatened to lock her up if she continued. Miss Queen Braiding Salon was only open for four months but the investigators had raided her eight times. The police often parked their cars outside her shop while they took long breaks. Consequently, Robinson's customers stopped coming.

At the center of the licensing debate were questions of economic opportunity for African-Americans, particularly women, and control over what many considered to be a cultural art form, braiding hair. Nothing was special about it; their mothers, and grandmothers for as long as any braider could recall had braided hair on the front porch, in the backyard, and the kitchen before they went to school. Many braiders, who mostly were religious women, began to gather in churches and at various salons at night to discussion the injustice. One particular female minister, Reverend Frances Brown (not her real name) from Watts, California, who also wore braids, became involved after the Samantha Ryan incident. Reverend Brown opened her church doors for meetings. The general consensus was that God was involved in the whole matter. Reverend Brown led the prayer services and told the group of braiders that God had given them a natural plantation, their scalp, natural seeds, their roots, and a natural crop, their chemical-free hair and no man had anything to do with it. Reverend Brown told them that God had given them heavenly *reparation* for the suffering that America would or could never repay. Many braiders, beyond the city limits of Los Angeles, saw the new wave of braiders and braid wearers across the nation as reparation for slavery because African-Americans being ashamed of their hair was a direct vestige of slavery, which backfired in the face of white America and created a hair craze from Madame C.J. Walker to a potential multi-billion dollar empire for African-Americans.

The cosmetology lobby insisted that public health and safety interest demand braiders be regulated. Braiders said the industry's position has little to do with health and safety and everything to do with economics—wanting to control a fledgling industry that had quickly become a promising source of mega-wealth for independent black women.

African-Americans in general saw the burdensome licensing requirements placed on the braiders as roadblocks to entrepreneurship. (In New York State, to be licensed, as a hairbraider, required 900 hours of training. New York created a separate license for natural hairstyling in 1992. But no cosmetology school in the state offered a course of study to complete such a license.) California's cosmetology code, similar to those in 48 other states, mandates that braiders like Samantha Ryan attend cosmetology school—at fees of up to $1200 for a nine-month to two-year program—during which time they would learn nothing about their chosen profession. Cosmetology schools did not teach African-style hairbraiding—or any method of treating black hair in its natural state—nor did they test it on licensing exams. Most braiders learned from relatives or friends; it was a cultural practice that extended back to Africa. Dreadlocks, on the other hand, roots were in Jamaica beginning as a religious belief in the Rastafarian faith. Both of the styles expressed a sense of renewed pride, neither required chemicals, and both were profitable.

The venom of self-hatred injected into the minds during and after slavery that caused African-Americans to distance themselves from the image of Africa was beginning to wear off. Many African-Americans believed that as more and more black women turned to natural hairstyles, less and less of their money went into the hands of the large chemically based ethnic hair industry. It was the powerful ethnic hair industry behind the sudden interest in shutting down braiding shops before the craze for natural hair grew out of control. Can you image the confusion that would be created if black people actually started loving themselves? Gradually many police would be out of work and black students would aspire an education in unheard of numbers. More than licensing fees were at stake for the states. There were also hundreds of millions of dollars at stake for the cosmetology schools and most of all; the hair relaxer industry was at risk of losing billions of dollars annually. The idea of black people taking pride in their natural hair was a threat to a lot of people. Who knows, if something like that got out-of-hand it could cause black-on-black crime to gradually decrease and God only knows what a financial burden that could cause the prison industry.

Cornwell v. California Board of Barbering and Cosmetology

On January 28, 1997, the Institute for Justice filed a lawsuit in federal district court in San Diego challenging California's cosmetology licensing statute and regulations on behalf of practitioners of African hairbraiding and other forms of natural hairstyling. The cosmetology laws needlessly stifle job and entrepreneurial opportunities and suppress a vibrant means of cultural expression.

The ramifications of this lawsuit extended far beyond the individuals involved. Occupational licensing laws throughout the United States restricted entry into hundreds of professions. Particularly at a time when welfare reform emphasized the transition from dependency to work, it was essential to curb regulatory barriers that impeded creation of jobs and enterprises. This lawsuit directly challenged the boundaries of state power to regulate entry into businesses and professions. Their attorneys claimed the braiders were an asset to welfare reform and society in general.

Welfare reform is the name for a policy change in the state-administered social welfare system to reduce dependence on welfare, as demanded by political conservatives. The reasons for instituting welfare reform usually include:

• objections to the cost of social welfare

• desire to minimize the culture of poverty fostered by the welfare system

• negative work ethics of people who live off welfare

• a perceived lack of incentive for welfare recipients to search for a job

Before welfare reform in1996, welfare payments were distributed through a program known as Aid to Families with Dependent Children (AFDC). In the 1980s, the program drew heavy criticism. There were numerous stories of "welfare queens", women who cheated the welfare system by receiving multiple checks each month and growing wealthy while not working. Many critics claimed that welfare bred a poor work incentive and a self-perpetuation "culture of poverty" in which ambitions focused on staying on welfare and avoiding productive work.

President Bill Clinton had promised to "end welfare as we know it" in his State of the Union Address. The welfare reform movement reached its apex on August 22, 1996, when President Clinton signed a welfare reform bill, officially titled the *Personal Responsibility and Work Opportunity Reconciliation Act of 1996*. The bill was hammered out in a compromise with the Republican-controlled Congress, and many Democrats were critical of Clinton's decision to sign the bill, saying it was much the same as the two previous welfare reform bills he had vetoed.

In this new climate of African braiders and natural hair stylists, hundreds of former single mothers once on welfare had discovered a profession that provided for their family. Women were anxious and proud of their new independence. Dr. Cornwell was considered an outlaw and an enemy of the state for training women in the art of Sisterlocks. Braids and Locks were becoming the new non-chemical "permanent."

The plaintiffs in the lawsuit filed in San Diego were Dr. JoAnne Cornwell, the American Hairbraiders and Natural Hair Care Association, and the Braiderie, a San Diego braiding salon. This lawsuit was a cornerstone of efforts to restore economic liberty-the right to work for an honest living as a fundamental civil right.

"The woman who follows the crowd will usually go no farther than the crowd. The woman who walks alone is likely to find herself in places no one has ever been before."

—Albert Einstein

The Art and Business of HairBraiding

Hairbraiding is more than a means of entrepreneurship; it is an important form of cultural expression. Ever since African slaves were brought to the United States, the characteristically textured hair of African-descended people has been an important facet of the badge of racial inferiority stamped upon African-Americans. As historian Noliwe M. Rooks recounts, in her 1996 book, Hair Raising, that both African slaves in the South and free African-Americans in the North were taught to view straight light-colored hair as the paramount expression of female beauty. Following emancipation, products and advertising directed toward black women was built upon this racial ideology. Rooks found that advertisements for skin lighteners and hair straighteners marketed by white companies during the late 19th and early 20th centuries suggested to African-Americans that only through changing physical features will persons of African descent be afforded class mobility and social acceptance by the dominant culture. Racial self-hatred promoted by such practices was an important bulwark of the Jim Crow regime.

In the minds of many African-Americans, the dominant standard of beauty continues to be defined in white terms, and black women (particularly professionals) have struggled to comport with this definition, often at great damage to their hair and self-esteem. Doing the natural hair revolution, traditional African hairstyles geared toward the natural texture and beauty of black hair emerged and steadily gained popularity. The hairstyles were remarkably artistic and individualized, and avoided the serious damage that can occur when hair is treated with chemicals and other artificial products. Dr. JoAnne Cornwell has said, "Our issues are significantly different than those our fore-mothers-aunts-sisters faced. Today, no one is making us not accept and celebrate what we really are on any level. We have the ability to set new standards based on our unique and stunning natural attributes, and it is high time we began seriously asking ourselves what symbols we are wearing on our heads."

Natural hair care has grown into a multi-million dollar industry, with specialized products and training. Because it requires fairly little capital and modest training, in a free and open market the natural hair care industry would have unlimited potential to provide entrepreneurial and employment opportunities, as well as popular services and products to millions of consumers.

HairBraiding and Occupational Licensing

Nearly 500 occupations are regulated by states, and about half of those require state licenses. Occupations requiring government licenses include not only the medical, legal, and other highly specialized professions, but also professions in which justification for restrictions on entry is virtually nonexistent, such as beekeepers, lightning rod salesmen, fence installers, and septic tank cleaners. In all, occupational licensing laws govern entry into about ten percent of all jobs in America. Barbers and beauticians require licenses in all 50 states.

Typically, licensing boards are comprised of members of the regulated profession with the coercive power of government at their disposal. As a result, licensing requirements often exceed valid public health and safety objectives, and instead are used to reduce competition from newcomers. As economist Walter Williams observes, these laws and regulations "discriminate against certain people," particularly "outsiders, latecomers and those without resources," among which members of minority groups disproportionately are represented.

Ironically, the licensing laws that restricted hairbraiders were put in place during the 1930s by hairdressers (today's cosmetologists), who at that time, were the renegades fighting an entrenched monopoly. Prior to the 1920s, barbers and cosmeticians (who performed skin care and some hair cutting) enjoyed an exclusive monopoly, bestowed by government through occupational licensing laws, over all types of hair treatment. Hairdressers were arrested in several states for violating the licensing laws. During that time, hairdressers organized their own trade association and sought to break the barbers' monopoly through lobbying and litigation. The following resolution, passed by National Hairdressers Association at its 1923 convention, parallels the hairbraiders' struggle of the 1990s:

Resolved, while expressing our good will to those engaged in business as barbers and repudiating any thought of encroaching on the domain of their work or of soliciting the patronage of men for work ordinarily done in the barber shop, we condemn the antagonistic legislation which would attempt to classify as barbers and subject to bar-

bers' laws those who are engaged in the practice of our profession, and we assert the right of engaging in all work ordinarily done in the hairdressing and beauty parlor on women and children, free from the domination of barbers' laws.

The cosmetologists ultimately succeeded in freeing themselves from the barbers' monopoly and obtaining a separate licensing process through which they then created a state-enforced cartel of their own that subjects everyone engaged in the care or styling of women's hair, skin, or fingernails to their domination. It is a cartel the National Cosmetology Association today fiercely protects.

The California cosmetology law is typical of licensing laws around the country. Enacted in the 1930s, the statute places regulation of all hairstyling under the control of the State Board of Barbering and Cosmetology, which is comprised of five public members and four members representing the professions. The board, in turn, issues and enforces extensive regulations, including 1,600 hours of prescribed training in approved cosmetology schools and an examination. Schools, instructors, and salons also must obtain licenses. In 1982, the Attorney General issued an opinion finding that hairbraiding is covered by cosmetology licensing requirements, even though cosmetology schools do not teach it and the licensing examination does not test it. The entire system creates a mismatch between regulatory objectives and realities. In the name of protecting public health and safety, the regulatory process licenses people who have no practical experience in certain services, yet forbids people who are proficient in those same services.

Hairbraiders and other natural hairstylists face special barriers under the licensing regime. Neither the prescribed cosmetology course nor the examination covers hairbraiding, but they do require extensive training and proficiency in hairstyles and techniques (such as the use of chemicals) that are unrelated to hairbraiding. The effect was that in order to lawfully offer hairbraiding services, a person must take a nine-month course costing several thousand dollars and pass an examination, neither of which has anything whatsoever to do with the services that would be offered to the public. Nor can hairbraiders viably operate their own training programs: their curricula would not qualify for licensure under the cosmetology laws, nor would their graduates qualify for the licensing examination, even if they are completely proficient in the services they wish to offer to the public. And without a license, hairbraiders cannot lawfully offer their services to the public regardless of proficiency. No separate or specialized license is available for braiding, even though separate licenses are offered for others who specialize in nails, skin, or electrolysis.

As a result, most braiders are compelled to conform to the arbitrary ruling, give up their profession, or to operate outside the law and, ironically, outside the reach of health and safety regulations. The authorities generally have turned a blind eye to home-based salons. However, when braiders attempt to go "legitimate" by applying for capital or opening salons outside their homes, they find their efforts barred by the absence of a license. Obviously, neither entrepreneurs nor consumers were served well by the current system.

The Controversy Continued

The lawsuit challenged the constitutionality of subjecting hairbraiding and natural hairstyling to the cosmetology licensing laws. The plaintiffs did not object to legitimate health and safety regulations-indeed, they had developed their own training and safety standards but did object to a system that seeks to destroy and illegitimize their livelihoods. In terms of her own business, Dr. Cornwell planned to open her own salon and expand her training program for thousands of others, which of course were illegal under current laws. "I think it is a crime and tragedy that what I do has to be underground," says Cornwell, and she is determined to lift the barriers.

These were precisely the sorts of barriers that prompted the creation in 1995 of the American Hairbraiders and Natural Hair Care Association (AHNHA) by Taalib-din Uqdah. Uqdah and Pamela Ferrell the proprietors of Cornrows & Co., a Washington, D.C. salon. Ferrell published a self-help text entitled, Let's Talk Hair: Every Black Woman's Personal Consultation for Healthy Growing Hair. After fighting for more than a decade against District of Columbia bureaucrats who were trying to close their business, Uqdah and Ferrell decided to help others involved in similar predicaments. The association provided assistance to natural hairstylists nationwide on licensing and regulation issues and lobbies for deregulation. It published a newsletter, provides industry standards of practice and codes of conduct, and worked to develop an accreditation and certification program. Its primary mission was to protect natural hair care providers from burdensome legislation that prevents them from earning a living.

One AHNHA member that encountered severe regulatory problems is the San Diego-based Braiderie, a partnership comprised of Ali and Assiyah Rasheed and Margurite Sylva. Ali Rasheed is an entrepreneur with an extensive business background in the San Diego area. His wife, Assiyah immigrated from Senegal 18 years prior to the incident in search of a new life. She arrived with no skills, but has worked her way up the economic ladder, gained American citizenship, and managed the Braiderie's day-to-day operations. Margurite Sylva also from Senegal is a licensed cosmetologist and a master braider.

In 1994, the trio decided to open a salon, expanding Margurite Sylva's existing small business. They opened a location in San Diego, and then added a second in Oceanside. They also planned to open a salon in Senegal to facilitate a braid training exchange program. The Braiderie provided opportunities for braiders, most of whom are immigrants from Senegal and Guinea. The braiders lacked the time or money to take an expensive nine-month cosmetology course and therefore were unlicensed, although they are completely proficient in braiding. The salon ever received a consumer complaint. Nonetheless, the Board of Barbering and Cosmetology cited the Braiderie for "aiding and abetting" the unlicensed practice of hairbraiding. The salon appealed the citation.

Ali Rasheed said of the government's intrusion, "Hairbraiding offers employment opportunities for people who don't have education or skills." Nonetheless braiders begun to surface in San Diego working in mainstream hair salons or operating their own small salons. But they watched this controversy closely to see what would happen. As AHNHA's Taalib-din Uqdah explains, the effect of oppressive licensing laws is that the natural hair care industry has been clandestine.

7

Black-on-Black Racism

While the court battle to decriminalize braiding hair and natural hair care was being gallantly fought in civil court, in the court of public opinion magazine columnist and readers were buzzing with viewpoints. Below is an excerpt of an article discovered online written by Earl Ofari Hutchinson.

Nappy and proud?

This is the typical magazine ad targeted to a black female audience.

"The type of black woman who would wear red [hair] has confidence and style."

—Today's Black Woman Magazine, advertisement

A controversy long confined to African-Americans publicly exploded in recent weeks, when black 17-year-old Michelle Barskile of North Carolina made national news because she could not attend her sorority's debutante ball. That story broke just after Ruth Sherman, a white elementary school teacher in New York, had to flee her school under heavy fire from black parents.

Barskile's offense? She wore her hair in a dreadlocks style that her sorority chapter deemed unacceptable. Sherman's offense was reading passages from noted black author and scholar Carolivia Herron's book "Nappy Hair" to her mostly black and Latino students. The parents claimed she was demeaning African-Americans.

The ads in magazine targeted at black women continue to send messages of straight and relaxed hair is the way to happiness.

"Get gorgeous! Steal the spotlight with this glamorous unswept design!"

—Braids and Beauty Magazine, advertisement.

The great hair obsession among black women reflects the deep and compelling need by African-Americans to identify with and accept America's values and standards. The beauty-care industry has skillfully fed that compulsion with fantasies of physical glitter and social glamour and turned them into mammoth profits.

Hair-care product manufacturers have sold many black women on the notion that their hair is the path to self-esteem, success and sexual allure. A century ago the legendary Madame C.J. Walker built a multi-million-dollar empire on the premise that black women want to look like white women and that good hair is the path to independence and prosperity.

"Elegance, spiced with Southern flavor, begins with a mane awash in a golden blond shade."

—Today's Black Woman Magazine, advertisement

The Afro or natural look of the 1960s and the braid craze of the 1990s are touted as examples of black women rejecting white beauty standards. They aren't. The Afro style was short-lived and always more a chic fad than a revolution in black consciousness. Today's braided look is even more tightly tied to style and fashion trends, without even the pretensions of "black pride." Even many black women who sport the bald look are meanwhile fixated on matching the right clothes, makeup and earrings with the style. Many soon tire of these hair fads and retreat back to the straightening comb, extensions or a perm.

The great hair obsession is driven by the painful need of many African-Americans to conform to the dominant values of American society. And beauty, fashion and hairstyles are the most popular and perverse expressions of those values. Barskile and Sherman learned the hard way that many Africans still believe the fiction that good hair makes you, and nappy hair doesn't.

An Online Responses to Earl Ofari Hutchinson:
(12/07/98)

Had Earl Ofari Hutchinson bothered to do any research at all, he would have learned that women in "Mother Africa" have been braiding, coloring, straightening and (heaven help us) weaving their hair for centuries. I seem to recall one tribe of women in West Africa that actually handed down extension hair from one generation to the next. Shocking to think that these poor damsels were not aware that they secretly hated themselves and longed to be white women.

When black men stop shaving names and Mercedes-Benz symbols into the sides of their own heads, then and only then can they tell me what to do with my own, which I have been wearing "natural" for three years.

Hutchinson's article failed to mention that black men are at least partly responsible for the hair neurosis that many "sistahs" exhibit. When was the last time you saw a dark-skinned Nubian goddess, nappy hair and all, in any rap or R&B music video? For every black man that complements me on my naturally nappy hair there are at least 99 others who will openly disrespect me because of it, or roll their eyes and pray quietly to Jesus that "this child will run a hot comb through that mess."

I admit the black women I know are obsessed with their hair. We spend hundreds, even thousands, of dollars each year on products to care for it. The white women I know, on the other hand, are more likely to obsess on the size of their behinds. They spend hundreds and thousands of dollars on pills, potions, athletic equipment and surgery to get rid of it. If worse comes to worse, they starve themselves to death. I ask you now, which is more harmful?

—B. S.
St. Louis, MO

I agree with Earl Ofari Hutchinson that a white standard of beauty (in the way of light skin, straight hair and so on) has long been coveted by many African-Americans: It is a truth that is difficult to acknowledge. However, there is an acknowledgment and cognizance of our own pathology that exists today, and it is the first step to acquiring self-love and being proud of who and what we are. Because only when we are aware of the debilitating pathologies that the legacy of slavery has created can we begin to eradicate them.

Unlike Hutchinson, I believe we *have* come a long way. I am old enough to know that hairstyles such as "nubian knots," "dreads," "twists" or the assorted varieties of braided hairstyles, would not have been acceptable in the black community 20 years ago, let alone the white one!

These styles are not reflections of white society, by the way. They have roots in Africa. The same hairstyles Hutchinson says are an ode to American glamour and fashion consciousness were created on African soil by African women. The whole notion of "adornment" has its roots in Africa, from the ancient Egyptians to the current day Masai (who dye their long braids red by the way!). It is ironic indeed that African-American women who have a lineage that includes ancestors who created, for example, face painting, the kohl-lined eye and elaborate wigs of braids (Ramses wore hair extensions!) are today, in Hutchinson's view, "conforming" to a white standard by embracing wholeheartedly said adornments.

Historically, our freedom and love of self were oppressed to such an extreme degree that we tried to obtain a white standard of beauty, while rejecting our own. But that is changing. We've come a long way, and yes, we've even farther to go—but it would be ironic and sad indeed to make the assumption that our African lineage and history of glorious adornment plays no part in how we see ourselves today, and how we would like others to see us, or to negate the progress we have made.

Hutchinson should refrain from likening our desire to beautify ourselves to an obsessive compulsion, and see it more as carrying on a wondrous legacy, one that could not be stifled or oppressed.

—D. R.
Southfield, Mich.

In considering whether to wear a natural hairstyle, black women have to constantly think of how they will be perceived by bosses, supervisors and others. When we come to a workplace, we determine if the workplace is hospitable for us to wear our hair in whatever style and not be perceived negatively.

This is one of the main reasons why we don't go natural. Our creativity is stifled more by this society than any desire to copy white women's hairstyles. Look at the way black and white women dress: It's totally different. But we feel we have to conform in order to be not viewed negatively and to advance in our jobs. Also, because we were brought here from Africa with no combs or brushes, we had no way to care for our hair properly for hundreds of years. When Madame Walker came on the scene that was the first time we were able to take care of our hair properly. Thus, the obsessive way we view our hair.

—J. S.
Birmingham, AL

I'm a 45-year-old black woman and I still clearly remember being embarrassed as white second grade teacher read the fairytale, "Little Black Sambo" to our all black class. The other children didn't seem to mind. A week later the teacher read, "Black Beauty" and I hated that also because "Black Beauty" was about a black horse not beautiful black child. The next week she read "Heidi" a story about a lovable little white girl living with her grandfather. This experience made me desire to be white and hate being black. Since black people are so sensitive to things that white people dismiss as trivial importance, I think it would've been wise if the teacher considered the stigma placed upon African-Americans and is passed from one generation to the next. I would've been upset with the teacher also; perhaps not if she was black herself.

—T. V.
Kansas City, Kansas

In the college classes I teach, I have used the furor around <u>Nappy Hair</u> as an example of body politics. It illustrates why appearance is never simply an innocuous vehicle for each individual to express her or his identity. Hair is ideally suited to exploring the constraints of femininity, since it often represents power hierarchies among women based on class, race, and ethnicity. As Patricia Hill Collins pointed out in <u>Black Feminist Thought</u> (1990), blue-eyed, blonde, thin, white women can't be considered beautiful without black women with classical African features, dark skin, and kinky hair. In other words, the admiration of black beauty had to be heavily devalued in order to give exaggerated appreciation to white beauty. Given that two-thirds of African-American women today straighten their hair, any book celebrating nappy hair is bound to cause a stir. The slogan "black is beautiful" may have gained general acceptance across the color line, but the historical legacy of slavery and racism continues to make hair a source of contention, with different meanings for white people than for people of color.

—J. W.
Sacramento, CA

◆   ◆   ◆

Hair War, Stockholm Syndrome and The Brown Bag Test

Black cosmetologists began to lose customers to the braiders. Black women were beginning to wear braids and dreads in rapidly growing number nationally. The licensed beauticians' sentiments were strongly with the state—put them braiders out of business. Braiding hair at home became an undercover operation with all the secrecy of a drug house. Braiders peeked through peek holes before opening their heavily secured doors. They asked for passwords over the phone and spoke in code before they gave a caller an appointment. And in the typical tradition of police tactics to turn one suspect against the other, the DCA sought the aid of the cosmetologists to inform of braiders. The black community became further divided. In addition to the Bloods and the Crips drug wars, the cosmetologists and braiders were at hair war, but both were after turf.

Whenever a braider would get cited at her home or shop, she would suspect her rival the cosmetologist as the informant. In many cases the cosmetologists were falsely accused of siding with the enemy.

After slavery was abolished many African-Americans scrambled to leave the South only to discover that the South followed them. Their dark skin was an obstacle. African-Americans felt they had to convince whites that they not only respected them but also wished to look like them. Thousands of African-Americans severely damaged their skin with concoctions claiming to lighten their skin that white companies sold them through black newspapers ads. African-Americans also damaged their scalps with lye and other mixtures sold by whites that claimed to not only beautify them but also help them get accepted for a good job. Blacks begin to prefer to assimilate with white culture over their own and soon became the victims of what later became known as the Stockholm Syndrome. Today, many black comics and rappers seem to suffer from the Stockholm Syndrome as they berate black women as part of their career.

Stockholm Syndrome describes the behavior of kidnap victims who, over time, become sympathetic to their captors. The name derives from a 1973 hostage incident in Stockholm, Sweden. At the end of six days of captivity in a bank, several kidnapped victims actually resisted rescue attempts, and afterwards refused to testify against their captors. The most famous incident in the U.S. involved the kidnapped heiress Patty Hearst. Captured by a radical political group known as the Symbionese Liberation Army in 1974, Ms. Hearst eventually became an accomplice of the group, taking on the assumed name "Tania" and assisting them in several bank robberies. After her re-capture, she denounced the group and her involvement.

What causes Stockholm Syndrome? Captives begin to identify with their captors initially as a defense mechanism, out of fear of violence. Like slaves identified with the slave master and tried to please him or her. Small acts of kindness by the captor are magnified. Rescue attempts are also seen as a threat; since it is likely the captive would be injured during such attempts. Similarly, many slaves rejected Harriet Tubman's offers to aid their escape through the Underground Railroad.

It is important to note that these symptoms occur under tremendous emotional and often physical duress. The behavior is considered a common survival strategy for victims of interpersonal abuse, and has been observed in battered spouses, abused children, prisoners of war, and concentration camp survivors.

Some slaves sought to please the white man by betraying other African-Americans. Moreover, African-Americans called each other the same derogatory and demeaning names that whites called them, hence the word nigger, as a ill-fated attempt to assimilate the white man. Dark skinned blacks were snubbed by light skinned blacks because the light skinned felt superior and closer to white—totally disconnected from the fact that their every existence, most likely, came by way of a duty-bound or forcible sex act between a black female slave or domestic worker and a white man. Nevertheless, dark skinned African-Americans envied and reviled the light skinned black because the dark skinned African-Americans felt inferior. That was the white way of reenacting Bacon's Rebellion, where a third party turns two races or group of people against each other.

By the early 1900s, most African-Americans straightened their hair, hence appearing less black. African-Americans with naturally straight hair distanced themselves from darker skin African-Americans with coarse hair. Finally, sufficiently inculcated light skinned African-Americans formed clubs that excluded African-Americans darker than a brown paper bag, called The Brown Bag Test. Several decades later, when Black Power became vogue, light skin African-Americans were shunned and accused of not being black enough by darker African-Americans. Both desperate were attempts for a moment of superiority perpetrated by a victim upon a victim. However, the KKK never conducted a *Brown Bag Test* when deciding whether to lynch a black man or set him free. The white bus driver in Alabama in 1955 did not use a Brown Bag Test on (highly light skinned) Rosa Parks before he demanded that she give her seat to a white man or risk being arrested. And there was no Brown Bag litmus test used to eject Homer Plessy from the train in 1892. The Plessy vs. Ferguson Case established the "separate but equal" doctrine that pervaded life in the American South for over fifty years.

The cosmetologist and braiders continued their feud for years until the court battle was decided. It still took a while to reconcile the relationship but today braiders and cosmetologist work side by side. However, in the early days of Sisterlocks, Dr. Cornwell felt the sting of the Stockholm Syndrome from both braiders and cosmetologists. Unfortunately, there appears to be a difference of opinion on who exactly is the enemy. To some African-Americans in the hair care profession, Sisterlocks is just another competitor attempting to steal bread from their tables and their snub is purely that of any business owner trying to protect their investment. Dr. Cornwell feels that the enemy is not competition but poverty. The fact that Sisterlocks opens opportunities for black women across the country to become entrepreneurs is a threat to the monopoly that the ethnic hair industry has over the black community. Sisterlocks is also a threat to those that earn a living by encouraging black women to shun African styles and culture originality and continue to perpetrate a facade. "I don't take it personally," says Dr. Cornwell. "The braiders and cosmetologist are not resisting me; they're resisting change."

CROSS

by Langston Hughes

My old man's a white old man
And my old mother's black.
If ever I cursed my white old man
I take my curses back.
If ever I cursed my black old mother
And wished she were in hell,
I'm sorry for that evil wish
And now I wish her well
My old man died in a fine big house.
My ma died in a shack.
I wonder were I'm going to die,
Being neither white nor black?

* **I, Too, Sing America**
*
* by Langston Hughes
*
*
* I, too, sing America
*
* I am the darker brother, they
* send me to eat in the kitchen
* When company comes
* But I laugh
* And eat well
* And grow strong
*
* Tomorrow
* I'll be at the table
* When company comes
* Nobody will dare say to me
* "Eat in the kitchen." Then.
* Besides, they'll see how
* Beautiful I am—And be
* Ashamed
*
* I, too, am America

8

Hairbraiders Win Opening Round, and Personal Testimonies

Excerpt of press release: May 5, 1997

Washington, D.C.—Federal district court Judge Rudi M. Brewster last Friday (May 2) denied a motion to dismiss a lawsuit filed in San Diego by African hairbraiders challenging occupational licensing requirements imposed by the California Board of Barbering and Cosmetology.

"This decision marks an important triumph for the right to earn an honest living," declared Clint Bolick, litigation director for the Washington, D.C. based Institute for Justice, which represents the braiders. "The decision opens the way for us to prove that the tangled cosmetology regulations are irrational and unconstitutional."

The lawsuit was filed in January by Dr. JoAnne Cornwell, a stylist of African-American hair and chair of the Africana Studies Department at San Diego State University, and the American Hairbraiders and Natural Hair care Association. They challenge as barriers to economic opportunity the state's requirements of 1,600 hours of prescribed training and a licensing examination that deal with such subjects as eyebrow arching, chemicals, and cosmetics—but not at all with the specialized practice of African hairstyling.

Judge Brewster's 28-page opinion dismissed some of the plaintiffs and defendants from the lawsuit, but ruled that the braiders' claims have legal merit if they can prove them at trial. Observing that only four percent of the required curriculum relates to health and safety, Judge Brewster concluded that the rules place "an almost insurmountable barrier in front of anyone who seeks to practice African hair styling," the effect of which "is to force African hair stylists out of business in favor of mainstream hair stylists and barbers."

"In America, people have the right to earn an honest living," said Donna Matias, an Institute for Justice attorney. "This lawsuit seeks to vindicate that right by removing arbitrary governmental barriers to free enterprise. Such government regulations that exceed legitimate public health and safety objectives cut off the bottom rungs of the economic ladder."

VICTORY FOR CALIFORNIA BRAIDERS

CALIFORNIA

On August 18, 1999, federal court Judge Rudi Brewster (9th Circuit) ruled in favor of AHNHA plaintiff Dr. JoAnne Cornwell [80 Fed. Sup. 2nd 1101; Cornwell v. Hamilton Southern District of California], that braiders cannot be forced to go to cosmetology school where braiding is not taught, forced to learn from texts that do not teach braiding, forced to take a test on subject matter that does not pertain to braiding, forced to take additional courses in order to teach braiding, or forced to work or learn in a toxic chemical environment associated with a school or salon where chemicals are used, that have been proven to cause miscarriages, birth defects, infertility, cancer, and upper respiratory problems. On June 15, 2000, Governor Gray Davis signed SB-235 into law (effective 01/01/01), exempting hairbraiders from the cosmetology laws in the state.

Just as braiding shops made overnight entrepreneurs of hordes of newly immigrated African women, in the last decade many African-American women have learned to lock and make a full-time business of it. African-American stylists have stated that locking is the new sweeping trend in black hair, what braiding was before it. "A lot of people with locks have this spiritual feeling about their relationship with their loctician," says one natural hair stylist. "Once someone does your locks, they are very special to you. It's a unique feeling, more so than braids. Braiding is more elusive. It's not permanent. It's just a temporary solution. Locks are a way of life."

While braids are mostly hair that's not the wearer's own, locks are made by tightly twisting and retwisting together thin sections of natural hair until each section begins to grow as one mass, like dreads but with lots of thin strands instead of a few big bunches. Women who wear locks can style them a "mainstream" shape like a bob if they want, just as they can with relaxed hair. But as with braiding, no harsh chemicals are involved. Braiders and locticians both fall under the umbrella term of "natural hair care," but locticians see themselves as evolving beyond the braiders and consider ownership of their craft to reside in the African-American community. An African braider I talked to saw it the same way. "Locks, that's the black women's thing," she said. She wasn't planning on learning how to lock.

Excerpts from an online interview with Dr. Cornwell

I never intended to start a natural hair care business. Once I'd come up with this new hair technique; though, it attracted so much attention, I almost had no choice. I was approached constantly with questions and inquiries about how women could get their hair done like mine! The business grew out of an almost desperate need of our women to get free of 'that hair thing.'

During the 1980s I wore a short natural and loved it! But, I got tired of it after 8 years or so and because I wasn't aware of any other natural options, I went back to chemicals. Soon after, I became aware of locks as an option, but it took me at least 2 years to get the courage to go that way. Then it had to be my way, not the larger, traditional locks. That's when I began experimenting with what would eventually become Sisterlocks.

The big problem with locks for me was that there was no good way to start them. Also, the edges always looked shabby, shampooing disrupted the groomed look, and they were too large for elaborate styling. After roughly 2 years of experimenting with Sisterlocks, I found it solved all of these problems.

In 1997 a group of natural hair businesses teamed up with a DC public interest law firm and the director of the American Hairbraiders and Natural Haircare Association, and we filed suit against the cosmetology board in California. What prompted this was that some braiders were being targeted by the board and a number of them had gotten fed up with the fines, harassment and inappropriate interference of the cosmetology industry. My business was eventually identified as the ideal test case for this challenge. At the time, I didn't realize how devastating it would have been if we had lost! (I can remember after the fact saying "What was I thinking!!??") Anyway, after two-and-a-half years in court, we prevailed and got legal exemption. If you read the judge's decision you'll see that "Sisterlocks" is specifically named there, but in practice, ALL natural hair care businesses in California are now exempt, thanks to our victory. PLUS, since the victory was in Federal court, the precedent has been established for many other states as well.

Though it has been a source of pride, the case really had no direct effect on our business. Indirectly, I think our victory may have inspired more confidence about the legitimacy of natural hair care among average people. Maybe it also made more people feel it was safer to take our classes than they had believed before.

Today we have Consultants in around 35 states in the US, and 10 countries outside the US. We have approximately 1500 active Consultants at this time. I should note though, that Consultants are not employed by Sisterlocks. They run their own businesses, and the Sisterlocks Company does not profit directly when they perform our hair technique. Many think we're getting rich because there are so many Sisterlocks wearers. The truth is that unless people are purchasing products from us, we get nothing—except "bragging rights!" (smile)

I believe the majority of us know that relaxers are ultimately harmful to our health. Why do we continue with this behavior? For me it is plainly obvious, though I'm moved with sadness every time I think about it: Most of our women continue using chemicals and other means to alter their hair because, on some level, as a culture we have bought into the lie that our natural physical attributes are somehow inferior. We believe we have to cover them up or 'correct' them in order to be beautiful and feel good about ourselves.

We shouldn't use discussions about "other women" or "other groups" to diminish the fact that WE. African descended people (especially those in the Diaspora: ie. the US, Europe, Caribbean, Canada, etc.) still suffer to some degree from a 'victim' or 'oppressed' mentality. This is at the core of why we judge what we look like (hair, skin, noses, lips, etc.) against what we believe on some level we should look like. This produces a need to replicate the norm promoted by the majority culture: straight hair, light skin, narrow noses, thin lips, etc. I generally refrain from debating this point though. I find there is so much emotion and anger behind people's arguments (not surprising!) that these discussions can be counter-productive. I just walk through my life proudly and in love with myself—my hair, my nose, ALL of it—and I welcome people lovingly into Sisterlocks if they decide they want to do more to embrace their own natural selves.

The Inaugural issue of our Sisterlocks Lifestyle Journal contains a reprint of a chapter from my 1997 book (now out of print), <u>That Hair Thing and the Sisterlocks Approach</u>. The chapter is titled, "So, How Did You Come Up With This Idea Anyway? It gives a detailed account of the entire discovery process. Essentially, I experimented over a 2-year period (1991–1993) before coming up with Sisterlocks. The early years of my own Sisterlocks reflected the fits and starts of the creation process. My locks were irregular and full of bunching and random sizes. I can't really set a 'starting date' to my Sisterlocks because they were such a work in progress in the early years. ALL of the initial 5–6 inches of experimental Sisterlocks had to be gradually cut off over the years in order to obtain a uniform look once I had finally figured things out.

I have never measured my locks, but the longest ones are starting to touch the chair seat when I sit down. I trim my Sisterlocks every year to eliminate weak ends and unevenness.

When people fail to provide the minimum recommended maintenance for their Sisterlocks, they will most likely have problems. So many of our women are used to thinking about their natural hair just as something to tie other hair into, or attach hair pieces onto, or pin wigs to, or scorch, or 'fix' with chemicals. We're not that accustomed to what our OWN hair really needs, or how it REALLY looks when it is healthy, and things like that. Sisterlocks Consultants are trained to re-educate their clients in new ways of caring for their natural hair. Also, our product line is custom made for our own natural hair types. When people take care of their Sisterlocks properly, they will very easily grow more hair than they ever dreamed possible! (Individuals with diseases of the scalp, medical issues, drug-related hair breakage, etc. may have special issues, but this would be true for them regardless of the hair technique.)

Problems like hair breakage can have several causes from poor maintenance to reactions to medications and stress. An individual should always seek to discover why they are experiencing breakage before seeking a remedy. Generally speaking, having the hair in locks protects the individual hair strands more than if these strands were loose. In this way it can be good for hair that is weak and has a tendency to break. However, if the cause of breakage is internal, nothing external—not even Sisterlocks—will correct the problem. Also, if the person neglects their Sisterlocks they may eventually break as well.

Running the Sisterlocks business continues to be a challenge. I'm still confident though, that it will continue to grow and will one day really prosper!

We have not stopped developing our training program—just the opposite! We've taken the last couple of years to completely re-structure how we do things. We've also expanded our classes to four days. We have a class scheduled at the end of April in San Diego where we will be training six new Associate Trainers from around the country, plus one from Jamaica!

My typical day is hectic! Too hectic! I try to start each day with exercise though. I may go to the gym, or pop in an exercise tape at home. Then, I generally spend a few hours doing Sisterlocks work—not hair, but running the business side. (For many years I also maintained a client base, but today I only re-tighten a couple of friends.) My Sisterlocks duties range from meeting with staff, to working on product development, to coaching consultants by phone, to managing certification issues, to planning training classes and speaking engagements, and so forth. I generally schedule my university teaching for after noon. My time there is spent preparing classes and teaching, attending meetings, working with student assistants and meeting with colleagues. When I return home, it's Sisterlocks business again! Generally, I find I have to address issues that have come up during the afternoon while I was away. I try not to work into the evening or nighttime though. I like to keep that time for myself, even if I just choose to be a couch potato. My fun activities include salsa dancing (my partner and I are pretty good too!), hitting poetry spots and art walks, exercising and working in my yard.

Final word: For anyone wanting to learn more about Sisterlocks, I recommend two things:

- *We have an extensive website www.sisterlocks.com*

- *Get a copy of the "Sisterlocks Lifestyle Journal." There is an "Information Gallery" in every issue geared to newcomers and anyone curious about what they can/should expect from the Sisterlocks experience*

SISTERLOCKS WOMAN

From behind a subtle invisible shield
The Sisterlocks Woman has escaped
The hot and sweaty press and curl
To give her hair a carefree break
Give way to the conscientious sister
Unrestrained by chemical wax
She meets the world self-assured
Her roots can finally relax
She's not a slave to Hollywood
She's not bound by the subliminal spell
That shouts, "Other women are the heads of beauty
And Black women are the tails!"

The interlocking of hair creates unity
Symbolic of what every sister knows
Sisters must stand together for strength
No matter what the wild wind blows
Her spirit is not held captive
Her internal peace is not shaken
Because God stepped in; lifted her chin
And said, "My splendor shall not be forsaken"
He empowered her with the authority
To be the appraiser of her worth
Sisterlocks expresses her personality
The most envied woman on earth

Her skin tone is at-one-with the sun
There's radiance on her full lips
Even blind men can't ignore
The soft jiggle in her hips
Her love life is confidential
God foremost is her Rock
She's a confident Sisterlocks Woman
With a legacy of superior stock

Profiles, Interviews, and Personal Testimonies of Natural Hair Lovers

Loc's not just a hairstyle—it's a way of life.

By Yvonne Varner—New Jersey

My relationship with hair started at the age of 5 years old. My mother never learned how to do hair and this was good. She took me to the beauty parlor weekly with her. I had thick, long, and very well groomed hair. I knew that hair was important and most black women I knew believe it was their crown. I went through many changes and some painful. My hair was course and long. I would began with a Virgrol and a wash, then next a straighten comb. Oh there was no blow dryer in my day, just a dryer. My hair took at least 3 hours if you did not stop to let me rest. My stylist always had a standing appointment every two weeks. My mom dropped me off at the salon and returned 5 hours later. I even secured a job as the coke girl for the clients. This went on for several years. The Afro came out and I was set free. I had an Angel Davis Afro and I loved my hair. The whole family wore the Afro but my Afro was the best. I started to learn how to take care of my hair.

Then something happen! Ultra Sheen and my Mom adapted to the perm. Things started to go down hill. I received a perm at the age of 12. We went on vacation that summer from our home in New Jersey to Los Angeles, Las Vegas, and Mexico. I left with long straight hair and return with broken split ends. My mom could not help me, she could not even braid. I had to have a hair cut from my uncle the barber. Now I had an Afro and about four inches of hair. I sported this style for a year; lucky for me I had growing hair. My hair grew and I knew what I wanted. I wanted braids and my cousin was a master braider. I wore braids with and without extensions. I was saved.

Time passed and I was now 18 years old with a style of my own and a hair stylist. I went back and forth with perms and braids. After several years, I began to read and learn more about natural hair. I decided to Loc after I read an article about locs. I was a mother with a daughter of my own, Michelle. I never thought a perm was a solution to hair care for a young girl. I had a weekly regimen. I begin with washing then blow drying follow through with a warm electric straighten comb and ending with braids. I decided for myself to make an appointment with a salon that only did locs. I was determined to loc and I did not care who liked it. I had a haircut and was twisted. I was happy until I arrived home and my husband was not as happy. He referred to my twist as little worms. This made me a little uncomfortable but still determined to be different. I started to think about locking my daughter too. She was 6 years old and had a natural hair, which was healthy. I took her with me to the next appointment and the beautician twisted her hair. She looked as if she silk locked. My husband liked her long silky locs but did not have a clue she was locking. I never said anything until it was too late. Both my daughter and I wear traditional lock.

Sisterlocks was something I learned about later while I wore traditional locs. I learned to do locs over the years and became very good. My number one client was my daughter. I decided to go get a license for hair after being laid off from a job. I received a license and went to work as a Loc specialist in a salon. I was exposed to seminars and top stylists of natural hair. The Sisterlocks classes where offered in New York and New Jersey. I decided I needed to be trained to do Sisterlocks. I attended the class in the summer of 2005 and I am so glad I did. I decided I wanted to cut off my traditional locs and start Sisterlocks. I cut off my traditional loc in early 2006 and remain wearing a short natural. I plan to Sisterlock late March 2007. Loc's are not just a hairstyle but also a way of life.

Locks of Love By Michelle Varner—New Jersey

My locks are my lifeline. I am 16 years old and have been growing my locks since I was seven years old. My locks have been an extensive part my life from childhood to womanhood. My hair is a part of me. It is my personality and what makes me Michelle. When I was young I didn't understand what my hair was I thought it was simply just cool. As I grew older I realized that locking is an art and lifestyle. What I mean by lifestyle is one that is pure natural. Many times people have asked me if I could take out my locks. I answer, "Not unless I cut them at the root." They then proceed to give me a shocked look and ask me do I ever want to cut them. The answer I give them is the answer I have had for the past nine years, no. My locks are my individuality. Why would I want straight hair? I can do everything I can do with straight hair with my locks, naturally. The keyword is natural. The problem right now is too many females put chemical in their hair to have the appearance of straight silky hair. If God made us with curly, bouncy, beautiful naps that's what were supposed to have.

Black women need to embrace our hair. Natural is the way to be. If you don't agree with me ask yourself this question, why do most black women have short, damaged hair? I'll tell you why. Because they damaged their hair with chemicals for hair that is not theirs to begin with. So do I want to cut my beautiful locks?

No! I rather have a head-full of long waist length locks than have damaged hair. My locks are what makes me, me. It is the reflection of my personality. My locks are strong and don't break like my spirit. My locks have a few curves but always straighten out at the end—like my utter determination.

Most importantly, my locks are filled with love from the hand of my family the same as my heart. I say to you as long as I live I'm keeping my locks not dreadlocks because there is nothing dreadful about me!

DORIS GRAVITTE—Moreno Valley, California

I was born Doris Briggs May 18, 1956 in Los Angeles, California. Thru Sister-locks I have developed a family of associates and friends. The types of clients that seek out locks as a hairstyle are strong individuals that are accepting of a lifestyle change. We no longer are willing to accept being forced into styles that fail to identify who we are as a culture. We stand tall and proud in the sister and brother lock family. We offer a freedom to our people that we never had before. I've carried a lot of weight on my shoulders, enough for two. At last I'm becoming free!

I have a degree in cosmetology, and I'm a licensed locktician, plus own properties all over the United States. Some even fondly call me the Imelda Marcos of the Real Estate industry. I come from a family of women that practiced home health care. My Aunt Annie McNeal Ervin who was my grandmother's sister was a cosmetologist in West Helena, Arkansas long before I was born. My mother grew up in Arkansas reared under the training of Auntie Ervin pressing and curling my mother and her sister LeBertha's hair.

As I reached my teen years it became noticeable that I had picked up the skill of hair care. I started braiding my own hair by parting it down the middle and bringing the braids to the center part. Then I would roll the ends of the braids allowing it to develop into curls. Once I removed the rollers the next day I would take my fingers and intertwine the curled ends with the look resembling a Mohawk running from the crown point of the head to the back nape line. At that time in my life I was about twelve years of age. By the time I was thirteen the world was changing and natural hair care was on the change, although, the phase "Natural Hair Care" had not yet been coined.

The word got around my community that I could braid hair really good so my parents started letting me braid for revenue. My babysitter Sandy Reece was the first to influence me in branching out to accept business from various clients. She would bring parents with their daughters to my house for me to braid. As news begin to travel throughout, kids in the neighborhood would wait in the evenings on our front porch for me to come home from school to braid their hair.

By the time I got to junior high school the braiding business had prepared me with basic business skills, which landed me a job on campus at our junior high school working in the front office after school. I did not have much time for braiding in the afternoons so I had to limit my hair business to weekends only. Having my own money was a maturing factor in my up bringing. It taught me financial responsibility at an early age. When we were in elementary school we were introduced to a banking program as a part of our academic studies. Each week our parents provided us with an allowance of fifteen cents that went into an envelope that had a string we use to close it with. This envelope had to be given to our teacher on Thursday morning upon arriving to class. Before recess each Thursday the Brinks truck came to our school and picked up all the envelopes and took them to Wells Fargo Bank for deposits into our individual accounts. This taught me to save at an early age so when I made more money I looked forward to putting more money in my account. Each week when the teacher returned our envelopes the total amount of money was posted on a general journal printed on the envelope. This was certainly exciting to me.

As the seventies evolved the Jheri curl became a popular style in our community. My father took my sister and me to the corner barbershop for our first salon hairstyle "The Jheri curl". The dilemma we faced with this type of curl required the use of chemicals that altered the natural curl pattern of our hair. The chemical Thiogluculate was not our friend. We as black consumers found this out the hard way.

After, my twelfth grade year of high school, I attended CSUN-California State University Northridge. By this time the natural had become the common hairstyle especially for black college students. Looking back at some of my pictures I had photos with acquaintances in college such as Abby Lincoln who was awarded the academy award for "The Love of Ivy" with Sidney Poitier and another with the outspoken activist Stokely Carmichael of the Black Panthers all styling their naturals.

In 2005, I attended an Academy for Sisterlocks and Brotherlocks. This felt like the first day of the rest of my life. I finally found my place in the hair care industry. I no longer have to practice damaging and destroying the real texture of our hair by pressing, perming and relaxing. The technique of locking the hair is a process by which we protect the natural texture of our hair. In addition, we are able to maintain the natural curl pattern. No split ends, no tangles. This new phenomena continue to far exceed the expectations ever imaged in this society today. We have length were as we have always struggled with hair growth. Our lengths flow to our knees freely and no chemicals added. It is for every age group male and female. Locks do not discriminate any age group, manageable with any style.

The evolution of Locks has certainly changed my life giving me a newfound sense of self, identity and expression. I see the future of Locks influencing a new culture for black America. My message to our readers is that in view of all our struggles the object is to plan ones life for success, for if we fail to plan for success we have planned to fail. Thank you Sisterlocks.

Olufemi Alexander is a divorced mother of five and operates her hair business from her home in **Moreno Valley, California**. Olufemi, for many years wanted to be a homeowner and achieved her dream as an independent entrepreneur. She is a strong advocate for natural living. She is the only woman I've met who delivered all of her children at home with the assistance of a midwife.

Olufemi is a Certified Sisterlocks Consultant and also the owner of Naturally Yours Boutique. http://www.NaturallyYoursBoutique.com. She has practiced natural hair care for many years and knew that the Sisterlocks technique was something she had to learn. "It has been an asset to my career," Olufemi explains.

Aside from Sisterlocks, Olufemi is a spiritual person who reaches out to minister to the world through her website and CD designed to instill peace within the heart and soul of women.

Olufemi's CD is called Embracing Your Beauty ... From the Inside Out. It's a collection of affirmations for women set to music. She asks questions, "Are you determined to feel like a '10'? Would you like to rid yourself of all the stressors in your life and improve your self-esteem and confidence? Do you want to live an abundant life filled with inner peace, love and joy, take charge of your life and achieve greater success and personal development?"

Olufemi believes that even a beautiful natural woman wearing Sisterlocks or any other natural hairdo is incomplete without a strong spiritual foundation because, "as a woman thinks in her heart, so is she". Olufemi is now looking into expanding her hair business. She's desirous of opening a natural hair salon outside of her home where she can be the catalyst to helping others have a "spot" to do business. This project is a two-year project and one of many more to come.

Telifa 'Tee' Smith is a Certified Sisterlocks Consultant who owns a chic salon that she shares with another loctician in **Riverside, California**. "I first became familiar with Sisterlocks through a book called <u>Let's Talk Hair</u> by Pamela Ferrell," said Tee. "While flipping the pages, I spotted Dr. Cornwell's hairdo and knew right away that it was something unusual and fantastic that I wanted to know more about. That was in 1997. I took the Sisterlocks training the same year and been wearing Sisterlocks since then." Tee says that she had gone through a lot of hair changes in her life everything from press & curl to the natural, which she was wearing prior to becoming acquainted with Sisterlocks. Tee became a licensed cosmologist in the 70s. "I had long ago given up on relaxers," says Tee, "although many of my female clients in the 70s, 80s and 90s preferred it." Today Tee's clientele is exclusively Sisterlocks and Brotherlocks, which she prefers. You may locate Tee Smith in the official Sisterlocks referral directory.

Karen Southerland—Florida

Before I became a Sisterlocks consultant who is presently pursuing my certification, I had always had a career as an educator. I spent seven years in the classroom being a full-time advocate for children and how to guarantee their success in the classroom, on their standardized tests, and the most important of all, being a mentor who would remain as a permanent figure in their life. Often times, educators are people who are considered role models; and therefore, everything they do is under a close watch and/or scrutiny. Educators are definitely judged by everyone, in terms of political connections, where they live, what kind of car they own/drive, how they dress, and especially how they wear they HAIR. This is the criteria which one is used to determine whether an educator is magical with children and their success of learning, instead of how well they have a rapport with children, or motivate children to learn. Hair has been used as a way to categorize what kind of personality I have and dictates how I would relate to others and most of the time the individuals who have had the most difficulty in accepting Sisterlocks as a healthy alternative are the members of my own race—BLACK FOLKS!!!!

Even though I am an educator, I. like, most of my sisters, have had a long and endearing journey with my hair. I come from a rather conservative mother who views braids and hair weave extensions as post-1960s and the time of revolution or rebellion. I had to endure the pressures and impressions from her telling me not to discover my natural hair and how I would not be granted any job interviews. She advised me not to reveal my natural hair because I was making an entrance in the field of education where the applicants had to send photographs of themselves attached to the application. I was in college at the time and my hair had gone through trauma due to heavy blow drying, overlapping of chemicals and additional chemical reactions from the strong chlorine, which had not been mixed very well. This class had to satisfy a physical education requirement. Yes, this added insult to injury with thought of sacrificing my hair for a college course grade. Happily, I passed the class with flying colors, but what about my appearance and how would I feel about myself in the long run????

After my first encounter with chemicals and no longer being able to go to a hairdresser, I began to twist my hair. I was first introduced to the art of twisting hair by a sister I had met in college. Talia was a senior who had already made preparations to go to graduate school. Talia demonstrated to me that many successful Black individuals wear natural hair styles even though I had never encountered any at that time. She made me aware of the many products that I had collected over the past few months or longer; I did not need them, and they were simply a way to waste money. She would shampoo her hair once a month and re-twist sections when her busy scheduled allowed her to do so. This was not the most popular thing to do, but I did not care what others thought; because I wanted healthy looking hair like Talia's hair. I had one problem—the remaining perm that still existed in my hair passed the first inch from the scalp. The perm took the coiling pattern away from my hair, which caused the twist to slip. The perm also caused me to still need a product, like gel or hair lotion, which I had vowed not to buy any more. So, now, I have another problem—How am I going to get my twist to stay in my hair without product???? By this time, I had made major discoveries about my hair and skin.

I had learned from Talia if I cannot put the product on my skin, then it cannot go into my hair either. My skin no longer had acne problems because I had found the problem—THOSE UNNECESSARY HAIR PRODUCTS ON YOUR PILLOW THEN INADVERTENTLY ON YOUR FACE!!!!! My acne problem had been solved without going to the dermatologist, who in the past would only give me a prescription without revealing the cause of the skin problem.

I wore the twist until I graduated from college. My mother interfered by offering to pay for my hair salon visits. I agreed to go as long as the hairdresser did not perm my hair. My mother assured me that she would not do such a thing. Tonya had a way with the blow dryer. Tonya knew how to determine the right temperature of the blow dryer and use the brush at the same time. She would put my hair in a nice French roll and I really liked the way she took care of my hair. She was the best hairdresser I have ever had. Just like most, hairdressers relocate; and sometimes, are difficult to find. I lost touch with Tonya and never saw her again.

So I ended up searching for another hairdresser, but, in the meantime, doing my own hair. Every time, I had to prepare for a new job interview, I made sure that my hair was pressed for the interview. Afterward, my twists would reappear. I would have parents at conference time stare at my hair instead of listening to what was said about their child's performance in school. Interesting enough, the parent who was staring at me would have no hairline or breakage throughout their own hair. When they arrive at home, they would make statements to their child about my appearance.

The child would share this with me the next day. Now, this is the focal point of the child's education—MY HAIR!!!!!! I would make it a priority to redirect the parent and the student that education is the key. Members of my own race would talk badly about natural hair and did not mind/was unaware that their own hair was going through its own trauma. This parent did not view any of the positives, for example, my skin condition was immaculate; my hair was healthy and shining; my hair was bouncing and behaving, in the twist style. I could not dare advise this parent on being healthy because they felt they look good, even though they had no hairline; all that matters is—THEY HAD ACQUIRED THE DESIRED STRAIGHTNESS. My boss at the time had been a member of the other race, and did not have a problem with my hair until she got frustrated due to comments about my hair from MEMBERS OF MY OWN RACE—BLACK FOLKS!!!

Since then, I have found a new working environment in which I conducted an interview with my Sisterlocks. I am working in an environment where there are more black immigrants and less descendents of slaves in America. So, I feel that this contributed to the ease and acceptance of my Sisterlocks and appreciation for my honesty and good work ethics. I have since been asked to join an In-School Committee who designs curriculum that explores Black Migration and Members of the African Diaspora. I was honored and thanked God that I had finally ARRIVED!!! Sisterlocks have helped me to identify individuals who love themselves and in turn love others around them. My Sisterlocks have been helpful even though some had suggested that it would hinder my job and life possibilities.

Life with Sisterlocks has been rewarding. My hair has natural oils and this is my first time experiencing this. I never had a problem with hair growth, but I have had moments where hair loss is an issue. Sisterlocks addressed this problem without me having to go a trichologist. My dandruff problem alleviated itself under the Sisterlocks system. This system has created a haven for my hair to GROW!!!! I decided to have them a year and a half ago and have been pleased with the results ever since. I had one situation in the classroom where I had to go to a professional development workshop. As an educator/teacher, I had to leave substitute plans. I had also left a note on the board, where it said "A note from Ms. Southerland". My students shared with me the day of my return that some- one had drawn a perm box next to my name and some students found it to be funny. My quick and immediate response was," Well, I wish that perm box next to my name had remained there because I would have put a face on the board with only three hair strands sticking up on the top of the head. Also my illustra- tion would have shown the rest of the hair falling on the floor." "Students, I would suggest that you do research with the help of your science teachers on the study of (lye) or sodium hydroxide and the side effects of its toxicity" My stu- dents burst into laughter and my colleagues could not face me as I crossed paths with them in the hallway.

Lauren McDonald—Charlotte, North Carolina

I got my first perm at 15. I loved having long kinky free bouncy hair. I thought all of my hair problems were over. No more Afro picks, no more large tooth combs, no more struggles with combing my hair after shampooing or getting it wet. I had arrived. I had straight hair and I wore it proud. It kind of made me feel less black. I started to feel better than females who did not have perms because their hair did not look as pretty as mine. This went on for years until my hair began to weaken under the pressure of perming, blow-drying and the use of curl- ing irons. I wanted my hair to be natural again but the transition from a perm to natural hair was a bit much for me, as I had done this several times before. I would wear my hair natural then go back to a perm for convenience until one day I had the worse experience of my life.

After a touch up that was professionally done, I began to loose hair. I can't begin to tell you where it went. It seemed to melt away. I did not see it on my pil- low, or on my clothing, in my comb or in the sink. It just vanished over a 3-week period. The end result was almost total baldness. Yes I was bald around my hair- line, the nape of my neck and in sections. I had some hair, very short hair left on my crown. Needless to say I was overwhelmed which led me to be depressed. The little hair that I had left felt prickly like a man's 5 o'clock shadow. I wore a scarf or a wide headband to cover my baldness praying that my hair would grow back. I said to myself, "if my hair ever grows back I will never ever perm it again".

No one knew the pressure I was under because I covered it up well. I can remember one day my husband came home early from work and I was in the bathroom checking the progress of my, which had now become my everyday rit- ual. The look on his face said it all as he asked, "What in the world have you done to your hair?" I was speechless because now he could see what I was covering up for weeks. He was now aware of my hair trauma. All I could do was cry as I shared with him what had happened. I wouldn't wish this on my worse enemy if I had one. Not even the hairstylist who gave me the touch up. I'll never forget how it took me three months to call her to let her know. I couldn't bring myself to call sooner because I was devastated, shocked, overwhelmed from my hair loss. Nothing like this had ever happened to me or anyone that I knew. Yes, I heard horror stories of perms gone bad, but never considered in a million years that it could happen to me. When I told the hairstylist about my hair, she had the audacity to tell me that I had "alopecia". Alopecia! The nerve of her. Her words just added to my pain and made me angry. It took everything out of me not to take her to court.

It saddens me sometimes when I see others not embracing the natural beauty of their birth hair and wonder if they too would ever experience what I did. I often wonder what it would take to make them realize that heat and perms are no good for the hair. I see females with permed hair that is clearly over processed. I see them trying to hold on to those weak strands with grease and gels. I imagine the strands of hair screaming, "I'm not gonna hold on to your head much longer!" as they try to do all they can to make it look good. Some of them no longer have a hairline.

This horrific experience happened in 1993. I wore braids all of '94' and took hair vitamins throughout the year hoping that my hair shaft had not been com- pletely destroyed. I would dangle my head from the bed in an attempt to massage my scalp. I did every thing that came to mind in hopes of regaining my hair. I was desperate and longed for my long hair that I often tossed and ran my fingers through. In '95' when I stopped wearing braids I had hair again. I was a happy camper. I had the hair that I was born with, all natural and chemical free. I knew that I would never perm again but did not know what to do with this head full of natural hair. It was too long for an afro and I didn't dare cut it after all I had gone through.

Though I admired locs, I never considered them. They appeared to be heavy and monotonous with no styling options. In Jan. '98' I was introduced to Sister- locks. Wow. The amazing thing is that I went to find out about them not for me but for a friend who had to work that day. When I saw how beautiful they were I was awed. I knew I had to have them and ended up getting them the following weekend. While they were being installed suddenly about ½ way through the process, I panicked and said, "oh my gosh what have I done? I wondered if I made the right decision. That was over 9 years ago and I have no regrets. Not even one.

I never thought that my hair could be so beautiful without chemicals, combing, heat and grease. My hair has grown longer than I could ever imagine. It is so healthy and full of life. I've learned to embrace my nappiness through Sisterlocks. I turn heads wherever I go. Some people don't believe that all of this hair on my head is actually growing out of my head. They are amazed when I say yes it is all mine, every strand, every inch. Some of them try to touch it to see if they can determine where or how it is extended. These are the doubters who find it so hard to believe that my hair could grow this long so quick. These are strangers, people that I don't even know. Some people are bold enough to ask what are they? When I tell them, they usually follow with, how did I get them so small and how do I maintain them?

My Sisterlocks cascade down to my backside and I wear them proudly. I can style them if I choose to or leave them as they are. Most times I just let them flow. I love my Sisterlocks. Wearing my hair in Sisterlocks is the best thing I could've done for me and my hair. I feel so free and liberated. My Sisterlocks are so much a part of me that I forget that I have them until I see someone curiously staring or admiring them. Permed hair never gave me this much attention. Not that I was looking for any then or now. Dr. Cornwell says "Come Home to Sisterlocks", and to this I say thank you JoAnne for inviting me.

My Hairitage: A Journey to Sisterlocks
by Mae Brooks—Chicago, ILL

I, **Mae Brooks (Maevette Lavinia Allen-Brooks)**, age 30, answer to the call of wife, mother, daughter, sister, aunt, niece, mentor, and friend. Singing, dancing, writing, creating, laughing, and acting are things I enjoy. I am a strong advocate of civic duty and strive to do my part by volunteering and educating whenever I can. What makes my life most rewarding is knowing my life's mission—to share acceptance and honor the purpose in my life and in others. A native Chicagoan of African decent, I pride myself in assisting brothers and sisters throughout the Diaspora with their natural hair needs. I create textured styles including twists, locs, and braids which offer my clients an array of versatility without the use of extensions. As a cultural artist I embrace the African-inspired art form of hair-locking most dearly. The live canvases I employ demonstrate my passion for the art. With over ten years of experience, I often reflect and revisit the road I've traversed thus far.

Maevette Lavinia Allen was the last-born and the only girl of the Polk-Allen clan. The year was 1975. She had thick nappy hair, which her mother Willie Mae, kept groomed in Afros, puffs, braids, or twists. Occasionally, Willie Mae would get out the pressing comb and olive oil, which made little Maevette scream to the top of her lungs just from the heat approaching her ear. Since Willie Mae was an older parent, she decided that she would eventually need a more manageable hair maintenance system for her little girl. One day Maevette came home from the first grade and was met with a very warm invitation to the basement of their house on 93rd and Paxton. Maevette was used to getting her hair done in the kitchen, so this was a treat for the six-year old—so she thought. When Maevette got down in that basement, her mom mixed together a bottle of liquid and some white cream that stank to high heavens! It was a mild relaxer, a concoction designed to relax all the kinks right out of her hair. Little did Maevette know that this would lead to years of scalp burns, hair damage, and unhappiness.

From the early 1980's to the late 1990's, Maevette wore relaxed styles. She styled her own hair at home but went to the shop for relaxer touch ups and was told, "When you feel the burn, let me know." She had no idea that she was subjecting her scalp and hair to traumatic experiences every time she went to the shop. Doing hair was a hobby that Maevette first took up with her dolls. The styles varied from braids to twists to ponytails. When she started experimenting with her own hair, she expanded her creations to asymmetrical bobs, flips, mushrooms, crimps, and other styles which required blow dryers, spritz, and curling irons. Eventually, Maevette would move on to relaxing her own hair, and when she ran into trouble, she would go to the shop for a fix. While in college, Maevette continued the cycle of relaxing and styling but found a stylist to do the relaxing and styling for her. As time went on, Maevette noticed that she had suffered some permanent nerve damage in the back of her head from a weave track she had ripped off her scalp some years ago after her attempt to loosen the weave bond with oils and conditioners as a former stylist suggested had failed. She also realized that compared to a seventh grade picture of herself she had found, her hair was considerably thin. When she asked her present stylist if her hair would ever get thick like that again, the answer was, "No." Disheartened and distraught, Maevette sulked around, pondering what she was going to do about her hair.

While studying Theatre Arts and Music in college, she landed a job at a popular science museum where she served as a tour guide and exhibit interpreter. In her misery Maevette was teased at work because she wore her hair slicked back in the same boring ponytail everyday. A male coworker eventually approached her and asked her if she ever thought about wearing her hair natural. Maevette embraced the idea and decided that natural would be best instead of fighting to keep her hair in a way that was not naturally hers to keep. Soon after, she sought out a girlfriend on campus and asked her how she transitioned from relaxed to natural hair. Maevette went out the next day and copied what her friend had done, thus returning to work with long, flowing, spaghetti-like crochet braids. Well, Maevette was a laughing stock, and the same male coworker approached her again with pointed interrogation. She simply replied, "I'm going natural. The braids are my transitional style." The male coworker then said, "So, you're going natural and then what?" Maevette answered, "I don't know. I never thought about that." "Have you ever considered locs?" he asked. "No," Maevette replied. "Well, I'll get you some information and you decide," he stated as Maevette went on about her day. At the close of the day, Maevette had forty pages of information to consider. Those forty pages changed her life.

After reading, praying, meditating, and bugging the heck out of everyone she saw with locs, Maevette decided that locs were the way to go. The book she read suggested three ways to start locks: comb coils, two-strand twists, and braids. Well, Maevette couldn't figure out how to do the comb coils, and she couldn't quite imagine how braids would transform into locs. So, she decided to try the two-strand twists, for she had learned how to do them from a fellow Festival worker in Winston-Salem, NC, the Summer of 1999. It was now Fall of the same year, and about 2–3 inches of her hair at the base was kinky from the new growth, and the rest was straight from the relaxer. Following a painstaking 15-hour session, Maevette had her first set of locs. The twists were neat and nicely parted into pencil-size squares. She used a hand mirror and a hallway mirror by the front door of her childhood home to check and recheck the parts so they'd be perfect. But Maevette was not prepared for the initial reactions.

Some of the theatre majors exclaimed that Maevette was locking for a fad. Actually, a debate arose among her peers as to whether she was going to keep them or not. Her theatre professor even stressed that it would be hard to land a professional acting gig with locs. Maevette's preacher brother called her choice a fad, "... like the fro's of the 60's and 70's and the braids of the 80's." Folks talked about the twists at the base looking cool but taunted her about the stringy ends. She had planned to loc her hair at the roots and gradually cut off the straight ends, but she panicked. In the middle of the night Maevette cut the relaxed ends off and just left the kinkier twists near her scalp. She received a few compliments after cutting off the ends, but when she washed it, it all came down. Maevette was upset and realized that she didn't give her hair enough time to do its thing. Well, she rocked a 3-inch Afro for about a week and a half until the frustration of finals made her snap.

Maevette thought that maintaining an Afro would be easy, but that style took her an extra 15 to 20 minutes to groom. No one told her that braiding it at night would make it more manageable in the morning. So, one day after classes she started grabbing hair and twisting it wherever her hands lay. This time, she was going to wear the two-strand twists with the freeform parts until the end of finals and take those down to do the perfect parts again. As the days went by Maevette received so many compliments with the freeform parts that she decided to leave those twists in and let them lock from there. Meanwhile, the male coworker who initiated her quest had been watching the transformation unfold month after month. Soon after, he asked Maevette if she could maintain his locs because he had a hard time coordinating with his loctitian's schedule. She said, "I barely know what I'm doing with my own locs. How do you expect me to do yours?" He replied, "Come on sis. I have faith in you. Please, just do me this favor." Maevette agreed and said, "Okay, okay, I'll do it. But let me connect with this sister on campus who's a loctician so I can get some pointers and have some structure to what I do."

After getting in touch with the chemistry major that was also an established loctician, Maevette went to her house to watch her work and took plenty of notes. Following a short dialogue at the end of the session, Maevette made a fifty-dollar investment and purchased combs, clips, a dryer, shampoo, conditioner, oil, and a few other things the sister suggested. Her first client, the male coworker, was happy that Maevette did the research. When he examined his freshly maintained locs in the mirror, he said, "It's all good" in Swahili and told Maevette he'd be contacting her again real soon. Two days passed, and the male coworker called saying his play sister was in a hair crisis. She had extension braids over relaxed hair, and when she took the braids down, her hair came out. Maevette spoke to the play sister on the phone and informed her that she only knew how to start locks using the two-strand twist method. The young lady said she wasn't choosy, just as long as Maevette could do something with her hair. Well, something was done, Maevette wasn't sure of the outcome, but client number two was pleased and was willing to go along for the ride.

During that time, a year had passed since Maevette started her locs for the second time. She landed a professional acting gig at a well-known African-American theatre company on the Southeast side of Chicago. At the audition she met a Jamaican man with locs whom she would soon date and cohabitate. The Jamaican was impressed with the work she did on her own locs and took pride in watching her work on her two clients. He recognized a God-given talent and asked Maevette if she ever thought of going into business for herself. She said, "No." Then, without second thought, the Jamaican laid out an elaborate marketing plan. He and Maevette took to the streets like Bonnie and Clyde, posting flyers on streetlamp poles, mailboxes, bus shelters, and storefronts. Maevette went door to door to different businesses like traditional beauty shops that didn't offer her services, African braid shops, African apparel shops, and vegetarian restaurants. The response was very slow at first, so she maintained a traditional nine to five and did locs part time.

Maevette eventually realized that the two-strand twist method only worked for longer hair, so she called a friend who showed her how to do the single strand comb coil twist. Maevette practiced and practiced until it became second nature. Now, she could expand her services and slowly evolve into the one they called "Mae." Each summer she made a point to go to every black ethnic festival in Chicago and pass out flyers. More people started calling, and word of mouth took flight. As her popularity grew Mae had a chance to deal with almost every texture of hair imaginable. The thorn in her side was brothers and sisters with naturally wavy, curly, or straight hair. She tried the twist methods and even tried braiding, but she just couldn't keep the hair together to lock. In the summer of 2002 Mae took a locking course to learn a technique that was sure to work on finer textures of hair. At the end of the course she was certified and well-learned about product knowledge, parting patterns, scalp diseases, shampoo procedures, and advanced locking methods. The Jamaican felt the class was a waste of time, but when it came time for the artsy two to open a shop after she quit a law firm to do locs full time, he proudly boasted that a certified loctitian was on staff. After three and a half years, personality differences dissolved the relationship. The professional bond fizzled also. The shop was lost. Mae was in hiding. The Jamaican reared his ugly head, and an order of protection was established.

Mae was devastated. The relationship with the Jamaican lasted a half year longer than her first marriage on paper. Her daughter had just come to live with her as she was with her dad and paternal grandma while Maevette was finishing school. A single father appeared in Mae's life in the midst of the drama, seeming to be the answer to said prayers. The two would soon marry, and Mae's daughter would gain two brothers. Concurrently, Mae moved from shop to shop, gaining and losing and gaining and losing customers. "When will this cycle end?" she constantly asked herself. God granted her request through one of the sons she inherited upon her marriage to Mr. Brooks. It was revealed that the son had health challenges that required specialized attention. Additionally, Mae's elderly father—Mojo, the first black Mailman of the Year in the City of Chicago (1972)—lived with the family also and needed looking after from time to time. So, Mae decided to work from home, and her clients adjusted well.

Presently, Mae considers herself a cultural artist who works on live canvases. She believes the art form of hairlocking to be African-inspired and worthy of being preserved. An overachiever since early on Mae has always sought to challenge herself. After achieving status as an experienced loctician, she decided to take the Sisterlocks™ training in May of 2006. She wanted to be versatile within her art form and provide services to wearers of all kinds of locs. Taking the training was no easy task. Mae had to find a proxy to look after the children on certain days while her husband went to work. She executed a letter writing campaign to let all the authorities know what was going on.

Mae's four-day Sisterlocks training was at a hotel in Chicago near the O'Hara Airport. Her mother-in-law was gracious enough to pitch in at the hotel to watch the youngest baby and the two older children on non-school days. Fortunately, the two-year old was away out of town with his birth mom. At the close of the third day of training, her mother-in-law had to leave unexpectedly. Mae couldn't get her overnight assignment done, for all of her time was spent keeping up with the children. By the time her husband made it to the hotel, everyone was exhausted and ready for bed. On the fourth and final day, Mae went to class anyway in faith that things would work out. Everything turned out fine, and she forged some dynamic friendships that she hoped would last a lifetime.

It's now December 2006, and I, Mae Brooks, age 30, am awaiting certification from the Sisterlocks™ Home Office in San Diego, California. The previous story spans seven years of my cultural artistry, but I started working with natural hair during my first job ever as a shampoo girl over fifteen years ago. Since completing the Sisterlocks™ training, I've acquired quite a few clients through direct marketing and word of mouth. Some Sisterlocks™ consultants do not do traditional locs, so I've received referrals for traditional services also. A few people found my name on the Sisterlocks™ Trainee Registry, and I am humbled and truly grateful. What has helped me the most is believing in God, believing in myself, being surrounded by positive people, and having a supportive family. I am proud of my [hairitage] and this journey to Sisterlocks™. I hope it inspires others to embrace change and to follow their dreams. One of my dreams was to get a space that would accommodate my business and my family. Well, my family and I have been afforded the opportunity to move from a three-bedroom apartment to a five-bedroom house.

I Love My Hair. Natural hair. Chemical-free hair.
By Adrienne D. Abraham—Wichita, KS.

My first encounter with Sisterlocks was from my mother. She absolutely loves her Sisterlocks and would not trade them for the world! She talks that way with others who know not, including myself. It was this dialogue that moved me to be trained in Sisterlocks.

I was already beginning to move towards natural hair, being ever so tired of perming, touch-ups, curling and pressing; all of these methods used to straighten my hair just to discover that I was the only one who wanted straight hair! My hair certainly did not care to be straight and that fact was confirmed every time the need for a touch-up arose. My hair did not want to be straight!!

In 2002, my mother and I journeyed to Atlanta, GA for the Sisterlocks training session. I was feeling good and was very excited. I had not permed my hair for over 6 months and felt compelled to do so for this trip. I had no idea what I was getting myself into.

When we arrived in Atlanta, after checking into our hotel, we went the site for the training. We took our seats and the women with Sisterlocks started to fill the room. Immediately I felt like an idiot, an outsider. Like I did not belong there. An intruder. I was so disappointed in just perming my hair because I knew I would have to start over again in letting the perm grow out. I was convinced. NO MORE PERMS!!

Those women with Sisterlocks were proud! You could feel that they all absolutely loved their hair and would not go back for anything. It was BEAUTIFUL. It was breath-taking. That picture makes a statement—there is no fear in going natural. It should be embraced.

That was over three years ago and I have worn my hair naturally since. And I love it! I can't see going back to perms or straightening my hair. I would and do recommend Sisterlocks or Natural hair to any sister who is ready to be freed from the chains of processed/straightened hair.

GO NATURAL!

WHEN NAPPY DIDN'T MAKE ME HAPPY
By Keshia Harrell

It was November of 5th grade, and my mother and I were in the hair supply store. As we walked up the hair-straightening aisle, I figured this was as good a time as any.

"Mom, can I get a perm?"

"Perm? What you want a perm for?"

"To make my hair straight."

"Girl, you don't need no perm. Your hair is fine."

"But all the other girls in my class have perms and I don't want to be the only one with kinky hair."

"Your hair isn't kinky. It's curly and it's natural."

I wasn't going to win this argument. "OK," I sulked.

I felt like the only girl in the 5th grade without straight hair.

Mom usually did my hair in ponytails. She sometimes braided my puffy ends and left a swoop of remaining hair falling on my right cheek and three little braids in the front covering my big forehead. Other times she'd box braid my hair all over. But I went to a school where the majority of students were White or Hispanic, most with long hair. Some had naturally straight hair. But even the Caucasian and Hispanic girls who had curly hair straightened their hair.

They made me feel like I wasn't as pretty as they were because my hair wasn't as long or as straight. They made comments about my "short and kinky" hair. Some girls asked me, "Why is it like that?" Like it was abnormal. I told myself that they didn't know what they were talking about. But in 5th grade, the few girls in my school with kinky hair got perms to straighten their hair. Some wore it with a part in the middle and curled under at the ends. Others wore it half up, with the back out and drop-curls at the ends.

Why Don't You Get a Perm?

"Why don't you get a perm?" some girls occasionally asked me. I felt left out.

On top of that, every magazine I saw for Black females made me feel like I had to have straight hair too. I resembled the sad girl in some ads' "before" pictures.

And even though my mom said my hair looked fine natural, the smiling girl with her new and improved permed hair in the "after" picture succeeded in making me feel like my kind of hair wasn't acceptable. Mom or Grandma would press my hair to make it straight on special occasions, like picture day at school or friends' birthday parties. Grandma would stand over the stove, heating up the black metal hot comb over the fire. After testing how hot the comb was so it wouldn't burn my hair, she'd pull it through a section of my hair with clear hair grease. My hair was soon straight and slick.

Hair Pressure Increased

The following year, the pressure increased. When I began 6th grade in my new junior high, my classmates teased me about my wild hair.

"Yo, Keshia, you'd be pretty if you did something with your hair," one of the boys in my class told me.

"You look like an African!" said Mareena, one of my classmates. "It's so kinky."

"I am African," I told her. "African-American."

"No, you look like you're straight from Africa."

"OK," I thought. Was I supposed to take that as an insult? Africa is where my ancestors are from.

Nearly Came to Tears

Despite her ignorance, though, Mareena's comment hurt. I felt like an ugly outcast. That night, I nearly came to tears as I thought about what she'd said. But I told myself, "Don't cry. Only the weak cry. Their words or thoughts don't affect me."

I was hurt that I was being judged by something so trivial, but I wanted to be accepted. So I tried again to convince my mother and grandmother to let me get a perm or relaxer.

"No, Keshia, you don't need a perm. Do you want your hair to fall out? Then you won't have to worry about getting a perm," Grandma said.

"OK," I pouted. But I still wanted straight, flowing hair like Keshia Knight Pulliam, who played Rudy, one of the daughters, on The Cosby Show.

Then a couple of months later, my aunt asked me to be a bridesmaid in her wedding. [See sidebar.] At the wedding, all my female cousins and aunts were talking about how much easier it was to have a perm. I guess that influenced my grandma and mother, because before we went back to New York, I got my hair permed. I was so happy to be sitting in that big black leather salon chair. "When this is all over, I'll be 'pretty,'" I thought. "No one will make fun of me."

I closed my eyes as the beautician matted the chemical-smelling white cream into my hair. After a couple of minutes, though, I felt a burning sensation on my scalp. "It's burning!" I screamed. It felt as if the perm was eating my hair out from the roots. The beautician hurried over and started to rinse the cream out. I saw a few patches of hair in the sink. A little more came out as she combed. But it was all worth it to me. My hair was straight. The beautician pulled my hair into a bun, stuffing it to make it look big. I was happy. I went back to school thinking, "Finally. I'm going to fit in with the rest of the girls."

Straight Hair Not So Glorious

"Keshia, you finally got your hair permed," they said. I was ecstatic about not being teased anymore. Even the boys noticed.

"It's about time you did something with your hair," some said. "Shut up!" I yelled back. Why couldn't they just keep their comments to themselves?

After two weeks of straight hair, I realized that my perm wasn't as glorious as I thought it would be. I felt a little worse about myself because I'd changed to be accepted by others. Plus, after I took my bun out, my hair was straight at the roots and puffed out and frizzy at the ends. I wanted to scream. My hair still wasn't straight.

Suffered Through Hot Comb

"What happened to your ends?" my classmates asked. "Whoever permed your hair didn't leave it in long enough."

"Shut up!" I wanted to scream.

No matter how much I conditioned or put a flat iron through my hair, it still frizzed up. And my mother and grandmother decided against letting me keep my hair permed because of hair breakage and the burns. But I still wanted my hair to be straight. So when my perm grew out, I learned how to use the hot comb on my own. I lost a lot of hair during my time of learning. I had a habit of leaving the hot comb on the stove for too long and not testing it. I'd put the comb to my hair and hear a "sizzzzzling" sound followed by the pungent smell of burnt hair. I looked in the mirror and wanted to cry. Once, I singed my hair so badly that I ended up losing a big chunk of hair from the middle of my head. That was enough of hot combs for me.

Turned to Braids

So I taught myself to braid. At first, my braids came out crooked and bushy at the ends, but I got better since I also used my little sister's hair to practice. (She didn't mind.)

People still made comments about my hair. "I like your hair," some said. "You didn't braid it tight enough," others said.

For a while, the positive comments made me feel good. And the negative comments didn't hurt as much as they did before. I was becoming a little more confident in myself, so their opinions didn't matter as much.

High School

Still, on my first day of high school, it felt like all the girls had just walked out of a beauty parlor. They had wraps, weaves, braids and curls. My hair was in a semi-straight, semi-frizzy ponytail on top of my head. I felt like an outcast once again.

Got Sick of It All

So, for most of my freshman and sophomore year, I suffered through hot comb and curlers. At the beginning of my junior year, I was looking in the mirror thinking of how I was going to do my hair for the first day of school. Suddenly, I got sick. Sick of burning myself. Sick of having to get up in the morning to do it. Sick of my hair frizzing up when it was rainy or humid. Sick of worrying about what people would think of it. Sick of conforming to make other people happy.

So I started to braid it again. Accepting my puffs was hard. I'd get up in the morning and look in the mirror and worry about what people would think. Even now I have to repeatedly remind myself that I shouldn't worry about what others think and that if I like my hairstyle, then that's all that matters.

My Mood Determines My Hairstyle

Now I'm a high school senior, and people still stare at me because of my hair and ask, "Why don't you do something with it?" I do my hair depending on my mood. If I'm tired and I don't care, I leave my Afro-puff in a ponytail on top of my head. (People have compared it to a bird's nest, but I've grown to love it.) Other times I braid it. And sometimes when I get bored with my puffs and braids, I press my hair, just for a different look. After years of looking in the mirror and getting upset about my reflection, I realized that it wasn't me who didn't like my hair. It was the people who teased me, the sitcom actress, the girl on the magazine cover.

Now I know that I don't have to be beautiful in the societal sense; I can be beautiful in the ME sense. I don't look like every other girl in my school, and I like it that way. Sometimes, though, I still feel "ugly" because of my hair, like when I read an *Ebony* or *Cosmo Girl Magazine*. But then I think, "Whose standards of beauty say you have to have straight hair to be beautiful?" Not mine. That makes me feel better. I no longer have daydreams of looking like Keshia Knight Pulliam; I'd rather look like Keshia LaToria Harrell. Myself.

My Journey to becoming a Sisterlocks Consultant
By Jennifer P. Edwards—Washington, D.C.

My name is Jennifer Edwards and I am currently a freelance hairstylist, living in Washington, DC, and I am 29 years old. I first stumbled upon Sisterlocks when my cousin told me about a natural hair show. She sent me the link for the shows website. I explored the entire site because I was fascinated with all the classes that were offered on learning natural hair.

There was a link on that site for Sisterlocks, so I clicked on the link. From there I was in awe. I had never heard of them nor had I ever seen them in person on anyone, but they were beautiful. I explored the Sisterlocks website for a while until I saw how much it cost to take the class. And that's where my interest ended. How in the world was I going to come up with $1000 and be able to take the time off from work to take the class?

A few months later my cousin called me because she wanted to get her hair colored. She further explained that she was getting Sisterlocks done and needed to do the coloring before the locks were put in. We sat and talked for hours about Sisterlocks, how long it would take to get them done, and the cost. She also lent me her book by Dr. Joanne Cornwell. About a month later my cousin got her locks done and they looked great!

A few months after that my best friend, Tonya, came to visit me in DC. While she was here we did a lot of sightseeing. As we were doing this during her visit, I kept seeing people with Sisterlocks. I'd just walk up to them and ask if they had Sisterlocks and how long they had them. Each person I saw looked absolutely beautiful. After I did that to about three different people, my best friend asked what was I doing and what Sisterlocks was. I gave my brief description of Sisterlocks and sent her to the website. When Tonya returned home she called me and asked me about Sisterlocks again. She told me that she was interested in getting them done. I again told her to go to the website and go to the consultant's page to find someone in her area that does them. She said" no, I mean have you ever thought of doing them, you know taking the class and offering them". I said to her, "did you see how much it cost?" At that point she proceeded to say, "Well, if I'm going to end up paying $400–$600 to get Sisterlocks, I might as well pay for you to take the class and you become my consultant for life". I was speechless. All I could say was "stop playing, you're crazy". She said, "and you already know this, so what's the problem". She and I have been friends since we were 13 years old, so I knew she was serious. And when she puts her mind to something she, it happens. She continued to suggest that I take the class that was being offered a few weeks from then in Atlanta. I further knew how serious she was when she even knew that there was still an opening in that class. I told her that I had to think about it and get back to her. The next day I had done a great deal of thinking and decided to go for it. How often does a chance like this to come around? We all pray for small miracles all the time. This time mine came from an angle that I've known forever. I called her and said, "how about Detroit in July".

So now I've been given this gift that I'm so excited about that I'm telling everyone what Tonya is doing for me.

I tell my sister, who has had traditional locs for years, about it and she told me to tell Tonya that she will help her pay for the class. And when it is the right time I would give my niece, who at the time was 3 years old, Sisterlocks. That sounded good to me, so I reported back to Tonya with the news. She immediately said, "No! You tell your sister that she can pay for the hotel and airfare, the class is mine." If that wasn't the funniest thing, my two "sisters" fighting over what they were going to do for me. When it rains, it pours ... wow.

July rolls around, and I get the time off from the salon where I was working at the time. The class blew me away. It was fantastic! Every night I went to my room with a headache because of all my new knowledge. By the last day of the class I was still hungry for more, while at the same time lacking the desire to touch another silky or relaxed head of hair again. I wanted to kick myself for not learning more about natural hair. All I knew was how to cornrow, and that I had learned only a few years prior. Once I got off the plane back in DC, reality set in. As much as I wanted to only do natural hair at the time, I was still a stylist at a salon in Northern Virginia. As luck would have it, some things transpired at the salon and I chose to leave. I would not have had the courage to do so if I had not been armed with my Sisterlocks training. Being a Sisterlocks consultant gives you the freedom to have your own business and be your own boss. After I left the salon I did just that, created my business. As a freelance hairstylist, I travel to my clients to provide a variety of services. I offer hairstyling for weddings, proms and pageants, as well as Sisterlocks.

Sisterlocks classes are offered in different states throughout that year. As a benefit to Those who have taken the class, they allow you to register into any class at a great discount. Since I first took the class in Detroit, I have also been to New Jersey to take a few days of the class again. I'm thankful to be able to do this. It helps to keep things fresh in my mind. And also it is good to get input from different trainers and updates from home office. I am grateful to Dr. Joanne Cornwell for creating Sisterlocks, and also to my personal angel, Tonya, for giving me the chance to be a Sisterlocks consultant.

My Life Experience Leading to Sisterlocks
Reneá T Henry—New York, NY

Like so many African American women, I have had a complicated relationship with my hair. These days we are in love—a mature, satisfying love. I respect my hair and it respects me. We provide for one another in ways other women only wish their hair would. We complement each other. Everyone can tell we are in love. But it took some time and effort for us to get here ...

Since 2002, I have had Sisterlocks and in May 2006 I became a Consultant Trainee. I found Sisterlocks after committing myself to learning more about the ways black women relate to their own beauty. I marvel at the ways black women wear their hair. There is no end to the creativity. Sometimes no end to the lengths black women will go to try and make their hair conform to an ideal standard or beauty. For some women, the way they wear their hair is simply cosmetic. But for others, hair styling becomes an outward manifestation of a deeply rooted cultural struggle for affirmation and self-realization. My experience falls somewhere in between.

As a young girl, my hair was styled by my grandmother, a licensed cosmetologist. I got weekly washes, and on special occasions my hair was pressed and curled with hot marcel irons. In between, my mother created elaborate styles with geometric parts, fancy barrettes and tight two-strand twists. Having my hair done meant sitting still, being tugged and, once the style was complete, taking care not to mess up the handiwork. I didn't know how to comb my own hair. In fact, I wasn't allowed to 'play' in my hair. So I didn't.

My grandmother gave me my first relaxer. It was a very mild one, but it started the next phase of my hair journey. Once my grandmother died, I had to enter an open marketplace for hair care. My mother had to find someone to keep up the maintenance of the chemical process and, unlike that with my grandmother, my relationship with these people was wholly impersonal. At the same time, I started gaining other insights about the way people perceived my hair. While my mother and grandmother often talked about my hair being thick or taking so much time to style, I could never remember them making negative comments about my hair. As I became a teenager, I realized that a girl's hair was part of how people decided whether she was beautiful. Having hair that was not straight was not beautiful. My grandmother may have relaxed my hair for any number of reasons, but I felt compelled to maintain the relaxer because by the time I reached high school, I had gotten the message that my hair needed 'fixing.'

Unfortunately, the 'fix' was often more trouble than I wanted. For one thing, my hairstyle conflicted with my active lifestyle. Besides living in an extremely hot, humid climate, I was taking dance classes more than twelve hours a week. As soon as I had my hair done, it was undone. Sweating, restyling ... it was a pointless cycle. So I started cutting my hair shorter and shorter under the misguided notion that less hair would be less work. It wasn't. My hair became increasingly more high maintenance. I found out that having short hair was not seen as beautiful and I got negative feedback or worse, no feedback or affirmation from my peers about my beauty at a time I sorely wanted it. Luckily for me, in retrospect, I did not abandon my passion for studying dance because my hair became an increasing nuisance. But I knew girls who abandoned sports or other pursuits because it was not 'ladylike.' They dared not exert themselves in anyway that might take away from their appearance or draw negative remarks.

As far as hairdressers went, there was no confusion between my grandmother's loving care and the haphazard service I often got in salons. Bad haircuts, chemical burns, curling iron mishaps, I had it all. I spent hours waiting on overbooked stylists who didn't seem to understand that I had somewhere else to go and needed to keep my appointment time promptly. Out of frustration, I finally took matters and the blow dryer into my own hands. Things got worse before they got better. But I taught myself how to do a decent roller set and even got brave (foolish!) enough to try more than a few colors. I finally started playing in my own hair, literally taking matters back into my own hands.

Once I went away to college, I set out on a path that led me back to natural styles and ultimately to Sisterlocks. I went to a predominantly white university and was often too cash and time strapped to find a stylist to maintain my relaxer. After a couple of harrowing episodes with at-home perm kits in the dorm shower, I started wearing braid extensions. No longer tethered to my curling iron, I could go weeks, even months without worrying about my hair ... Well, not months (!)

I discovered when my hair got hopelessly matted after too many neglected weeks. Instead of fretting, I just cut it all off!

There underneath it all was my natural hair. For the next ten years or so, I tried every braid variation known to the Diaspora ... box braids, silky locs, two strand twist extensions, cornrows, you name it, I had them. I learned all about Kanekalon, French Refined, and 2B. But every six weeks—I learned!—I had to remove my 'hair' and start over.

By this time, I had moved to four different states and each time had to track down a dependable, skilled braider. I had grown weary of late nights spent unbraiding my hair in front of the television. And I had enough of neck cramps and lost weekends getting my hair redone. I vowed never to braid again. But what next! I was wit's end trying to figure out how to care for and style my natural, unprocessed hair. The styles I tried were time consuming and, according to my mother, unflattering. All I knew were the childhood techniques of my youth. I started to regress. I was wearing Afro puff ponytails and barrettes again! One day in a panic of weakness, I ducked into a salon and got my hair pressed. I looked like a movie star when I left, but what was I going to do when I went to the gym or took a shower? It only took a few days for the teenager in me to put her foot down and refuse to modify her lifestyle for a hairstyle. Rather than leaning on my own limited understanding, I started, for the first time researching natural hairstyles. With the same intensity I focused on my career in African American studies, I honed in on natural black hair care. You'd think I would have done so long before. But I had put precious little thought into my hair beyond keeping it presentable.

Why did so many black women shy away from wearing their natural hairstyles? Why did so many black women alter or conceal their hair altogether? It seemed like everything I had ever learned about African American culture had been preparing me to explore and embrace what would come next. I don't even remember where I first saw Sisterlocks. But I approached slowly. Growing up in the South, I had been exposed to any number of stereotypes about locked hair. While I didn't believe the negative generalizations, I didn't exactly identify either. It just didn't resonate. After my last press and curl though, I revisited every style technique I had ever seen and serendipitously came back to Sisterlocks. And this time my mind and heart was open. Here was a technique that offered all the beauty and versatility I had loved about my braid extensions without the torture of undoing them and also celebrating the natural texture of my hair. By now a professional, I easily dismissed all the suggestions I might suffer repercussions on my job for wearing locks. The more I considered Sisterlocks, the more inevitable they seemed for me.

By the time I slid into my consultant's chair to get my Sisterlocks installed, I felt as if I had taken a 360-degree journey. And it only continues. Having learned so much about natural hair and our perceptions of it, I wanted to continue. So when I had the chance, I decided to learn the Sisterlocks technique myself. Never again will I feel disconnected from my hair and my own beauty. It is in my hands and subject to my own influence. I now have the best of all worlds. No matter how I style my Sisterlocks they always fully represent the beauty and possibility of my natural hair texture. Rather than coaxing and damaging my hair to achieve different looks, changing my hairstyle is now only an exercise in imagination. My hair is healthy and strong and beautiful. We do not fight or struggle or despair with each other, we only grow more abundant. And after an initial spell of infatuation, I am no longer unduly obsessed with my hair. I no longer fret how it will behave when we go out. If a style experiment fails, I go on—still confident. Most days, I don't give my hair a second thought; I know its fine. And that's exactly as it should be. It took awhile, but my hair and I have discovered that we are perfect for one another. Despite what anyone else may think, we complement each other perfectly. I would not change my hair and it doesn't change me ... no matter how I style it. If you saw me, you could tell that I take good care of my hair, but it does not overpower me. It is not fussy or overworked. It doesn't fight me or cry out for help. I don't smother it with products or torture it with chemicals and heat. We enter the room together. We provide for one another in ways other women only wish their hair would. We complement each other. Everyone can tell we are in love.

"It takes more courage to be yourself than the courage of a soldier on the battlefield."

—Prof. Cornell West—Princeton University
On Tavis Smiley Show
1-13-07

9

Root Profit

"The significant problems we face cannot be solved at the same level of thinking we were at when we created them."

—Albert Einstein (1879–1955)

The concept of root profit is transforming your perceived natural liability into your natural asset. Take Muhammad Ali (formerly Cassius Marcellus Clay, Jr.) changed his name after he became a Muslim in the. In 1964, Ali failed the Armed Forces qualifying test because his writing and spelling skills were sub par. However, in early 1966, the tests were revised and Ali was reclassified 1A. He refused to serve in the United States Army during the Vietnam War as a conscientious objector, because "War is against the teachings of the Holy Qur'an. I'm not trying to dodge the draft. We are not supposed to take part in no wars unless declared by Allah or The Messenger. We don't take part in Christian wars or wars of any unbelievers." Ali also famously said, "I ain't got no quarrel with those Vietcong" and "no Vietcong ever called me nigger."

Ali refused to respond to his name being read out as Cassius Clay, stating, as instructed by his mentors from the Nation of Islam, that Clay was the name given to his slave ancestors by the white man. By refusing to respond to this name, Ali's personal life was filled with controversy. Only a few journalists (most notably Howard Cosell) accepted his name change at that time. The adoption of this name symbolized his new identity as a member of the Nation of Islam and provoked hatred by white America and ambiguity among blacks. Ali was essentially banned from fighting in the United States and forced to accept bouts abroad for most of 1966.

The government charged him with violating the Selective Service Act. After a long court battle, Ali was convicted of draft evasion and sentenced to five years in jail and fined $10,000 fine, but in another lawsuit in 1970, a judge ruled that Ali could still box professionally. The next year, Ali won his legal battle when the

U.S. Supreme Court said he was not guilty of draft evasion. Suddenly black people loved him but whites were steaming. In part the hatred of Ali stemmed from his religion and his public denouncement of the white man and their American standards of beauty.

According to the 1977 movie "The Greatest" where Ali played himself, his first wife's irresistible attraction for cosmetics, provocative clothing, and rejection of Islamic doctrine led to their 1966 divorce after two years of marriage. The same scene was played in the 2001 movie "Ali" starring Will Smith. Nevertheless, Muhammad Ali became the most popular person of any race in the world during the zenith of his career and even into his retirement. Muhammad Ali slowly rose from the most hated black man in America by whites to the most loved regardless of his consistent rejection of American beauty standards for black women.

There was a time when the Japanese were the most hated people in the United States. The Attack on Pearl Harbor was a surprise attack on Pearl Harbor, Oahu, Hawaii. It was launched on the morning of Sunday, December 7, 1941 (Hawaii time) by Japan's 1st Air Fleet against the U.S. Pacific Fleet and other US armed forces stationed there at the harbor and also on the other side of the Oahu island. The attack spurred the US into entering World War II. US casualties were heavy and included 2,403 dead; 1,178 wounded; 4 battleships, 3 destroyers, 3 cruisers, and 188 planes. Japan casualties, by contrast, included 64 dead, 1 captured, 29 planes and 4 submarines. Japanese American Internment was the forced removal of approximately 120,000 Japanese and Japanese Americans (62 percent of whom were United States citizens) from the West Coast of the United States during World War II. While approximately 10,000 were able to relocate to other parts of the country, the remainder—roughly 110,000 men, women and children—were sent to hastily constructed camps called "War Relocation Centers" in remote portions of the nation's interior. President Franklin D. Roosevelt authorized the internment with Executive Order 9066, which allowed local military commanders to designate "military areas" as "exclusion zones", from which "any or all persons may be excluded." This power was used to declare that all people of Japanese ancestry were excluded from the entire Pacific coast, including all of California and most of Oregon and Washington, except for those in internment camps.

In 1944, the Supreme Court upheld the constitutionality of the exclusion, removal, and detention, arguing that it is permissible to curtail the civil rights of a racial group when there is a "pressing public necessity." Americans hated *Japs* and sworn never to purchase Japanese products—NEVER!

However, Japanese filed lawsuits and some compensation for property losses was paid in 1948, but most internees were unable to fully recover their losses. In 1988, President Ronald Reagan signed legislation, which apologized for the internment on behalf of the U.S. government. The legislation stated that government actions were based on "race prejudice, war hysteria, and a failure of political leadership" and beginning in 1990, the government paid reparations to surviving internees. In 2007, Toyota sales were 13% higher in the United States than Ford and General Motors. Americans buy more Japanese cars such as the Lexus, Cambry, Avalon, Corolla, Tercel, Sienna, FJ Cruiser, Paseo etc. As a result, Americans have made Japanese cars the number seller in the United States.

Another example of turning your perceived negatives into root profit is the plight of big women. Big women were once perceived as unattractive but big women got together and started a BIG BEAUTY WOMEN Network. All around America there are Big Beauty Women Clothing Stores, size plus models and big women nightclubs and health spas. These women refuse to give anyone permission to make them ashamed of themselves any longer, and they are receiving the profits, not their skinny oppressors. There are several black celebrities that rose from dire circumstances and used the thing that plagued them the most as a rope to pull them out of their pit of pain and into wealth.

When the ugly side of life dumps manure on you, don't waddle in it—make fertilizer and sell it on the open market. Mo'Nique, comedienne and actress, chose to do the latter. In her book, <u>Skinny Women Are Evil</u>—*Notes of a Big Girl in a Small-Minded World* (2004) Mo'Nique turns her experience of being ridiculed about her robust frame into a humorous book that hit the New York Times Best Seller's List. In <u>Skinny Women Are Evil</u>, Mo'Nique strips away the stigma of being weight-challenged and introduces a new vocabulary in which F.A.T. is FABULOUS AND THICK. That is root profit!

Everybody knows about the cruelty of slavery upon black people but what many have not considered is how ex-slaves turned their pain into big profits. The plight of the sharecropper was just a fine hair above slavery. The disadvantage lays in the fact that the black laborer worked the field and grew the crop and the white landowner kept the books. When it came time to spit the profits the landowner usually cheated the illiterate laborer. By the time the landowner deducted the expenses of living on the farm, the taxes, the cost of expenses; all kind of made up expenses, the laborer ended up with only a few dollars above his debt and sometimes he was left in debt to the landowner, which compelled him to work another year. Black folk would sit on the front porch of their shack in the evening and play their harmonica, guitar, or fiddle and sing about their pain, which gave birth to the Blues. From the book <u>Trouble in Mind</u> (1998) by historian Leon F. Lit-wack, I've extracted an original song. Check out the words and see how they turned their pain into profit. This is an excerpt from a song that ended up selling a lot of records.

Well, it makes no difference
How you make out your time
White man sho' to bring a
Nigger out behin'

Chorus:
Ain't it hard? Ain't it hard?
Ain't it hard to be a nigger, nigger, nigger?
Ain't it hard? Ain't it hard?
For you can't get yo' money when it's due

Lemme tell you, white man
Lemme me tell, honey
Nigger makes de cotton
White folks get de money

Ef you work all de week
An' work all de time
White man sho' to bring a
Nigger out behin

The settlement placed the black tenant and sharecropper in a vulnerable posi-tion. Since most were illiterate, they could not challenge the figures or the con-tractual arrangement. "Well, you had to take their word for it," Kelly Jackson recalled in <u>Trouble in Mind.</u> "What they said, you couldn't argue with them. You better not 'spute them. They would tell you at the end of the year you just have to take what they say. You couldn't ask question." If literate, the laborer still dared not question the settlement, if he valued his job or his life. "I have been liv-ing in this Delta thirty years," a Mississippi sharecropper revealed, "and I know that I have been robbed every year; but there's no use jumping out of the frying pan into the fire. If we ask any questions, we are cussed, and if we raise up we are shot, and that ends it."

You may work on the railroad
You may work on the freight
You may get up in the morning
And work till late

You may work around the house
Till the big settling time
It makes no difference
You are coming out behin'

Many men and women left the drudgery of sharecropping and became professional Blues singers like Robert Johnson, Lighting Hopkins, Muddy Waters, John Lee Hooker, B. B. King, Alberta Hunter, W. C. Handy, Sippie Wallace, Billie Holiday, Bessie Smith, Lucille Hegamin, Ida Cox, many, many more. After the murder of a black man in Tennessee a blues singer wrote these lyrics, which was sung in juke joints.

Tom Moss was an innocent man
He was at home in bed
Teacher of a class in Sunday School
Was shot through the head

Oh me, oh my, Lord have mercy on me
Oh me, oh my, Lord have mercy on me

They are roaming the streets with guns
Looking for us to shoot
All we can do is pray to the Lord
There is nothing else we can do

All black singers, including gospel, are rooted from the Blues because they gave us the Blues before they gave us religious. Speaking of gospel, very few accomplished individuals exemplifies root profit like the black preacher. Slave masters gave slaves Christianity to discourage them from uprising and brainwash them into humility; however, the slaves and ex-slaves could not pray in the same area of the church as whites. There was a separate section for blacks, usually in the balcony while the white preacher whooped and hollered about love and going to heaven. It was racism that created the black church. The early rationale for slavery was based upon the idea that Native Americans and Africans were not Christian. Faced with Africans that had converted to Christianity, in 1664 Maryland passed a law that baptism into Christianity did not free a slave. That did not deter slaves from becoming Christians. In Christianity they saw hope. Certain scriptures, I imagine, let them know that God had a better plan for them; for example: Deuteronomy 28:13—*And the LORD shall make thee the head, and not the tail; and thou shalt be above only, and thou shalt not be beneath.* From the same Christianity that slave masters used to further enslave Africans backfired and churches became slave's main gathering place for planning, plotting, and praying for freedom.

We are a people with superb resilience. No matter how low we have been, no matter the odds against us, as Maya Angelo says in her poem, *and still I rise.* Today seventy-five percent of African-Americans in America are Christians. The most popular preachers in America are black pastors and many have mega-sized congregations and are renowned worldwide such as: Rev. Creflo Dollar, Rev. Eddie Long, Rev. T. D. Jakes, Rev. Frederick Price, Rev. Bill Winston, Rev. John Cherry, Rev. Juanita Bynum, Rev. Floyd H. Flake, Rev. Beverly 'Bam' Crawford and hundreds more, and ex-rappers like Rev. M.C. Hammer, Run Simmons from Run DMC, ex-actors like Desmond Wilson, and Rev. Clifton Davis each with their own nationally televised Christian ministries, books, seminars, and major conferences.

"You don't get in life what you want but you get what you are.
Use your passion to become millionaires"

—Les Brown
Motivational speaker and Author
Black Enterprise Report
1-14-07

Hundreds of major gospel singers and writers was ultimately created from the roots of racism such as Mahalia Jackson known as 'The Queen of Gospel Song,' and Tommy Dorsey known as 'The Father of Gospel Music.' These early artists expressed their pain of white oppression through Christian songs and became the favorites of royalty worldwide. Black churches are responsible for the establishment and support of many black colleges, major charities, civil rights leaders such as Reverend Martin Luther King, Jr., and black politicians such as Ohio Secretary of State Kenneth Blackwell. If the whites had not pushed Christianity down the throats of slaves much of the wealth of African-Americans today would not exist.

The antidote for the venom of delusional self-hatred is knowledge of self, which will inculcate within us a vision of who we were, whose we are, and where we need to go. This vision is jump-started with an understanding of our history. For our history is not something that is to be discarded as useless, worthless or obsolete, but is vital to our very survival as a people. Amos N. Wilson writes in his book, <u>The Falsification of African Consciousness</u>: "When we get into social amnesia—into forgetting our history—we also forget or misinterpret the history and motives of others as well as our motives. The way to learn of our own creation, how we came to be what we are, is getting to know ourselves. It is through getting to know the self intimately that we get to know the forces that shaped us as a self. Therefore knowing the self becomes knowledge of the world. A deep study of Black History is the most profound way to learn about the psychology of Europeans and to understand the psychology that flows from their history. If we don't know ourselves, not only are we a puzzle to ourselves; other people are also a puzzle to us as well. We assume the wrong identity and identify ourselves with our enemies. If we don't know who we are then we are whomever somebody tells us we are."

Many black women were ashamed of their hair as a child but few turned the stigma of her hair into a goldmine; however, Caryn Johnson aka Whoopi Goldberg did. Whoopi once said in an interview, "The first person I ever saw with dreads was Rosalind Cash, and I remember thinking she looked incredible, but I didn't consider it for me then," she says. "I was wearing my hair in a little natural and I used to braid it. And then one day, much later, I just got tired and I said, 'You know, I'm never taking these braids out.' But for so long my particular package was alien to everybody."

During her 1984 one-woman show, that Whoopi Goldberg picked author Bebe Moore Campbell (1950–2006) from the audience to play-off-of in one of her sketches. She skipped out onstage with a white shirt draped over her head, speaking in the pip-squeak voice of a child: "Hi, I'm 9, and this is my long, blonde hair," she announced, veering in Campbell's direction. Campbell sat mortified on the front-row, watching her approach. "Here I come," Whoopi muttered under her breath, staring at Campbell with a steely gaze. In an instant Whoopi had lured Campbell on the stage. "Your braids are so pretty," she gushed, as she bent over and stroked the cornrows Campbell wore at the time. "Don't they call you nappy head?" she asked pointedly. "Not anymore," Campbell shot back. Campbell later said in an *Essence Magazine* article, "It was, as they say of religious conversions, a defining moment. A look passed between us of recognition, understanding, shared pain. The audience roared."

Today, as she did more than two decades, Whoopi Goldberg hair manages to captivate audiences. The dark-skinned, dreadlocked woman, who has grossed Hollywood billions of dollars at the box office, unashamedly adorns her ever-present dreads. Goldberg has been recognized as well for her humanitarian efforts on behalf of children, the homeless, human rights, substance abuse, and the battle against AIDS. In 1995 her hands, feet, and signature braids were pressed in cement outside Mann's Chinese Theater in Los Angeles, and in 2001, she received a star on Hollywood's Walk of Fame.

Richard Pryor, who many considered a comedic *genius*, made a fortune by putting a comedic spin on his less than desirable roots. Root profit at work. Early in his career, Pryor used the word 'nigger' like bullets being fired from a machine gun. Perhaps his background made him think like a nigger and ultimately made him believe that he was a nigger. The Bible says in Proverbs 23:7—*For as man thinketh in his heart, so is he*. Ralph Waldo Emerson once said, "The ancestor of every action is a thought." Pryor acted like a nigger, called himself a nigger, and subconsciously became a nigger. He considered 'nigger' as part of his heritage, the roots of his existence in America ... then he reconfigured it to his advantage; although, it made the more subdued society uncomfortable, they snuck into record stores and bought his albums in massive numbers, which included, *That Nigger is Crazy* and *Bicentennial Nigger*. Pryor also created a popular skit called *Supernigger*. While Pryor gained great financial wealth, his personal life was a carousel of pathological episodes.

Later in his career after a trip to Africa in 1991, Pryor vowed to stop using the word nigger, which was the word that propelled him to stardom and earned him the dubious title of comedic genius. However, by that time, 75% of the black comics around considered the word nigger their comedic meal ticket, their membership into the proverbial and unofficial Raw Comics Club, and ultimately their passport to fame.

On November 27, 2006, (after Michael Richards, a white comic, got national scorn for using a barrage of racial slurs including the word nigger on an audience of black heckers at the Laugh Factory in Los Angeles) Paul Mooney, another comedian notorious for using the word nigger, (former comedic writer and friend of Richard Pryor) vowed to stop using the word. Nevertheless, less than two weeks later, black comedian, Damon Wayans was banned from The Laugh Factory, according to news reports, when he used the word 'nigger' 16 times in his 22 minute act. He reportedly later said regarding the club owner, "No white man is going to tell me not to use the word. It's part of our heritage." He seems to be unaware to the fact that many black national and community leaders, educators, and women groups have consistently pleaded for black comics and rappers to stop using the word, especially as entertainment. But what else can you expect from a man who reportedly in 2001 attempted to trademark the word 'Nigga' for a line of clothing. Fortunately, the Trademark Office has denied Wayan's application but he seems adamant to see impressible black youth wearing his Nigga clothes with the word Nigga on their T-shirts, caps, and jackets, which of course would set a national trend among the sequacious hip-hop generation. This attempt is root profit at its worse and would surely violate the Law of Reciprocity. The means would not justify the end. However, Wayans seems apathetic to the psychological harm his venture would create. Some celebrities are proof that talent and integrity are not synonymous.

In the field of sports, root profit can be seen everywhere. We all realize that black athletes are dominant in any sport that they were allowed access as a child. Baseball, basketball, boxing, and track are inexpensive to pursue; therefore African-Americans enjoyed such activities as a child and later excelled in high school sports, which led many to an athletic scholarship. Of course, there was a time when African-Americans were not allowed in any of the aforementioned professional sports. Most star black athletes came from humble beginnings; this was especially true prior to the 1980s. All they had were their natural instincts; no previous training. This is particularly the case in boxing. Black men were considered by white society as criminals, street thugs, and destine for prison. Unfortunately, many black males lived the life that white people prophesized. Many acquired street-fighting skills and many went to prison; however, from the streets and prisons came several world-boxing champions.

John Arthur Johnson (1878–1946), better known as Jack Johnson and nicknamed the "Galveston Giant", was an American boxer and arguably the best heavyweight of his generation. He was the first black Heavyweight Champion of the World, 1908–1915. For more than thirteen years, Jack Johnson was the most famous, and the most notorious, African-American on Earth. That started it all for black men in the boxing arena.

Ever since Joe Louis became heavyweight champion of the world in 1949 until 2006, there have been approximately sixty heavyweight champions of the world and approximately five out of six of them were black men. These men fought from their heart. They battled their way from gang infested neighborhoods, crime, prisons, and poverty to become world champions. Fighting was all they knew because of who they were and who they were had a lot to do with racism. White fighters went into boxing for the sport; black fighters went in for survival and to vent a deep-seated anger against whites, even if his opponent was another black man. That was the difference. When a man is fighting for survival and revenge, he will defeat the man out for the sport of it every time. Speaking of anger, George Foreman was a very angry heavyweight fighter.

"There has never been an athlete in the history of American sports who has so totally transformed his image from thug to hero. George Foreman became a jovial pitchman, and in the process recaptured the heavyweight championship at age forty-five. He will be missed." (The Boxing Times-1997)

Apart from his ads for Meineke Mufflers, Foreman also tours the world promoting his George Foreman Lean Mean Grilling Machine. Interestingly, Foreman has made more money from his grilling machine contracts than he made during his entire boxing career. He has also suggested that he's better known for the grill than he is for his boxing. The grill has become world famous as a fat reducing inexpensive fast cooking household item. The grill slogan is "knock out the fat" (even though the makers of Foreman's grill have shown no evidence that using the grill significantly reduces the fat content of foods over normal grilling methods.) Since it was first sold in 1995, over 55 million grills have been purchased. Foreman has made well over $150 million from the sales of his grills. This is more money than he made during his long boxing career.

Foreman won't say how much he has made as a product endorser, but he doesn't dispute a published estimate that his lifetime earnings are about $240 million—three times what he earned in the ring. In 1999, Salton bought the rights to use his name and selling skills in perpetuity (which means even when he's dead) for $127.5 million in cash and $10 million in stock. It stands as one of the biggest endorsement deals for any athlete. Under the original '95 deal, Foreman had a right to about 40% of the profits from the grills, which range in price from $20 to $150. At the height of its success, Foreman received $4.5 million a month in payouts, says Salton CEO Leonhard Dreimann. In 2004 Foreman began marketing the George Foreman brand of "Big and Tall" clothes through the retailer Casual Male. His clothing features "comfort zone" technology, which expands and contracts as the wearer's weight fluctuates. Foreman went from an antisocial, uneducated, thuggish, street fighter to become a well-respected role model and multi-millionaire, that's root profit.

An eagle does not escape the storm. It simply uses the storm to lift it higher.

—Author unknown

10

Black Hair Care Film Documentary

Black hair care business moved into hairweaves in the early 1990s. Human hair was originally a niche market for cancer victims and suffers of alopecia but suddenly hairweaves became an accessory for every beauty supply store in the black community. By the late nineties, 1.3 million pounds of human hair valued at $28 million were imported from countries like China, India, and Indonesia, where poor women sell their hair by the inch. Once the hair arrives in America, already sterilized and styled, it goes on to wholesalers who sell the goods to beauty supply shops, beauty parlors, and hair retailers. Previously controlled by Jewish merchants, the human hair business is now dominated by Korean immigrants, many who barely speak English.

To see a video and documented proof of how much control Koreans have over the black-beauty supply industry login at www.youtube. com/group/reformationblackhair on the Internet. Watch three videos; (1) Black hair I update July 2006; (2) Black hair II update July 2006; and (3) Black hair documentary part four.

I randomly visited 17 beauty supply stores in Los Angeles. As it turned out only 2 were black owned and 15 were non-black, mostly Korean and/or Asian owned. There were oblivious anti-theft mirrors in all of the stores and several stores even had armed security guards on duty. All of the stores had signs warning that the owner would prosecute theft to the fullest extent of the law. I don't blame the merchants for protecting their merchandise from pilferage; however, it seems clear to me that many African-Americans cannot afford to keep up the cherished image presented to blacks by the cosmetic industry. This obsessive madness of ethnic hair products is also the catalyst to the criminal justice system for many black teens.

African-Americans are the most economically disenfranchised people in America, yet their inferiority complex is responsible for the wealth of many corporations. There was a time when African-Americans at least owned a share of the business. Today none of the major ethnic hair manufacturers are black owned and very, very few beauty supply stores in urban communities.

Korean/Asian beauty supply stores boast that 99% of their customer base is black. I don't know of one black-owned business that can boast of a 99% Asian customer base not even if they owned a gasoline station in the heart an Asian community. Even if there is a popular soul food restaurant in the block, they seldom, if ever, go in to patronize. I realize that many Asians do not have the same diet as black people but in the name of maintaining a good relationship, they could at least wander in once a year and order a green salad or cup of coffee. Of the few black banks that exist, I seldom seen an Asian in line with a deposit slip but I have seen dozens of African-Americans with deposit slips in various Asian banks. Neither have I seen an Asian woman receiving a manicure from a black manicurist. Manicures and pedicures received by black females provided by Asians is another one-sided relationship. I only point this out as a fact—not bigotry. Asians have the right to do business anywhere they please but blacks need to be aware of the unilateral dynamics involved.

However, the fact the Asian people support each other before they support others is no reason to resent them. As a matter of fact, I would like to duplicate their commitment. They are in a foreign country that is prejudice against their people. If they didn't have a good plan to survive, their position in this country would be disastrous. Most likely Asians are acculturated with certain values that follow them throughout their lives, anywhere in the world. The same holds true with Jewish people. Both ethnic groups are discriminated against in America and if it were not for their stick-togetherness, racism in America would have stomped them perpetually into poverty. Their history in this country is atrocious; nonetheless, while I applaud the ingenuity of Jews, Asians, Latinos, and other minorities in the United States, my financial loyalty should begin in my mirror—not theirs.

Since the onset of African America history, women have been to forerunners of progressive change. As observation reveals repeatedly black women are increasingly the predominant readers, consumers, voters, worshippers, nurturers, most effective complainers, and promoters of justice. As far back as Harriet Tubman and the Underground Railroad, black women have been a formidable political force. However, it remains the innate duty of black men to adamantly support and protect black women and the interest of the race. Black men must not allow black women to stand-alone against the American standard of beauty. Black men have unintentionally become the most influential gratuitous promotion for the ethnic hair industry by sending the message to black women that they prefer them in hairweaves, wigs, and chemically straightened hair.

Today black women of social conscience are faced with three choices, which are (1) to adopt the beautiful styles on natural hair much as various locks, or (2) strongly encourage your beautician to buy black owned products, (3) to purchase their hair products from black manufacturers and from black beauty supply stores.

Misinformation Can Become a Way of Life

A whopping percent of Americans are classified as overweight. American holds the dubious distinction of having more fat citizens than any other country in the world according to the World Health Organization. American health standards misguided its citizens hundreds of years ago regarding healthy eating habits. By American standards of health a person should eat three times a day to maintain optimum health. This information was passed from one generation to the next. A nation embraced this doctrine. Now in nearly every home in America the standard of eating habit is three times a day. Every restaurant in America looks forward to the breakfast, lunch, and dinner crowd. Americans eat because it is time to eat not because we are hungry.

Health experts today warn us that we are eating too much. Health experts now recommend that we eat much less, which is difficult because we are under psychological bondage. Even though we now know that we were given false information in elementary school most of us continue to eat at least three times a day. Most overweight people and most black people grew up with erroneous information that has become a psychological addiction. If you never want to get an idea of how difficult it is to convince a hairweave wearing black woman to denounce her superficial hairstyle and embrace her natural hair then go to McDonalds during lunch hour and try to convince a fat person to denounce hamburgers and fries and eat an apple for lunch.

Today, millions of Americans spend billions of dollars each year on diet books, diet pills, and weight loss programs. There are health clubs open 24 hours a day, 7 days per week with personal trainers on staff. There are surgeries to remove fat and surgeries to shrink stomachs, and surgeries to wire the mouth shut. The American standards of health mislead America many, many years ago just as the American standard of beauty have been doing for many, many years.

African-Americans also spend billions of dollars annually on products claiming to make them naturally beautiful. Everyone in America lives in a world of overeating and a world of superficial beauty and if you embrace the lie it will cost you dearly.

There are other misconceptions passed off as truths. Want another revelation? When you were in school, you were taught that there were nine planets. Right? Well, in August 2006 there was a major astrological discovery and as a result Pluto was demoted from a planet to a dwarf planet. According to scientific data, dwarf planets are *not* planets. Therefore the information that the world has accepted as fact is false; there are really eight planets—not nine.

American standards of beauty have a long record of using psychological warfare on insecure people around the world and then, once sufficiently indoctrinated, an observant opportunist comes along and sells the psychological miracle-healing antidote. Most of the miracle-healing products are based on the stigma of being dark skinned. The skin whitening cream market earns billions annually.

"A lie told often enough becomes the truth"—*Vladimir Lenin*

Not comfortable in your own skin? Lighten up!

If you can't beat the system, try to join it. It is a worldwide phenomenon, affecting Asians, Africans, Indians, and other non-European peoples. Women, of course bear the brunt of the pain in this racist syndrome, as the cultures attach light skin tone to the highest standards of feminine beauty. Amina Mire, a university professor in Toronto publishing part of a doctoral dissertation in a special report for <u>Counterpunch</u>, *Pigmentation and Empire: The Emerging Skin-Whitening Industry*, does an excellent exposé of the health risks posed by products created and distributed by multinational corporations that profit handsomely from this sickness. The pursuit of the American standard of beauty has been the destruction of a large range of nationalities, ethnicities, and cultures of people worldwide far beyond the affliction of the descendants of African slaves in American. Even the most unlikely suspects are the victims of white-madness. Below you will find excerpts of Mire's dissertation.

At least in the United States, racially white eastern and southern European women have used skin-whitening in order to appear as 'white' as their 'Anglo-Saxon' "native" white sisters. In the United States, women of color also have practiced skin-whitening. Many of the early skin-bleaching commodities such as Nodinalina skin bleaching cream, a product, which has been in the US market since 1889, contained 10 per cent ammoniated mercury. Mercury is a highly toxic agent with serious health implications. According to Kathy Peiss, in 1930, a single survey found advertising for 232 different brand names of skin-bleaching promoted in mainstream magazines to mainly white women [that's right, white women] consumers in the United States. [Aging white women often develop dark spots on their face, hands, and bodies referred to as liver spots and in the All-American tradition to maintain youth and perceived beauty they, too, become victims of the Frankenstein Monster white people created.]

For example, almost all the medical literature published by western medical and dermatology journals offer us women of color as victims of the dubious desire for unattainable corporeal whiteness. This same unattainable desire is often reinforced with horrifying images of the damaged faces and bodies of women of color after using cheap skin-whitening containing toxic chemical agents such as ammoniated mercury, corticosteroids, and hydroquinone.

Some of the leading transnational corporations engaged in the 'trafficking' of skin-whitening products have extensive e-business domains. Often these companies set up Internet domains and e-shops in specific countries such as China, Japan, South Korea, Thailand, Singapore, Indonesia, just to name a few. [Even Asians are chasing the white-madness.] In addition to such e-business sales drives, extensive use of the Internet allows these corporations to avoid both the negative political implications and legal regulatory restrictions they could face if they were to openly promote skin-whitening commodities in North America and European markets.

The ethnic skin-whitening products which target poor women, around the world, particularly black women, including women of color living in North America and Europe, are relatively cheap but often contain highly toxic chemical agents such as mercury, hydroquinone and corticosteroids.

In Europe and North America, the 'ethnic" skin-whitening products are usually sold in 'ethnic-oriented' grocery stores and "beauty" salons. Many of these low end' but toxic skin-whitening products are manufactured in the Third World and are imported both legally and illegally to North America and Europe. Even though the western health authorities are well aware of the health risks associated with these toxic skin-whitening products they have taken very little if any, action to control their importation or to regulate their sales.

The other, more robust trend is the marketing of expensive skin-whitening products to affluent Asian women in living in Pacific Asian countries such as Japan, Korea, China, Thailand, Singapore, Malaysia, Indonesia and others. This represents the largest slice of the skin-whitening global market.

Partly because of the covert nature of the trafficking and informal circulation of toxic skin-whitening commodities, it is hard to gain accurate estimates of the market share of the 'low end' but highly toxic skin-whitening market. Similarly, because the 'high end' and, presumably less toxic skin-whitening commodities targeted to whites are promoted under the purview of *'anti-aging therapy,'* it is as difficult to gain an accurate or even a generally reliable estimate of the North America and European market shares of skin-whitening products targeted to white women. However, in Asia, where the skin-whitening market outside of Europe and North America is anchored, in 2001, in Japan alone, the skin-whitening market was estimated to be worth $ 5.6 billion. According to the same report, the fastest growing skin-whitening market in Asia is China. In 2001, China's skin-whitening market was estimated to be over $ 1.3 billion.

Based on the readily available mass of online advertising for emerging 'high end' skin-whitening products by transnational corporations, these products claim that they can 'improve' the 'appearance' as well as the 'health' of users. These skin-whitening commodities have powerful pharmaceutical properties; they can penetrate the skin and suppress the synthesis of the skin pigment, melanin. Indeed, the suppression of 'dark' pigment, melanin, is listed as an explicit example of skin-whitening health promotion benefits. Frantz Fanon wrote about the "corporeal malediction" of dark skin and here's the antidote! The damned of the earth can thus swiftly alleviate their condition by peaceful, albeit commercial means.

"In many of the advertisements for skin-whitening 1 come across during my research," said Mire, a discursive link is made between youthfulness and whiteness and whiteness and racial superiority. Second, in these advertisements, the aging process of white women is often implicitly racializing by the construction of 'hyper-pigmentation,' 'age-spots,' 'dull' skin tone,' as signs of "pigmentation pathologies". Consequently, skin-whitening advertising directed to white women often promises to 'cleanse,' 'purify,' 'transform' and 'restore' white women's 'smooth' and 'radiant' youthful white skin. Such advertising tries to expand the skin-whitening market with the covert rhetoric of racializing aesthetics. One recurring theme which runs through most of the promotional ads for skin-whitening posted at Asia registered Internet sites is the claim that skin-whitening cosmetics can transform the 'yellow' skin tones of Asian women to flawlessly 'radiant' white. These advertisements often deploy the visual technique of 'before' images of 'unhappy,' 'dark' faces of 'Asian-looking' models and 'after' images of smiling 'whitened' faces of the same models.

"I now want to take the reader to the Internet-based advertisements for skin-whitening products by the world's largest cosmetics company a leading promoter of new skin-whitening cosmetics the L'Oreal cosmetics company. L'Oreal's advertisements for skin-whitening products posted at Internet sites run by L'Oreal subsidiaries such as Lancôme, Vichy Laboratories and L'Oreal Paris systematically deploy a mixture of racializing rhetoric and dazzling visual images.

"Many of these advertisements which are directed mainly to Asian women use images and narratives with implicit references to the aesthetic 'inferiority' of 'dark' and 'yellow' skin tones of Asian women. In these ads, this implied is often reinforced with illustrations of the pathological nature of 'dark' and 'yellow' skin tones of 'Asian-looking' models. [L'Oreal enjoys an extremely large and loyal African-American customer base.]

"With over $14 billion sales in 2003, L'Oreal is the largest cosmetics company in the world. The company can be best understood as an economic 'super-structure' consisting of, at least, 12 major subsidiaries such as Lancôme Paris, Vichy Laboratories, La Roche-Posay Laboratoire Pharmacaceutique, Biotherm, L'Oreal Paris, Garnier, L'Oreal professional Paris, Giorgio Armani Perfumes, Maybelline New York, Ralph Lauren, Helena Rubinstein skincare, Shu Uemura, Maxtrix, Redken, SoftSheen-Carlson. Not all of the above listed L'Oreal subsidiaries deal with the promotion of skin-whitening cosmetics. However, this extensive list of L'Oreal subsidiaries illustrates the company's economic power and structural complexity. L'Oreal is also a 20 per cent shareholder of a major French based pharmaceutical firm, Sanofi-Synthélabo.

"A recent merger worth 60 billion dollars with another European based pharmaceutical firm, Aventis, makes Sanofi-Aventis the third largest pharmaceutical company in the world behind Pfizer and GlaxoSmithKline. I emphasize the financial link between Sanofi-Aventis and L'Oreal cosmetics in the present work partly to highlight L'Oreal's close connection with the pharmaceutical industry [as well as the movie industry, which was discussed earlier]. Skin-whitening, in this context, can be thought of as a lucrative 'spin-off' both for L'Oreal as well as a way to valorize research and development of pharmaceuticals outside the highly regulated biomedical domain."

BI-White:The skin Pigmentation ID
Source: http://www.vichy.com/gb/biwhite.

The ad reads:
More than half of Korean women experience brown spots and 30 per cent of them have a dull complexion. Over-production of melanin deep in the skin that triggers

brown spots and accumulation of melanin loaded dead cells at the skin's surface create a dull and uneven complexion. Vichy Laboratories has been able to associate the complementary effectiveness of Kojic Acid and pure Vitamin C in an everyday face care: BI-White.

Another L'Oreal advertisement for skin-whitening brand is called White Perfect. This particular skin-whitening brand is sold in L'Oreal's Asian markets and online e-shops. In that way, those who live outside Asia can purchase this and other L'Oreal skin-whitening brands over the Internet. In this ad, the racist aesthetics of "White-Perfect" reinforces the biomedicalized intervention of Asian women's skin coded by the sign of "Melanin-Bloc.

It is ironic that the cosmetic companies and movie industry sets the standard of beauty and then sell the female public the products to measure up. It is a perfect example of buying bandages from the beast that mauled you. Think about it ... if a beast is in the business of selling bandages it cannot stay in business unless customers are mauled on a regular basis. People are so easily manipulated, that I guaranteed you that if the ethnic hair industry (which includes the movie industy) decides to start promoting the beauty of black skin and short wooly hair and broad noses and spent several billion dollars per year for 20 years in the ad campaign, the world would begin to look quite different. All the super star female actress and models (who are the most powerful beauty standard for women) would be dark with short laniferous hair. Women would began having plastic surgery on their noses to look as African as possible and skin darkening cream would be the fasting selling product in the world.

I remember when black people with big lips were teased (by other black people) because the movie industry vicariously told us through their black buffoon actors that big lips were part of being black, ugly, and stupid. However, gradually the movie and cosmetic industry decided to call big lips luscious and full lips. I never heard the words luscious or full regarding big lips before the 1990s. Suddenly, big lips, the same lips that were ridiculed in racist caricatures throughout the centuries were in vogue. The same lips that until recently kept beautiful African-American women off the pages and covers of slick women's magazines. The lips that were the butt of racist jokes in millions of living rooms, boardrooms, ballrooms and private dining rooms and maligned so savagely that some most African-Americans were ashamed of them are now luscious. Yes, it is those same big, thick, full, luscious lips that are now all the rage, so much so that white women are running to doctors, begging to have their thin bird lips enlarged. I empathize with the manipulated white puppets that are seduced by media power.

"It's a fad that has become very popular," says Dr. Pearlman Hicks, a black plastic surgeon in Long Beach, Calif., who has noticed the trend among white women, especially in Hollywood but also elsewhere in the nation. "I'm not surprised that white women now want larger lips," says Dr. Hicks. "Beauty standards are moving more toward homogeneous definitions. Beauty is not necessarily blond hair and blue eyes any more. Now the models, especially in French publications, are so homogeneous that you can't tell what their background is. This ethnicity is becoming the new standard of beauty, and Caucasians are having their lips enlarged, attempting to become more exotic, more beautiful."

Other specialists agree, "It used to be full lips said you weren't white, Anglo-Saxon Protestant, which was considered negative," Dr. Arnold Klein, a Beverly Hills dermatologist, said in *U.S.A. Today*. "Now full lips are considered attractive, evidence of our shrinking global village." He and other dermatologists and plastic surgeons report that lip augmentation has been increasing among celebrities for years. And on magazine covers and in fashion and beauty layouts, women with big, voluptuous, richly-colored lips have replaced those with ribbon-thin lips. Today, the white stars, as well as ordinary women, want full mouths like the beautiful black women and men they once ridiculed. I never dreamed that someday the American standard of beauty would reverse and *my kind* of lips would be vogue. There are many pouty-mouthed white stars such as Michelle Pfeiffer, Julia Roberts, Kim Basinger, Brigitte Bardot and Sophia Loren, Angelina Jolie all of whom have been praised for their big, sensual lips that a few decades ago the same lips on black people were considered a laughing matter. Actress Julia Roberts' generous lips and broad, alluring smile has inspired legions of women to rush out for collagen and Botox injections. "My lips are so big I don't have to think about it, do I?" says Roberts. "But anything anybody does to make themselves look nice, more power to them."

Actress Barbara Hershey has admitted having her lips enlarged, and Cher, Madonna and a number of other entertainers and models are sporting the new puckered look. Whether or not the stars are using cosmetics or surgery to plump up their lips is a sensitive issue with many. Miss America Marjorie Judith Vincent also admits that she was at one time ashamed of her lips. "When I was younger, I remember—to be honest—that I didn't at first like my lips," says the third African-American woman to bear the coveted title that is synonymous with American beauty. "My lips were not the standard of what society said was beautiful at that time. I didn't think about it that much, but I felt some discomfort with my lips. But I'm not ashamed any longer, now I'm proud of my physical appearance," she says with confidence. "It is something I came to be comfortable with a long time ago, long before I became Miss America." Imagine that! Miss America was ashamed of her lips until society said it was okay to have big lips because the cosmetic and movie industry decided to call them luscious. But here again is manipulation. Don't allow yourself to be flattered or made ashamed of something that you had nothing to do with. Do not judge me by my lips but the words that come from my lips—that is what I am responsible for. India Arie sung, *I am not my hair* perhaps she should add another line that explains *neither am I my lips.* Society is fickle. If you continue to be so easily lead, one day the cosmetic and movie industry may decide that you should wear a designer shoebox on your head and you will be glad to do so and readily snub those that do not conform.

Never doubt that a small group of thoughtful committed citizens can change the world.
Indeed, it is the only thing that ever has.—Margaret Mead

I saw a movie in the 1960s starring Burl Ives. I don't remember what it was about but the title was powerful, it was called, "Let No Man Write My Epitaph." Isn't that a powerful statement? Let no man write my epitaph seems to say that you should write your own present, future, and tombstone. Why would you allow another person with an ulterior motive to decide your fate? During the Jim Crow era racist laws and policies controlled African-Americans. What's the difference in being controlled psychologically by companies that promote beauty products based on the African-American inferiority complex, which they created?

Sometimes I wonder how people, especially women, were duped into thinking that their body is a canvas for *body art.* God creation of woman has worked perfectly. Women have always been able to attract the opposite sex. Whose idea was it that she needs body art? Does the flowers in your garden need *pedal art* to improve it? Physical beauty is highly overrated. On one hand, most women resent being treated as objects but on the other hand, they accept by exploitation of the tattoo craze. It is like the materialistic person's pursuit of more and more things. They can never have enough.

According to a 1/09/07 TV documentary called "Addicted to Plastic Surgery" on the *WE Channel* (a channel dedicated to women) many women's obsession with the American idea of beauty has developed into an addiction. The show was centered on Beverly Hills plastic surgeons and their patients. Several of the women interviewed (all white—most under forty) were recipients of at least five cosmetic surgeries at different times. A 71-year-old woman, once married to actor

Gig Young, had received so many surgeries by so-o many doctors that she wouldn't remember the number. All of her earlier photographs showed her as a beautiful woman who had no need for cosmetic surgery in the first place. All through the show she desperately sought additional cosmetic surgery, which she was turned down by every doctor that saw her deformed face. Other women in their twenties admitted that they were addicted. One particular young married woman with children had already put her family in over $100,000 worth of debt and still argued with her husband that she wanted another nip and tuck to feel good about herself. During the course of the program, a belly dancer, admitted to having several liposuctions. The camera followed her to her doctor's office where she insisted on another one. The doctor finally agreed to schedule her for the procedure, although she wanted it right then. He later said that liposuction operations were the number one requested surgery in his business. "Young women feel they must have a perfect abdomen," he said. "Some men are also obsessed with plastic surgery."

Fashion Industry Yanks Our Chain

The fashion industry yanks us around also. Every day there's new fashions. The outfit you bought yesterday is out of style next month and you must have the latest. That cycle will continue throughout your lifetime. You will never be in fashion more than a few months, until you are out of style again, if you are easily manipulated.

Pajamas used to be reserved for the privacy of your home. Remember? Females seldom opened their front door in pajamas unless covered by a robe. However, the fashion industry has approved pajamas in public. As a result, males and females are seen in public in pajamas and fluffy slippers. Some schools have Pajama Day while others have banned students from wearing pajamas to class.

I remember when blue jeans were blue and fashionable—not faded or bleached out—remember that? There was a time when nobody would intentionally wear torn and ripped jeans other than a bum. But the fashion industry decided *vintage* jeans are in and brand new looking jeans are out. And now old beat-up, faded, and torn jeans are more expensive than the new undamaged crisp blue old-fashioned originals.

The American standard of beauty defies and challenges God and discipline as it dangles hard to resist temptations. Those of weak conviction are lured astray. The Bible says in John 15:12—*This is my commandment, that you love one another as I have loved you.* The American standard of beauty teaches us not to love one another but the shame each other into conforming to beauty standards set in place by forces other than God. If we loved one another as Christ loved us, we would not ridicule someone because of their innate physical feature, neither would insecure folks feel compelled to get nose jobs, breasts implants, tummy tucks, hairweaves, eye-widen surgery, use skin whiteners, and lose dangerously amount of weight to be accepted. This corrupt world would have you alter your body in a desperate attempt to be accepted. God didn't require us to cover ourselves with tattoos, facial and body piecings, and/or cosmetic surgeries to be loved. It is crucial that we (African-Americans in particular) learn to keep the main thing—the main thing, which is love for yourself because you are commanded to love your neighbor as you do yourself. However, if you have been manipulated to not love yourself then you can never fulfill God's commandments of love.

Asians and the American Beauty Standard

Asians are increasing seeking to remake themselves to American beauty standards. As reported in *Time Asia Magazine* 7/29/02—The culturally loaded issue today is the number of Asians looking to remake themselves to look more Caucasian. It is a charge many deny, although few would argue that under the relentless bombardment of Hollywood, satellite TV, and Madison Avenue, Asian's aesthetic ideal has changed drastically. "Beauty, after all, is evolutionary," says Harvard psychology professor Nancy Etcoff, who is the author of <u>Survival of the Prettiest:</u> *The Science of Beauty*—not coincidentally a best seller in Japan, Korea, Hong Kong and China. Asians are increasingly asking their surgeons for wider eyes, longer noses and fuller breasts—features not typical of the race. To accommodate such demands, surgeons in the region have had to invent unique techniques. The No. 1 procedure by far in Asia is a form of blepharoplasty, in which a crease is created above the eye by scalpel or by needle and thread.

In the U.S., blepharoplasty ranks near the top for Asians. In Taiwan, a million procedures were performed in 2001 double the number from five years ago. In Korea, surgeons estimate that at least one in 10 adults have received some form of surgical upgrade and even tots have their eyelids done. (That reminds me of the African-American women that take their tots to the beauty salon for hair relaxers, perms, and hair weaves.) In Japan, noninvasive procedures dubbed "petite surgery" have set off such a rage that top clinics are raking in $100 million a year. The government of Thailand has stopped plastic surgery except in emergencies.

In Elsewhere in Asia, this explosion of personal re-engineering is harder to document, because for every skilled and legitimate surgeon there seethes a swarm of shady pretenders. Indonesia, for instance, boasts only 43 licensed plastic surgeons for a population of about 230 million; yet an estimated 400 illicit procedures are performed each week in the capital alone. In Shenzhen, the Chinese boomtown, thousands of unlicensed "beauty-science centers" lure hordes of upwardly mobile patients, looking to buy a new pair of eyes or a new nose.

The results are often disastrous. In China alone, over 200,000 lawsuits were filed in the past decade against cosmetic surgery practitioners, according to the *China Quality Daily*, an official consumer protection newspaper.

Philippians 2: 14–16—*Do all things without murmuring and arguing, so that you may be blameless and innocent, children of God without blemish in the midst of a crooked and perverse generation, in which you shine like stars in the world. It is by your holding fast to the word of life that I can boast on the day of Christ that I did not run in vain or labour in vain.*

Too beautiful for prison: No jail time for Tampa Teacher Debra LaFave

Americas' obsession with beauty evades the criminal courts as the lawyer of a female guilty of having sex with a minor male argues that his client is too beautiful for prison. Children are dispensable in the view of her lawyer. The molester is this case was one of a rash of white female schoolteachers accused of having sex with young boys. However, the emphasis on this molester was her blonde hair and nice looks, which softened public outrage, as it would have been against an adult male teacher upon a minor female student. Before teaching, according to the molester herself, she was promiscuous as a teen, raped as a preteen, explored glamour modeling, had low self-esteem, bouts of depression, and finally turned to illegal drug use. Below is a summary of the story that made international news:

A former Florida teacher Debra LaFave who was arrested in June 2004, pleaded guilty in November in Tampa to having sex with a 14-year-old male student who attended the middle school where she taught in Florida's Hillsborough County, will not have to stand trial on additional charges because prosecutors dropped those charges.

"I am very remorseful," LaFave said at a news conference in Tampa. LaFave said she has bipolar disorder and is receiving therapy for the mental disorder. Her attorney said last year that LaFave would be in danger in prison because she was so beautiful. It appears her attorney's statement that Lafave was "too beautiful" to go to prison came true. As for Debra LaFave, she is now free to profit financially from her notoriety. She was sentenced to house arrest with limited privileges to leave home for a few hours a day.

Under the plea agreement reached with the Hillsborough prosecutors, LaFave, 25, was sentenced to three years of house arrest and seven years probation. She faced additional charges in neighboring Marion County for having sex with the same student during a trip there. Prosecutors in Marion County agreed to the same plea because the boy's parents said they did not want him to have to testify at what was expected to be a widely covered and televised trial.

11

Conspiracy Against Black-owned Cosmetic Companies and Black Consumers

The Rev. Jesse Jackson and other black leaders met with executives of Revlon Group and demanded that the company sever its ties with South Africa because of apartheid. Revlon executives had called the meeting to seek to end a two-week boycott organized in protest of comments in *Newsweek Magazine*. Rev. Jackson said the boycott would continue until Revlon had divested its business in South Africa, improved its hiring record for minorities and altered its strategy for TCB, a chemical based hair care product exclusively for African-Americans, which produced a curly hair look. Rev. Jackson demanded that Revlon altered it marketing strategy for the hair product that was the craze of the black community at the time. Although Rev. Jackson charged that the company was practicing unfair sale tactics, the meeting centered on insulting remarks make by a Revlon executive.

The comments made in *Newsweek* that prompted the boycotted occurred in November 1986, when Irving Bottner, president of Revlon's professional products division, told *Newsweek*, "In the next couple of years, the black-owned businesses will disappear. They'll all be sold to white companies." He added, "We are accused of taking business away from the black companies, but black consumers buy quality products—too often their black brothers didn't do them any good."

The implication was that African-Americans clearly preferred doing business with non-black businesses. So Rev. Jackson and a few other African-Americans got mad. In February 1987 Rev. Jesse Jackson staged a mock funeral at The House of the Lord Pentecostal Church in Brooklyn, NY and over 400 mourners attended and tossed into the empty casket their products manufactured by the Revlon Company in protest of the statement make a few months earlier by its president. The African-American mourners vowed to bury Revlon and would not allow "the MAN" to take over an industry that was rightfully a black inheritance.

By 1988, as Bottner predicted, white-owned companies dominated more than 50% of ethnic hair care market; however, Revlon, Alberto Culver, Helene Curtis, and other majority white-owned companies were not content with majority control. They wanted to fully control the multi-billion-dollar ethnic hair industry. By the end of the eighties and into the nineties, the ethnic hair-care industry had not slipped away from black ownership completely but nearly completely. George Johnson and his wife of 38 years, the last major holdout company, divorced and as part of the settlement Johnson relinquished Johnson Products ownership to his wife. In 1993, Joan Johnson sold the company to the white-owned Ivax Corporation for a reported sixty-seven million dollars. That marked the end of an era, which would never be regained because of African-Americans loyalty, according to an L'Oreal marketing report.

At the horizon of the new millennium, the black hair-care industry had loss all of the monopoly as it enjoyed over a century prior. It is amazing that none of the early female pioneers (Annie Malone, Madame C. J. Walker, Madame Sarah Washington, and others) of the industry sold their ownership to white companies, which I am sure was after them to do so. Perhaps it was because these businesswomen had a higher motivation than money. They were role models and inspiration for thousands of black women to become entrepreneurs. They saw a need for the race to become financial independent of white domination. Today, the manufacturing side of the industry is practically owned by large white-owned corporations. Johnson Products was sold again in 1998, to white-owned Carson Products. Soft Sheen Products, started in 1964 by Edward Gardner an African-American former elementary school principal in Chicago, was sold in 1998 to French cosmetics giant L'Oreal. And Pro-Line Corporation, once owned by African-American businessman and major philanthropist Commer Cottrell was sold to Alberto Culver.

In 1900, Booker T. Washington edited a volume entitled <u>A New Negro for a New Century</u>, in which he stated, *"The African-American woman can prove to the world that Negro Womanhood when properly treated and educated will burst forth into gems of pure brilliancy unsurpassed by any other race."*

Ethnic Hair Products Report From Mintel, a Major Market Researcher

Who is Mintel? Mintel is a global supplier of consumer, media, and market research and intelligence. For more than thirty years Mintel's services have provided unique insight that have a direct impact on the success of their corporate clients. Mintel helps companies discover opportunities, monitor competitors, develop products and services, and hone their marketing and advertising efforts. Mintel Reports provides a rigorous analysis of market landscapes and a performance forecast for each category. You may check out Mintel at www.mintel.com or go online to (PDF) Hair Styling Products US 02.

The pdf file is 110 pages; however, I didn't read nearly that much, I scanned through a few pages and excerpted approximately four or five paragraphs; you may review the entire report on the Internet by inserting 'Ethnic Hair Products Report From Mintel, a Major Market Researcher' in your browser. The following is an excerpt of some of the information contained there regarding black hair care products as it pertains to African-Americans. I underlined and/or highlighted in bold some of the more eye-opening statements.

John Frieda—Founded in 1990, Wilton, Connecticut-based John Frieda Professional Hair Care holds the distinction of owning one of the most popular hair styling product, showing 2001 sales of over $35 million from its Frizz-Ease product. The company's brands include frizz-ease, sheer blonde, beach blonde, ready-to-wear, and relax, a line introduced in 2001 to specifically address the needs of *black hair*. Unlike the majority of hair styling products found in FDM channels, John Frieda owes much of its success to drug store sales, which goes back to the line originally being introduced in drug stores before it reached nationwide distribution. According to the company, drug stores account for 50% of sales, while mass merchandisers and supermarkets account for 30% and 20% respectively.

In August 2002, it was announced that The Andrew Jergens Company, the U.S. subsidiary of Japanese soap-maker Kao Corporation, would buy John Frieda Professional Hair Care, Inc. for $450 million.

L'Oréal—Established in 1909, L'Oréal is the world's largest cosmetics company. The company is broken up into four divisions—consumer (hair care, skin care and makeup), professional (salon hair care), luxury (beauty products and fragrances), and active cosmetics (dermo-cosmetic products). The company's U.S. hair care brand names include L'Oréal Studio Line, Studio FX, Bodyvive, Colorvive, Curl Vive, in addition to a number of hair color, makeup and designer fragrance lines. **Recognizing opportunities present in the black hair care market, L'Oréal acquired Soft Sheen in 1998, and with it came the mass-market Optimum line and salon-exclusive Mizani, which both include hair styling products as well as shampoos, conditioners and relaxers.** Further in that direction, the company purchased Carson in 2000, and added its ethnic hair care products to its stable. The company also acquired Kiehl's. Since 1851, and its prestigious line of hair, skin and body care products, and Matrix Essentials, a salon line of hair care products, in 2000. In 2001, L'Oréal opened the L'Oréal Institute for Ethnic Hair & Skin Research in Chicago, a center dedicated to generating information for the general public, as well as scientists and doctors, on various ethnic personal care issues. (I guess that's a good thing that they have scientists and doctors looking at our skin and scalps before that push chemical based products and cause damage as in the early 1900s.)

Further cementing its position in the broader hair care market, L'Oréal USA took on a number of salon-only hair care products with the acquisition of ARTec Systems Group in 2002. The company reported sales of $12.2 billion in 2001, up 2% from 2000, and L'Oréal's North America business accounted for some 32% of total sales. Consumer product sales (hair care, skin care and makeup) accounted for more than half of all sales.

Alberto-Culver—Based in Melrose Park, Illinois, acquisition, as well as invention, has been the key to Alberto-Culver's success. The company's first product was Alberto VO5 Conditioning Hairdressing, created in the early 1950s and still on the market today. TRESemmè, sold on the premise of being salon-quality products at FDM store prices, was acquired in 1959. This was followed by the introduction of Alberto VO5 hair spray in 1961, and Alberto Consort hair spray for men in 1965. **Though the company already owned two black hair care lines—TCB (mass market) and Motions (salon-quality)—Alberto-Culver continued the trend of mainstream companies acquiring small black hair care companies with the acquisition of Pro-Line in 2000. The acquisition made Alberto-Culver the number two ethnic hair care products company in the world, according to the company's annual report.**

Alberto-Culver reported U.S. sales of $1.94 billion in 2001, up from $1.70 billion in 2000; total company 2002 sales were $2.65 billion, up from $2.49 billion in 2001 (fiscal year-end is September 30). While its Sally Beauty Supply chain contributes over half of company sales, the company credits 2001–2002 sales growth to the introduction of the TRESemmè Hydrology line.

Sally Beauty Supply began as one store in New Orleans in 1964. Today, Sally Beauty is the world's largest distributor of professional beauty supplies. Sally Beauty currently owns and operates more than 2,400 Sally Beauty Supply stores worldwide, including stores in 48 states, Puerto Rico, Japan, Germany, the United Kingdom, Ireland, Mexico and Canada. In 1969, Alberto-Culver acquired Sally Beauty Supply.

African-Americans Can Barely Afford the High Prices of Black Hair Products

The black hair care products companies "legitimately" earn an exuberant profit from the unnecessary chemically based hair accessories. The manufacturers' markup is 300% to 500%, which is free enterprise; however, it is illegal to monopolize a product or corner the market so that you can fix the prices as high as to want. When a major company buys out all the competition, it is no longer a free market. Such companies are in violation of antitrust laws, or competition laws. These are laws that prohibit anti-competitive behavior and unfair business practices. The laws make illegal certain practices deemed to hurt businesses or consumers or both, or generally to violate standards of ethical behavior. Government agencies known as competition regulators regulate antitrust laws, and may also be responsible for regulating related laws dealing with consumer protection.

L'Oreal has been charged with violating antitrust laws by the United States Government, which includes raising prices beyond the reach of the market. Their feeling is since the customer has nowhere else to go they can charge whatever they want. This price fixing causes many black kids and adults go to jail everyday for shoplifting hair products. You will have an opportunity to read an excerpt of the court documents in the next chapter.

To purchase the hair relaxer, conditioner, gel, and other accessories, which is needed approximately every 6 weeks, could easily cost $25 or more. Twenty-five dollars doesn't sound like much to a working adult but unemployed preteens, teenagers and single moms also want long silky hair. Most drug store managers in Los Angeles can tell you that they can hardly keep the ethnic hair products on the shelf, and in many cases there is no record of the sales. It is common knowledge that store employees treat black people, teens especially, as suspected thieves. The manager of a major supermarket in Los Angeles told me that ethnic hair products are stolen more than any other single item in the store followed by liquor then food. He told me that there were approximately four to eight shoplifters apprehended per month, usually female teenagers with hair products or accessories. The problem was solved when he put all of the ethnic hair products in a locked glass case. However some black community members complained to corporate but corporate supported his decision. A drug store manager in Los Angeles told me that she have a different employee per shift, seven days per week, assigned to monitor the ethnic hair products. She said that teenage girls were the biggest problem. "It's a Catch-22," said the white female manager, "some try to purchase the stuff with their Electronic Benefits Transfer or EBT [an electronic food stamp account] and when that fails their only other option is to steal it."

The following is a copy of a group email that I received in October 2006:

CVS Drug Stores and Black Hair Products

In some CVS stores, of all the hair care items vended there, only those marketed to African-Americans are tagged with anti-theft devices. This is a follow up to the e-mail, which I sent on Friday. On today, I went to my neighborhood CVS store to personally see for myself if the news reports of this national drug store profiling African-Americans by placing anti-theft devices on only Black hair care products were valid. After arriving at this store, I looked at both expensive and none expensive White hair products and I found NO anti-theft devices. I then looked on the boxes of both expensive and not expensive Black hair care products. What I found was shocking! ONLY Black hair care products had anti-theft devices on them. I immediately went to the store management and asked why did only the Black hair products have these devices? The store manager looked like a 'deer caught in the headlights of an approaching car.' He said White hair products also had the anti-theft devices. I asked him to walk please walk to the aisle with me and show me the White hair care products which had these anti-theft devices and he refused escort me to the aisle and show me and he was not able to tell me of any White hair care products which had the anti-theft devices on them! I immediately turned in my CVS cards and respectfully told this manger I would NEVER shop in this store and that I would inform all of my family, friends and Internet friends of this. I am now keeping my promise to inform each of you of this dirty, hidden, secret ploy of this national drug store CVS.

In early May 2006, this denunciation of racial profiling by pharmacy giant CVS began circulating on the Internet. According to news segments we found, the charge appears to have a basis of truth—in some CVS stores television news reporters visited, only hair care products meant for African-American consumers were security-tagged; the other kinds available on the shelves bore no such tags.

As reported by *News Channel 7* in Spartanburg, SC: "We bought hair care products from the CVS/pharmacy store in Boiling Springs. The hair relaxers for African-American women have security tags. Similar, more expensive hair straighteners for Caucasian women did not" and "We bought these boxes of 'Just

Five' hair color from the same shelf at the CVS store on Chesnee Highway in Spartanburg. The two for African-American women have security tags. The one for Caucasian women, no tag."

However, it was pointed out this had not been the case in every CVS visited. "That's two out of three CVS stores in Spartanburg and one out of eleven CVS stores in Greenville. The other CVS stores tagged hair products for both whites and African-Americans, or none of them."

A similar piece aired on 5 KCTV in Kansas City, MO. According to its investigation of ten area CVS stores (Olathe, Shawnee, Mission, KCK, Prairie Village, KCMO, Northland, and Independence), security labels were affixed only to products designed for African-Americans. The investigation found the same practices were not used at other drug stores like Osco and Walgreen's.

When called upon by the reporters from each of these news agencies to answer their findings, CVS explained it places security tags on products that are shoplifted the most. However, a follow-up piece by *News Channel 7* reported: "We checked with law enforcement to see if these hair care products have been reported stolen at the stores where we found such tagging. The Spartanburg County Sheriff's Office tells us over the last year thefts of sleeping pills and stuffed animals have been reported at a CVS on Chesnee Highway in Spartanburg and thefts of unknown items have been reported at this CVS in Boiling Springs. The Greenville Sheriff's Office tells us there have been no shoplifting reports at the CVS on Roper Mountain Road, but that often retailers don't report minor theft because they don't realize it's happened right away."

The South Carolina NAACP plans to ask CVS to change the way it tags its hair products.

In recent years several large chain retailers have been the targets of lawsuits charging them with unfairly treating minority customers as thieves, with plaintiffs claiming that the stores engaged in racial profiling and accused minority customers of shoplifting despite a lack of evidence that any thefts had occurred.

Theft of retail goods is a problem of almost unimaginable proportions. In 2001, the National Retail Federation estimated shoplifting cost retailers $10.23 billion, up from $8.45 billion in 2000. A 2003 University of Florida survey of 118 major retailers found that shoplifting cost retailers in the United States more than $10.7 billion in 2002, which is more than $29 million a day.

Drug stores are particularly prone to "shrinkage" (the retail industry's term for merchandise theft) because the goods sold in such establishments are generally small and easily pocketed. Some retailers, such as CVS, combat the light-fingered with Electronic Article Surveillance technology, an anti-shoplifting system that involves attaching electronically detectable tags to merchandise. It is these tags that are the subject of the current rumor about hair care products intended for African-Americans.

In the next chapter is an excerpt from court document regarding the United States versus the major ethnic hair product companies, namely L'Oreal and Carson. It's an antitrust case where the government is trying to stop those companies from monopolizing the ethnic hair market and price fixing. The government is trying to protect African-American women who are the disproportionate consumer and victims of the industry's tactics, just as Rev. Jesse Jackson tried to stop the deceptive marketing practices of Revlon three years earlier. I only excerpted the areas where African-American women were mentioned and the part that detailed the penalties and remedies. Especially notice the statements highlighted in bold and/or underlined. To read the court document in it's entirety (16 pages) insert *US v. L'Oreal* in your browser on the Internet. You will be angered by the blatant disrespect show by the ethnic hair industry to their most loyal and easiest manipulated customers.

IT'S NOT EASY BEING BLACK

by Richard O. Jones

Black folks used to say, "Take it easy"
But it's not easy being black
Folks don't take time to ask a fellow's name
They just say, "What's up Jack!"

It's hard for a black person to borrow money
The banks assume they won't get it back
So they have to go and rob somebody
I tell you ... it's not easy being black

And all black people can't dance!
The way white folks expect
And every now and then you do meet one
That can pass a credit check

It's not easy being black
Everyone expects you to be cool
And arrive to the meeting on CP time

And be the first to break the rules

Black preachers are expected to jump over the pews
And all the women expected to kick and holla'
The children put a dime in the collection plate
And the grown folks put in a dollar

All black folks wanna go to heaven
That's why so many get saved and that's a fact
And at the Pearly Gate they all can testify
O' Lord ... it wasn't easy being black

12

United States District Court District of Columbia, United States of America

Plaintiff,
v. Judge Royce C. Lamberth
L'OREAL USA, INC.,
L'OREAL S.A.,
and
CARSON, INC.,
Defendants.
Civil Action No. 1:00CV01848
Filed: August 8, 2000

COMPETITIVE IMPACT STATEMENT

The United States, pursuant to Section 2(b) of the Antitrust Procedures and Penalties Act, ("APPA") 15 U.S.C. §§ 16(b)-(h), files this Competitive Impact Statement relating to the Proposed Final Judgment submitted for entry in this civil antitrust proceeding.

I. NATURE AND PURPOSE OF THE PROCEEDING

On July 31, 2000, the United States filed a Complaint alleging that the acquisition of Carson, Inc. ("Carson") by L'Oreal USA, Inc. ("L'Oreal") would substantially lessen competition in violation of Section 7 of the Clayton Act, as amended, 15 U.S.C. § 18. The Complaint alleges that Carson and L'Oreal are, respectively, the nation's largest and third largest suppliers of adult women's hair relaxer kits sold in the United States. The proposed acquisition of Carson by L'Oreal will result in L'Oreal's controlling three of the top five selling brands and approximately 50 percent of adult women's hair relaxer kits sold through retail channels in the United States. As alleged in the Complaint, the elimination of Carson as a significant competitor substantially increases the likelihood that L'Oreal will raise prices of adult women's hair relaxer kits post-acquisition, thereby harming consumers.

Accordingly, the prayer for relief in the Complaint seeks among other things: (1) a judgment that the proposed acquisition would violate Section 7 of the Clayton Act; and (2) permanent injunctive relief that would prevent Defendants from carrying out the acquisition or otherwise combining their businesses or assets. At the same time the Complaint was filed, the United States also filed a proposed settlement that would permit L'Oreal and L'Oreal S.A. to complete their acquisition of Carson provided that certain assets are divested to preserve competition. The settlement consists of a Proposed Final Judgment and a Hold Separate Stipulation and Order. The Proposed Final Judgment orders Defendants to divest the *Gentle Treatment* and *Ultra Sheen* brands and associated assets to an acquirer approved by the United States. Defendants must complete these divestitures within ninety (90) calendar days after the filing of the Complaint, or five days after notice of the entry of the Final Judgment, whichever is later. If Defendants do not complete the divestitures within the prescribed time, then, under the terms of the proposed Final Judgment, this Court will appoint a trustee to sell the brands and associated assets. In the event a trustee is appointed, the Proposed Final Judgment provides that the trustee shall have the right, upon approval by the United States, to divest Carson's manufacturing facility in Chicago, Illinois. The Hold Separate Stipulation and Order, which this Court entered on July 31, 2000, and the Proposed Final Judgment require Defendants to maintain the products sold under the *Gentle Treatment* and *Ultra Sheen* brands as an economically viable part of an ongoing competitive business, with competitively sensitive business information and decision-making relating to the products sold under the two brands kept separate from L'Oreal's other businesses. Defendants have designated two Carson employees to monitor and ensure their compliance with these requirements. The United States and Defendants have stipulated that the Proposed Final Judgment may be entered after compliance with the APPA. Entry of the Proposed Final Judgment would terminate this action, except that this Court would retain jurisdiction to construe, modify or enforce the provisions of the Proposed Final Judgment and to punish violations thereof.

II. DESCRIPTION OF THE EVENTS GIVING RISE TO THE ALLEGED VIOLATION OF THE ANTITRUST LAWS

A. The Defendants

1. *L'Oreal S.A. and L'Oreal USA, Inc.*
L'Oreal S.A., a French corporation based in Paris, France, is the world's largest hair care and cosmetics company, with operations in over 150 countries and over 42,000 employees. Last year, L'Oreal S.A. reported over $10 billion in worldwide annual sales and $11 billion in total assets. Among L'Oreal S.A.'s wholly owned subsidiaries is L'Oreal USA, Inc. ("L'Oreal"), a Delaware corporation headquartered in New York, New York. Both L'Oreal S.A. and L'Oreal manufacture and market such well known brands as *L'Oreal, Lancome, Maybelline, Laboratories Garnier, Redken 5th Ave NYC, Ralph Lauren Fragrances, Giorgio Armani Parfums, Biotherm* and *Helena Rubinstein*. Soft Sheen Products, Inc. ("Soft Sheen"), based in Chicago, Illinois, is a wholly owned subsidiary of L'Oreal. L'Oreal acquired Soft Sheen in 1998. Soft Sheen makes and sells ethnic hair care products, **which are products primarily formulated for, and marketed to, African-American consumers.** These products include hair relaxer kits, hair color kits, hair dressings, shampoos and conditioners. Soft Sheen's brands include *Optimum Care,* the top-selling retail brand of adult women's hair relaxer kits in the United States. It also sells retail adult women's hair relaxer kits under the *Alternatives* and *Frizz Free* brands.

2. *Carson, Inc.*
Carson is a Delaware corporation headquartered in Savannah, Georgia. Founded in 1901, Carson is a global leader in products **specifically formulated to address the physiological characteristics of hair of consumers of African descent.** Carson makes and sells a complete line of ethnic hair care products, including hair relaxers, shampoos, conditioners, hair oils, hair colors, and shaving cremes. It is the nation's leading manufacturer of adult women's hair relaxer kits, which are sold through retail channels under the brands *Dark & Lovel, Gentle Treatment,* and *Ultra Sheen.* <u>Carson reported worldwide sales for 1999 of approximately $169 million.</u>

B. The Proposed Acquisition

On or about February 25, 2000, L'Oreal entered into an agreement with Carson to purchase for $5.20 per share the common stock of Carson. The value of the cash tender offer is approximately $79 million. This proposed combination, which would substantially lessen competition in the sale of adult women's hair relaxer kits in the United States, precipitated the United States's antitrust suit.

C. The Hair Relaxer Industry and the Competitive Effects of the Acquisition

1. *The Relevant Market Is Adult Women's Hair Relaxer Kits Sold Through Retail Channels in the United States*

The Complaint alleges that the development, production and sale of adult women's hair relaxer kits through retail outlets is a relevant product market under Section 7 of the Clayton Act. **Hair relaxers are chemicals used primarily by African-American women** to straighten their naturally curly hair prior to styling. Unless an African-American woman with naturally curly hair relaxes her hair, any hair style she adopts, aside from a totally natural look, will be short-lived. By relaxing her hair, an African-American woman has more styling options. **Between 65 and 80 percent of adult African-American women routinely relax their hair, spending in excess of $200 million annually on hair relaxers and associated products.**

Adult women's hair relaxer kits are marketed specifically to African-American women for home use. Each relaxer kit typically contains everything needed to relax hair, including: (i) a complete set of instructions; (ii) gloves; (iii) two bottles of chemicals (the activator and relaxer base) that, when mixed, form the chemical that relaxes the hair (invariably the active chemical in relaxer kits is "no-lye" calcium hydroxide); (iv) a bottle of a neutralizing shampoo to deactivate the relaxer; (v) conditioners to repair split ends and make the hair appear thicker or fuller; and in some kits, (vi) a gel to protect against scalp injury.

There are no good substitutes for adult women's hair relaxer kits. The unique qualities and characteristics of these hair relaxer kits distinguish them from products such as hot combs and professional hair relaxers sold in bulk to beauticians. Because of the unique qualities and characteristics of adult women's hair relaxer kits, a small but significant increase in the price of women's hair relaxer kits would not cause a sufficient number of purchasers to switch to other products so as to make such a price increase unprofitable. Thus, the Complaint alleges that a relevant product market in which to assess the competitive effects of this acquisition is the development, production and sale of adult women's hair relaxer kits through retail outlets.

The Complaint further alleges that the United States constitutes a relevant geographic market within the meaning of Section 7 of the Clayton Act. L'Oreal's and Carson's adult women's hair relaxer kits are manufactured in, and sold and compete throughout, the United States. Virtually no adult women's hair relaxer kits are imported into the United States. A small but significant increase in the price of adult women's hair relaxer kits would not cause a sufficient number of purchasers to switch to hair relaxer kits manufactured outside the United States to make the price increase unprofitable.

2. *Anticompetitive Consequences of the Acquisition*

The Complaint alleges that L'Oreal's acquisition of Carson will likely have the following anticompetitive effects: (i) competition generally in the development, production and sale of adult women's hair relaxer kits would be substantially lessened; (ii) the actual and potential competition between L'Oreal and Carson would be eliminated; and (iii) prices for adult women's hair relaxer kits would likely increase. Specifically, the Complaint alleges that Carson and L'Oreal are respectively the nation's largest and third largest suppliers of adult women's hair relaxer kits, and together own three of the top five selling brands. L'Oreal's *Optimum Care, Alternatives,* and *Frizz Free* brands and Carson's *Dark & Lovely, Gentle Treatment,* and *Ultra Sheen* brands of adult women's hair relaxer kits operate as significant competitive constraints on each firm's prices for its brands. If L'Oreal is permitted to acquire Carson, the substantial competition between the two companies would be eliminated, and L'Oreal would have the power to profitably increase prices unilaterally for one or more of its brands of retail adult women's hair relaxer kits, to the detriment of consumers.

This acquisition would increase concentration significantly. The market for adult women's hair relaxer kits is highly concentrated under a standard measure of market concentration employed by the term "sunk costs" as used in this context includes the costs of acquiring tangible and intangible assets that cannot be recovered through the redeployment of these assets outside the relevant market—in other words, costs uniquely incurred to enter the adult women's hair relaxer kit market, and which cannot be recovered when a firm leaves the relaxer market or enters another market.

Economists, called the Herfindahl-Hirschman Index ("HHI"). In this highly concentrated market, with a HHI of approximately 2,100, L'Oreal has a share of about 17 percent and Carson has a share of about 33.5 percent of total dollar sales of adult women's hair relaxer kits through retail channels. After acquiring Carson, L'Oreal would dominate the market with approximately a 50.5 percent share, making it nearly twice the size of its next largest competitor. Following the acquisition, the HHI would increase by over 1100 points from approximately 2100 to over 3200, well in excess of levels that raise significant antitrust concerns. The Complaint alleges that entry is unlikely to be timely, likely or sufficient to restore the competition lost through this transaction. Barriers to entering this market include: (i) the substantial time and expense required to build a brand reputation to overcome existing consumer preferences; (ii) the substantial sunk costs for promotional and advertising activity to secure the distribution and placement of a new entrant's kit in retail outlets; (iii) the inability of a new entrant to recoup quickly its substantial and largely sunk costs in promoting its brand; and (iv) the difficulty of securing shelf-space in retail outlets. **Most hair relaxer kits introduced in recent years have been unable to gain significant sales within several years after entering. This is due in part to the degree of consumer loyalty and brand recognition for long-established, well-regarded brands such as Carson's *Dark & Lovely, Gentle Treatment* and *Ultra Sheen* and L'Oreal's *Optimum Care*.** To succeed, an entrant must gain consumer confidence and trust, *as hair relaxers contain powerful chemicals that may pose significant danger health risks, such as burning one's scalp and hair.* The assets to be divested are defined and described in the Proposed Final Judgment as the "Hair Care Assets." *See* Section II(D) of the proposed Final Judgment. These assets also include other products (in addition to hair relaxer kits) sold under the *Gentle Treatment* and *Ultra Sheen* brands, but exclude the *Precise* and *Perfect Performance* brands. *See* Section II (H) of the Proposed Final Judgment. The divestiture of other ethnic hair care products sold under the *Gentle Treatment* and *Ultra Sheen* brands will enhance the acquirer's ability to compete post-divestiture.

Developing a reputation for quality, reliability, and performance of one's hair relaxer kit generally takes many years of effort. In short, new entry into the development, production and sale of adult women's hair relaxer kits through retail channels in the United States is time-consuming, expensive and difficult, and thus is unlikely to deter Defendants from exercising market power in the reasonably foreseeable future.

III. EXPLANATION OF THE PROPOSED FINAL JUDGMENT

The Proposed Final Judgment requires significant divestitures that will preserve competition in the sale of adult women's hair relaxer kits through retail channels in the United States. Within ninety (90) calendar days after July 31, 2000, the date the Complaint was filed, or five days after notice of entry of the Final Judgment, whichever is later, Defendants must divest the *Gentle Treatment,* and *Ultra Sheen* brands and associated assets (including the "Johnson Products Co., Inc." and "JP" names) to an acquirer that, in the United States's sole judgment, has the intent and capability (including the necessary managerial, operational, technical and financial capability) of competing effectively in the business of adult women's hair relaxer kits. This relief has been tailored to ensure that the ordered divestitures restore competition that would have been eliminated as a result of the acquisition, and prevent L'Oreal from exercising market power in the adult women's hair relaxer kit market after the acquisition.

Defendants must use their best efforts to divest these assets as expeditiously as possible. The Proposed Final Judgment provides that the assets must be divested in such a way as to satisfy the United States, in its sole discretion, that the acquirer can and will use the assets as part of a viable, ongoing business engaged in the sale of adult women's hair relaxer kits through retail channels in the United States. Until the ordered divestitures take place, Defendants must cooperate with any prospective purchasers.
If Defendants do not accomplish the ordered divestitures within the prescribed time period, then Section V of the Proposed Final Judgment provides that this Court will appoint a trustee, selected by the United States, to complete the divestitures. Section V of the Proposed/U.S. Department of Justice
Antitrust Division
Litigation II Section
1401 H Street, N.W., Suite 4000
Washington, D.C. 20530

BEHOLD OUR BEAUTY
by Dr. JoAnne Cornwell

Beauty is in the eye of the beholder. What a moving and powerful saying. Isn't it ironic that so many of us live in a world where the image around us sends very different messages! From the time we become conscious of our environment, we are influenced in ways that can make us believe beauty is not for us to see and define and celebrate on our own terms.

At the same time, our mothers, daughters, aunts, and nieces, our cousins and neighbors bring beauty into our lives with the unsung but stunning dazzle, and reassuring softness of their features all wrapped up in skin tones that remind us that nature is still our mother.

The sometimes-sassy, sometimes-subtle elegance of their smiles lights our way in this life, and if we can see this—if we have not been numbed by the confusing influences that seek to define us—we come to be both humbled and honored by what our own reflections mean to us. We are beauty!

Mother to Daughter
by Richard O. Jones

Maturity has drawn me to this conclusion, my daughter
Motherhood is love on trial
God is the judge and jury
The evidence is in the child
Regardless of our flaws and clashes
Your very essence I do adore
And if I had a thousand hearts
I couldn't love you more

Take heed to my words, my daughter
It's my prayer they are benign
As a squirrel hoards nuts for the winter
Bury them in your mind
I've known victories and defeats, my daughter
I've known joys and the aches
I give you as a shield for battle
My triumphs and mistakes

Beneath the veil of this smiling society
Revolves an impassionate world
There're thorns in every rose bush

Shells without the pearl
Commit yourself to higher education
Endure the struggle of this temporary endeavor
Without a higher education, my daughter
Your struggle could be forever

Learn to laugh at yourself, my daughter
Make peace and happiness your strive
Disappointments are inevitable
Move on, heal on ... survive
You are more than a conqueror,
Though wounds of the heart cut deep
And yes there'll be times, my daughter
You'll cry yourself to sleep

Deploy the power of forgiveness
Never allow anger or grief to tarry
Unhealthy stresses are lurking at your door
They're quite heavy stones to carry
Treat your body as a temple, my daughter
Don't pollute it with acts you'll regret
The stars above are watching
Present them a tall silhouette

Spread your wings and fly, my daughter
You're an angel and meant to soar
But never get too lofty to apologize
If ever your manners were poor
There're many advisor in the parade of life
Consider the source of the voices
Are they riding on a magnificent float?
Or marching behind the horses

And should destiny make you a mother, my daughter
Know that motherhood is a noble fate
Give to your daughter the precious gift of
Your triumphs and mistakes

The Sisterlocks Lifestyle

(From Sisterlocks Lifestyle Journal—Summer 2006)

Have you ever experienced an episode or phase in your life when it seemed as if everything just fell into place? Maybe this had to do with a relationship, or family harmony, or relationships in the workplace. Maybe this had to do with money issues that, at least for the moment, just fell into place. Perhaps this had to do with some goal or accomplishment in your life that you were finally able to obtain.

Nearly everyone has experienced something like this at one time or another. No matter how much stress or tension or effort we have to deal with at other times in our ordinary lives, most of us can think of a period—however brief it might be—when we culd (dare I say it?) EXHALE!

Speaking for myself, when I think of the profound change that Sisterlocks has brought into my life, I liken it to something that just made a whole set of issues fall into place. The difference here is that this feeling of ease and 'perfect fit' didn't merely last a week, month, or year. Oh no, this feeling of relief, stability, and inner satisfaction has ground me since the inception of Sisterlocks.

Do I still have bills and stress over money? Yes. Do my friends still drive me nuts sometimes? Yes. Do I stress over how to make this business succeed? Yes. Do I still have issues with my co-workers from time to time? Yes. Do I still over-work myself at times and neglect my health? Yes. Sisterlocks did not fix all this; it's true. But there is an important distinction to make here. There are all things I must *do*, things I must cope with. However, these things, these issues and challenges, are not me.

Life, at its core, is not simply about what we do or what is done to us. It is more about who and what we are being while we are doing whatever it is we have to do, or coping with whatever challenges life throws our way. The kind of self-acceptance that comes when we—our women especially—accept our natural hair can propel us over a kind of threshold where we are put in touch with ourselves on a much more profound level than we have ever experienced before. When this happens, we tend to look beyond our hair care issues into other areas of our lives.

Now that the hair's right, are we eating right? Now that the hair's right, does our skin look healthy? Is there something we can do about those allergies? Are we comfortable with our weight? We've gotten the message that natural is best, so we're looking for more natural remedies for pain and illness, and appreciating the value of exercise as a natural way to strengthen and heal ourselves.

Now that the hair's right, what colors and textures best reflect the inner integrity we feel? We're taking a new look at our clothes, our nails, our accessories, and our jewelry. We're also looking at our environment as an extension of ourselves, and want to support those settings and practices, in our communities, that support our health and wellbeing.

The Sisterlocks lifestyle isn't a formula for living. It's more of a celebration of our journeys as we grow into a greater and greater love and acceptance of who we are, and discover how much fun it is to do this thing together.—*Dr. JoAnne Cornwell*

Epilogue

Inflicting the psychological bondage of the American standard of beauty in early childhood is a much easier task than breaking it in adulthood. The mind of a child is totally vulnerable to his or her environment. The same-sex parent is the greatest influence on a child. If the same-sex parent has a passion for academics, reading, sports, arts & crafts, music, or drinking beer, watching television all day and/or following every fashion trend promoted by popular culture, the child will grow up with a trait of the same values. It is imperative for parents to be aware of the psychological influence they project to their children. On a daily basis in any urban city or community young black girls, as young as three-years-old, can be seen proudly sporting long artificial hair.

Parents and adult role models should encourage a strong sense of inner beauty and downplay commercialized beauty and vanity. I have observed that most young girl's hair is a direct reflection of the older influential females in their life. No child was born hating his or her image; that is an acquired depreciation. I have sisters, daughters, granddaughters and a wife, none of whom inherited glamour by American beauty standards. I have witnessed the mental anguish upon many black females as it pertains to their hair and skin tone. We have all heard it said that *it takes a village to raise a child.* Just as that statement is true, it is also true that *a damaged village will raise a damaged child. Therefore it takes a healthy village to raise a healthy child.*

The popular media, celebrities, models, family members, friends, coworkers, classmates, and often their own village tightens the screw of inferiority embedded by the cosmetic, ethnic hair, and movie industry. However, a female adult or child can overcome such inferiority by a meaningful association with other black females dealing with the same issues. Females who want to learn to appreciate their natural beauty can go to several websites that promote natural beauty and hair instead of being manipulated into a world of scalp burns and hair breakage. Type one of these three organizations into your browser, click, and read the information on their websites: (1) *nappy hair affair, or (2) nappy hair stories* or (3) *nappturality.*

There is always a need for additional natural beauty advocates, which may begin to neutralize the astronomical number of American beauty standards advocates. After you get some information and self-confidence, gather as many natural-hair-loving friends as you can and start good self-esteem club. You will be amazed how fast it grows and broadens the perspective of the village. Get a catchy name for your club, a name that will alert the public what you stand for as a group. Your club credo and mission statement should include all or part of the following: to promote natural hair, uplift the spirit of black females, and do charitable deeds for the community, and enhance your financial opportunities. Start new chapters as you grow. Become a nonprofit organization and receive tax-deductible donations to defray your cost.

Warning: Do not become so holier than thou that your club restricts sisters without natural hair. Embrace them; love them, as Christ loves you. However, when your club has a guest speaker insist that it is a black female with natural hair. This is not discrimination. You are promoting the beauty and battling the stigma of natural hair; it would be counterproductive to invite guest speakers that do not represent what you are all about.

When people are held captive by any type of bondage, mental or physical, a certain amount of deprogramming must take place before they can be emotionally restored. Good psychologists are needed to help overcome a large variety of addictions. A good religious support group in many cases is a spiritual form of psychological aid and has restored millions of people. A strong spiritual connection is an indispensable asset in the life of everyone but especially African-American women. However, there are several men and women organizations besides church that will suffice.

A sisterhood that celebrates natural beauty should be on your list of possibilities for membership. Everyone needs his or her confidence restored from time to time. Such support is best found with an unwavering sisterhood that honestly can appreciate your journey as a black woman.

Statistics show that African-Americans suffer from depression and anger more than other ethnic groups because of their persecution in the world past and present. There are more hate crimes against African-Americans in the United States that any other group, including homosexuals. There is over twenty magazines on the market that are dedicated the black hair care or black women in general and not one of them specializes in natural black feminine beauty. Unity is the weapon to defeat oppression.

Nappy Hair Affair
by Linda L. Jones

There are several other natural hair sisterhoods that can be discovered on the Internet. Find the one right for you. One such sisterhood is called Nappy Hair Affair, founded Linda Jones, a college professor, and author in Texas. Jones founded A Nappy Hair Affair in 1998 as a response to African-American friends bemoaning the grooming and styling difficulties they faced as they embraced natural and African-inspired hairstyles. "I had a number of friends ... who were lamenting not being able to find or afford someone to help them do their hair," she explains. "One day, I invited some friends over to my house so we could help each other groom our hair. From that first gathering, A Nappy Hair Affair and 'Hair Days' were born."

A Nappy Hair Affair is best known for sponsoring grass roots hair grooming sessions called Hair Days. These are gathering where sisters come together with others who understand their natural hair care needs and their choice to embrace a style more in keeping with their culture. Hair Days, which have fostered a spirit of bonding and support, have become so popular since I held the first one at my home in May 1998 that they are being held in several U.S. cities. We also have a Hair Day network in other countries. But A Nappy Hair Affair (ANHA) is about so much more than hair. It is about reclaiming and respecting our culture. We have been conditioned to hate one of our most unique characteristics-our hair in its most natural state. We have been conditioned to accept European standards of beauty and to reject our own. ANHA exists to cause a shift in such negative mindsets and promote a positive image of people of African descent. We do it through support, affirmation and education.

Ask activist Linda Jones what life is like these days, and her answer is likely to be "hairy." Not just because she's one of the nation's leading proponents of the natural hair movement for African-American women. It's all the *other* hats Jones wears, weaving efforts as a published author, a social advocate, a teacher, a media consultant and a performance artist into a vocation—and avocation—unlike any other. "I guess you could say that I'm a purveyor of my culture," asserts Jones, a former *Dallas Morning News* reporter turned *Chicken Soup* series essayist. "Whether I'm writing or teaching or speaking, I'm working to dispel misperceptions of what it means to be a person of color."

Jones devotes the lion's share of her time to running her own independent media consultancy, Manelock Communications (www. manelockcommunications.com). Through Manelock, Jones provides professional writing and media relations services for clients ranging from aspiring new authors to a Plano yoga shop. She also freelances for a range of publications, including *People* magazine. In addition to her "day jobs," she teaches—everything from English and creative writing courses for Upward Bound students at Richland Community College to developmental writing at Brookhaven College.

Asked about the disparate nature of her varied portfolio, and Jones quickly summarizes: "The common thread is blackness and a desire to push what is positive about my culture," she explains. "Some people say, 'I'm a writer or a teacher or a speaker first. *Then* I am black.' Not me. I was born black. That came first. Those other things came later." She's also quick to dismiss questions about the challenge of juggling so many balls. "I'm lucky," she asserts. "It isn't always easy but I'm able to make a living doing what I like to do, how I like to do it. How many people can say that?"

Young Woman Turns Offensive Insult into an Affirmative Affirmation

As a junior high school student in during the 80s, **Angela Coleman** experienced the usual derogatory remarks my other African-American girls regarding her hair texture. It was a common thing for black kids to nearly come to blows over being called nappy headed. There was also strife in those days for being considered too dark skinned or too light skinned. One day a girl made a discouraging slur about Angeles's kitchen (referring to the short hair at the nape of the neck), which was a code word for 'let's fight!' Angela heard and saw such incidents repeated throughout her youth. The experiences stuck with her.

Perhaps it was Angela's major in psychology, bolstered by her classes in African-American studies while at Princeton University, nearly a decade later, that gave her an historical understanding of the depth of inferiority as it pertained to African-Americans. She also discovered that their placement on the totem pole of the American standard of beauty was nonexistence. Although Angela was brought up in a household where black culture and pride in your black heritage was instilled she never realized until a student in college the psychological burden unfairly placed on black girls and the stigma of their unappreciated beauty. After graduation, Angela made a commitment to be a part of the solution in promoting the good self-esteem in black girls.

Ultimately, in 1994 Sisterhood Agenda was founded in Durham, North Carolina. Angela and her staff of dedicated individuals are devoted to the enrichment of African-American girls. One of the programs through Sisterhood Agenda is called "A Journey Toward Womanhood." In this program the young ladies learn to appreciate themselves and not get caught up in the lies and misleading information in the media that pays little homage to black pride and beauty. The young students develop a love for themselves, their unique hair, skin, and facial features. African-American communities throughout American would be empowered by other organizations modeled after Sisterhood Agenda because without such programs the damage instilled by the American standard of beauty could be a life sentence.

The organization also addresses the health, cultural, social, and economic concerns of women and girls of African descent. The mission of Sisterhood Agenda is achieved through the research and development of new initiatives and programs. For more information regarding Sisterhood Agenda go to website: www. sisterhoodagenda.com

SUGGESTIONS

To break the psychological bondage of American beauty standards a positive progressive action must be implemented on a city, county, state, national, and global basic. The epidemic of shame is broadcasted worldwide; therefore any antidote must go worldwide beginning at your front door. Every effort to the cause of uplifting the heads and spirits of women and men of color will serve as an inspiration to others. Let's begin small by paying compliments to black women who appear to be without chemically treated hair, even those of elementary school age. Just smile and simply say, "Your natural beauty is so refreshing." Such compliments can only be paid by a female in order to convey the proper message. Compliments from men can be easily taken out of context. When you see women who are conservatively dress (as opposed to provocatively dressed or overly exposed), smile and said, "It's so nice to see an elegant lady." These small courtesies will give encouragement.

Natural Makeovers by Natural Hair Salons

It would great if Natural Hair Salons put signs in the windows advertising NATURAL MAKEOVERS. (Not beauty makeovers.) Then have before and after pictures in the window. In the before picture, show a black woman with sores and burns in her head from chemically treated hair. In the after picture show the same woman after her natural hair is properly treated and grown into a stylish appearance.

Natural Hair Salon Owners Start Annually Natural Woman Contest (Be carefully not to said beauty contest.) Make the contest about the inner woman and the charitable things she does. Of course there should be fashion show but somewhat of an intellectual competition as well. Females must come to rely on their intellect more than their physical attributes as they have been subliminally trained to do.

Become a serious advocate of natural beauty and create a blog about breaking the psychological bondage of American beauty standards. Contact the Black Students Unions on college campuses throughout the USA and encourage them to invite more natural hair styled speakers to speak on the history of the assassination and revival of the black female image. Whenever a female celebrity with natural hair appears anywhere, encourage her with your attendance, which will gradually inspire more celebrities to wear natural hair. Start a natural hair club that is mobilized to raise funds for disadvantaged people. Feed the hungry, buy blankets for the homeless, etc. Volunteer at breasts cancer organizations and other charitable causes. Form free tutorial clubs to aid struggling students.

EARN MONEY BY PROMOTING NATURAL BEAUTY

Use this book as an additional fundraiser. Get the discount of a major bookstore. *NATURAL ... The BEAUTY 'N' Word* can be purchased at a discount up to 40% when you order 20 or more copies. Order 100 or more copies and receive 50% discount. Buyer must pay shipping cost. Resale the book at full retail cost and earn a 40% or 50% profit minus shipping cost and taxes. The sale of this book can boost the revenue for your church, club, school, or organization fundraiser. Contact author at least three weeks in advance of your scheduled event; however, the more advance notice the better. Contact the author by email at: richardojones1@verizon.net or www.literarysoulfoodcafe.
Inquire about the book fundraiser rates.

Nonprofit status

Natural: The Beautiful 'N' Word by Richard O. Jones is a literary project of The Literary Soul Food Café. The Literary Soul Food Café is an auxiliary of Quinn

Community Outreach Corporation (QCOC) a 501(c) (3) non-profit organization mobilized to promote tutorial and reading programs for youth and breasts cancer awareness in minority women. For a copy of QCOU's tax-exempt status number, contact the corporate office by mail at: Quinn Community Outreach Corporation—25400 Alessandro Boulevard #101—Moreno Valley, CA 92553 or contact the author at www.literarysoulfoodcafe.com.

About the Author

Richard O. Jones is a published author and poetry columnist for the A.C.C. Church and Community Newspaper in Los Angeles, CA since 1991 and Contributing writer for The Black Voice News in Riverside, CA since 2002. Jones was also a Crime Prevention Columnist for the Press Enterprise Newspaper in Riverside, CA from 2002–2003. Richard is a freelance writer and performs as a master of ceremony, poet and comedian.

In 1993 Richard produced his own public access cable TV show entitled, "Tips Against Crime." This was a format to interview ex-criminals, crime victims, and law enforcement officers on crime prevention tips, techniques, and procedures.

He has raised four daughters as a single parent after the death of his wife in 1981. Jones has been a mentor to male youth through various youth organizations in Los Angeles.

In 1994, Richard O. Jones appeared on the Oprah Winfrey Show as an anti-crime consultant. In 1996, he appeared on the Leeza Show, The Today Show, and four times as a crime tips advisors on UPN News 13 Crime Watch. Richard is also a contributing writer at the Black Voice Newspaper, in Riverside, and a motivational speaker at state prisons.

Jones' second book is autobiographical and entitled, "When Mama's Gone." This is the true dramatic story of a single male criminal parent raising four daughters as he struggles with his spirituality. Jones married in '99 and moved to Orange County, and united with Friendship Baptist Church in Yorba Linda. His membership at Friendship lasted until he and his wife and teenage son moved to Moreno Valley, CA one year later, at which time he united with A. K. Quinn A.M.E. Church. His third book, is entitled, "Embracing Monogamy in the Face of Temptation—The Black Man's Guide to Commitment." And his fourth is entitled, "YOU ARE TOMORROW'S HISTORY." His fifth book is entitled, "PARENTING THROUGH THE STORM," this is a survival guide for single parents. Mr. Jones taught a parenting class at Riverside Community College in the fall of 2001 and Feb. 2002.

More recent works is a Christian fiction entitled, "Church Member From Hell," "The Liberation of Aunt Jemima," a book of poetry dedicated to the African American spiritual woman, and a novel entitled "My Fifth Ex-Wife." Currently Richard O. Jones conducts a writer's workshop for youth through A.K. Quinn A.M.E. Church in Moreno Valley. His goal is to guide youth from their addiction to watching television and playing video games to realize their creativity through poetry, comedy, and becoming authors through The Literary Soul Food Café, a writer's workshop where he is the director.

Jones also serves as the treasurer for Quinn Community Outreach Corporation (QCOC) a nonprofit 501 (c) (3) nonprofit corporation. QCOC operates and oversees:

- Witness Project, a breast cancer education and screening program for African American and Latino women

- Free tutor programs for students

- The Literary Soul Food Café (a writer's workshop for youth and adults)

Other Books
By Richard O. Jones

Church Member From Hell—A Woman's journey from Damnation to Salvation

ISBN 0-595-26872-2
Published by iUniverse in 2003—paperback—356 pages—price $19.95
Telephone 1-800-288-4677
A Christian fiction set in the 1990s in the South during the dark history of black church-burnings. Main character is a woman raised and sexually abused in church-based orphanages. As an adult has seeks Christian counseling to overcome her nightmares and uncontrollable carnal urges.

My Fifth Ex-Wife—The Nuptial Trail of a Fractured Man

$18.95—ISBN 13:978-0-595-35866-3
Published by iUniverse in 2005—paperback—288 pages—price $18.95
Telephone 1-800-288-4677
A middle-aged man has a strange view to love and compassion for the women in his life. Created by his fractured childhood. He dismisses women for human flaws and is sure he's right until he marries a woman that shakes his reality a loose.

The Liberation of Aunt Jemima—A Poetic Tribute to the Spiritual Woman

ISBN 0-595-27154-5
Published by iUniverse in 2003—paperback—176 pages—price $15.95
Telephone 1-800-288-4677
Over 100 spiritual, humorous, love, and situational poems, written especially for the unique journey of African-American.

Embracing Monogamy in the Temptation—The Black Man's Guide to Commitment

ISBN 1-4208-7010-6 (sc)
Published by AuthorHouse in 2005—paperback—253 pages—price $14.95
Telephone 1-800-839-8640
www.authorhouse.com
Nonfiction. This is an instructional book for overcoming the fear of marriage. Biblical references are used liberally with an explanation of how to utilize them in personal situations. Young men are given the tools of wisdom needed for godly manhood and fatherhood.
All books can be purchased online at amazon.com or directly from the publisher. If you want to use books as fundraiser and purchased from 20 up to 500 books, you can receive discounts of 30%, 40% or 50%. Contact **richardojones1@ verizon.net** or **www.literarysoulfoodcafe**

Richard O. Jones is occasionally available for book signing and speaking engagements. Contact via email: richardojones1@verizon.net

Sisterlock Consultants and Trainees around the world

ALABAMA

Auburn Phyllis Harris **Bessemer** Tanya Fletcher **(Birmingham)** Vickese House, Vickie Brown House; Sharon L. Blanding-Starks **(Mobile)** Charlana Quiovers **(Montgomery)** Sheila Thomas

ARIZONA

(Phoenix) N'tosake Muhammad **(Sun Lakes)** Joyce Burks **(Surprise)** Chandra Hinkle, **(Tempe)** Nikki Butler

CALIFORNIA

(Altadena) Brook Green, Francesca Martin, **(Antelope)** Cheryl Anderson, **(Antioch)** Kimberly Allen, Barbara Bailey, Francine Powell, **(Berkeley)** LaKisha Bradley, **(Brentwood)** Ms. Adrian Robinson, **(Campbell)** Janice Charles, **(Carson)** Sheila Blow, Carina Callier, Linda Thomas, **(Compton)** LaJoy Baber, Shannon Grayson, Patrice Offord, Precious Stallworth, **(Corona)** Donna Harrison, **(Daly**

City) Bunnie Davis, Deborah Tutson, (El Cajon) Iris Gibson, (Fairfield) Lanola Smith, (Folsom) Theresa J. Reed, (Fontana) May Randolph (951-347-4147 or albertarandolph@yahoo.com), Octavia Wilerford (909-350-4366), (Foresthill) Tiffany Lair, (Gardena) Dianne Herbert, (Hawthorne)Tracy L. Davis, (Hayward) Phyllis McCoy, (Helendale) Paula Coleman, (Highland) Kimberly Bates, (Inglewood) Evelyn Y. Pegues, (La Mesa) Donna Gibson, (Lakewood) Laverne Smith, (Lemon Grove) Linda Brown, Adele G. Johnson, (Long Beach) Ben Burchall, Antoinette Knox-Smith, Jody Williams, (Los Angeles) Helen Brock, Geneva Brown, Mazell Brown, Dawn Burnett, Vivian R. Davis, Dora Garay, Osharye Hagood, Arlene R. Hill, Makilah Hubbert, Marilyn Hubbert, Fahmeeda Jabali, Tia Johnson, Zipporah Jones, Tashia Kinney, Phillip Lauth, Patricia A. Pine, Annie R. Smith, Erwin Thompson, Jacqueline Trotter, Rochelle Washington, Mellonease Wharton, Rozeena Williams, Javona L. Wright, (Menifee) Queen Spicer, (Moreno Valley) Doris Gravitte, Fredia Morris, Olufemi Alexander, (Oakland) Aesha Abdullah-Naeem, Nida Ali, Asia Bowden, Rebecca Jones, Ms. Charlie Martin, Kalimah Shuaibe, Adekemi Omotade, (Oceanside) Colleen Gooden, Eve Palkin, (Ontario) Njeri Ndicu, (Orange) Melanie Fields, (Pasadena) Maria V. Baber-Smith, Dawnelle Hawkins, Shelly Mays, Catherine Pulley, (Perris) Stacey Bolton, (Pittsburg) Peggy Lawson, (Poway) Peggy Troester, (Rialto) Kathy Harper-Duncan, Zebiydah Israel (951-965-6660), (Richmond) Rhonda Glenn (510-393-5572 or 510-835-7838), (Riverside) La Shawn Fenderson-Andy, Nicola Brown, Cassandra Nowell, Marnita Tinsley, (Sacramento) Rosalind Boyd, Shirley Rhodes, (San Diego) Lola Aldridge, Linda Childress, Patricia Ellis, Tiffany Farmer, Elizabeth Lewis, Evelyn Mathhews, Sharolyne Mills, Laini Patton, Netreia Peterman, Leondra Rew, Denise Seyfarth, Tsega Tesfamariam, Cheryl Samuels, (San Francisco) Monica Eskridge, Janice E. Gunn, Barbara A. Johnson, (San Jose) Janice Charles, (San Juan Capistrano) Diane Raibon, (Santa Clarita) Tracy Booker, (Spring Valley) Daphne Moyd, Donna Smith, (Stockton) Bridgett Turner, (Toluca Lake) Darlene Standifer aka Naima Obaitori, Twentynine Palms Lola Aldridge, (Vallejo) Jacqueline Candies, Kimberlee Monero, (Venice) Valonda Theus, Julia Walker, (Victorville) Deidre Mayes, (West Los Angeles) Roxanne Taylor

COLORADO

(Aurora) Mariam Bah; Janessa Brown, Fatoumata Cisse, Celvhone Law, Victoria Owokoya, (Boulder) Sheila Cooper, (Colorado Springs) Susan Thurlow, (Denver) Allea Ryan

CONNECTICUT

(Bridgeport): Marva King, Andrea Rowe **(Hartford)** Keturah Cook, Grace Stewart, Lorrice Stewart **(Meriden)** Carol Lomax **(Ridgefield)** Zu Byerly **(West Hartford)** Gail McClanahan **(Waterbury)** Lisa C. Clarke **(Windsor)** Gloria Dionne, Sheila Green

DELAWARE

(Bear) Donna L. Durrette **(Claymont)** Margaret A. Bowers **(Magnolia)** Pamela Faulk-Moore **(New Castle)** Dolores Minor, Kathryn A. Veney **(Newark)** Florinda Chaney **(Smyrna)** Angela L. Easley **(Wilmington)** Jovan Callis, Janice Henry, Yvonne Huntley, Willie F. Scott

FLORIDA

(Boca Raton) Crystal Spain **(Brandenton)** Ruby Clemons **(Brandon)** Erica Billouin, Tiffany Pate **(Coral Springs)** Tyrhonda Starks **(Coconut Creek)** Sheril Madden, Sandra Grimes **(Coral Springs)** Fatima Johnson, Kimberly F. Ramsay **(Ft. Lauderdale)** Talvia Vereen **(Ft. Walton Beach)** Teria Sims **(Goulds)** Helen Haynes **(Gulfport)** Rashida Strober **(Haines City)** Sandi Davidson **(Jacksonville)** Torey R. Spikes **(Jefferson South Bay)** Tina Marie **(Lake Worth)** Kathleen Abrahams, Gloria Boyd, Unie Thomas Jones **(Largo)** Melissa A. Lopez **(Lauderdale Lakes)** Iris Robinson-Griffin **(Lauderhill)** Dawn Creary, Joserine Pouncey-Davis, Karen Southerland **(Loxahatchee)** Stephan Sheriffe **(Melbourne)**Deidre Cannon, Christal Glenn **(Miami)** Tawanna Barnes-Kendrick, Sayblee Darsale, Marie Estime-Thompson, Stephanie Lee, Diane Linton, Donna McCree, Yolanda Newkirk, Chantal Saunders, Annette Shaw **(Miramar)** Amy Dehaney **(North Miami)** Patricia L. Deosaran **(Miramar)** Veronica J. Johnson, Nancy Randele-Durant **(N. Miami Beach)** Gaynell Christian, Sherri Grant **(Oakland Park)** Karlene Williams **(Palm Bay)** Greta Barner **(Pembroke Pines)** Barbara Douglas-Bullard, Sandra Hanchard, Glenda Laird **(Port St. Lucie)** Marilyn Azu **(St. Petersburg)** Angeal Battle, Chandra Lynn Golden, Gwen Purvis, Tonya Williams **(Sunrise)** Sheila Doblas **(Tamarac)** Jacqueline Ferreira **(Tampa)** Marie Brown, Evelyn C. Johnson, Bertha Mitchell, Linda Stokes, Errin Tice **(Titusville)** Tamu Roberts **(Valrico)** Pamelia Thompson-Denson, Zita Woodroffe **(West Palm Beach)** Cheryl Cash **(Winter Garden)** Dianne Nelson **(Winter Haven)** Brenda B. Richard

GEORGIA

(Acworth) LaVonne Johnson (Alpharetta) Claudia Harris (Atlanta) Shakeema Bell, Lendell Maddox, Jr., Patricia Bakr, Valinda J. Brown, Amber Carter, Trudy Hanna (Bogart) Jocelyn Bayliss; (Brunswick) Cathey Hazelhurst-Scott (College Park) Gail Tnomas-Lockman (Douglasville) Ernette Johnson, Thelma Mokwe (Fayetteville) Belinda Washington (Guyton) Alma P. Mack (Marietta) Khamila Knight **Marietta** Rhonda White (McDonough); Dawn Jennings (Norcross); Bobbie Cornett (Riverdale) Janet Rogers (Robbins Air Force Base) Joy Minor (Roswell) Cynthia Lucas (Smyrna)Dorothy Culpepper (Snellville) Sheila Barnes, Angela Boyd, Deborah Hines (Stone Mountain) Veronica "Roni" DeCoteau, Julia Stewart-Stackhaus (Union City) Sabriya Fields (Valdosta) A. Theresa Reaves

HAWAII

(Honolulu) Lillian Jones, Marlene Coach (Waipahu) Lornette Robinson-Stewart

ILLINOIS

(Bloomington) Felicia Kreul (Bolingbrook) Rasheeda Johnson-Coaks (Broadview) Roberta McGill (Calumet Park) Tony Carrington (Chicago) Joy Anderson, Maevette L. Allen Brooks, Annyce Armstead, Martha Donson, Sherita Eberhardt, Dianne B. Elizabeth, Rhonda Bowen, Paulette Brookes, Chantal Chablis, Shanna Dean, Barbara Garner, Octavia Hooks, Joy Morgan, Diana McNeal, Patsy Jacobs, Theresa Raines-McGowan, Dee Adra Simmons, Francia Street, Sonya L. Zeno (Chicago Heights) Nina Connors; (Country Club Hills) Binah Mohammed (Elmhurst) Eadra Brown (Harvey) Felicia Smith; (Joliet) Nicole Malonga (Maywood) Andrea Cook-Ellis, Georgette Bennett (Montgomery) Francine Powell (Romeoville) Cheryl McCord (Roscoe) Karen Bell

INDIANA

(Indianapolis) Adrienne Harris, Elicia R. Smith, Vonetta Robinson

KANSAS

(Wichita) Adrienne D. Abraham

KENTUCKY

(Louisville) Monica Echols

LOUISIANA

(New Orleans) Pamannie Davidson **(Baton Rouge)** Nomzamo Iyanu

MARYLAND

(Accokeek) Deborah McNair **(Altoskie)** Blossom Stewart-McCoy **(Annapolis)** Rose Miller, Jacqueline Watkins **(Baltimore)** Wyndolyn H. Alexander, Annette V. Bolling, Carol Cadogan, Malaika Cooper, E'vet Gundy-Flowers, Thelma Hawkins, Rosetta M. Jackson, Trulestine "Tee" Jefferson, Nicole Johnson, Caroline McCall, Lauren Neason, Venus Newby, Shannel Shell, Tasha Torain, Somari Toure-Pickett **(Bowie)** Shelley A. Brickey, "AZZIZA" Tiffany Roy **(Brandywine)** Vasti Williams, Joy Harley **(Capitol Heights)** Mary Clark, Ronnita Gunter **(Clarksville)** Karen M. Underwood **(Clinton)** Willa Ellis-Green, Miteshia K. Huff, Regina Zellars **(Columbia)** Doris Genus, Toni George, Teri Gilyard **(Forestville)** Carmel Owens **(Ft. Washington)** Cheron Hunt Ellison, Niko K. Gordon, Dorothy J. Powell **(Glen Burnie)** Sheryl Hood **(Hanover)** Freida R. Johnson **(Hyattsville)** Jennifer Massenburg **(Indian Head)** Yvette Anderson **(Issue)** Rosalene A. Krygar **(Kettering)** Tony Durrah **(Landover Hills)** Sabrina Carter **(Lanham)** Cykeithia Henderson, Brenda Lyn **(Largo)** Tammy Harkness, Doretha Ross **(Odenton)** Karen Hartridge **(Owings Mills)** Yasminah Abdullah **(Oxon Hill)** Shannon Evans **(Prince Frederick)** Anna Francis-Finch **(Randallstown)** Katurah Spence **(Silver Spring) (Springdale)** Kathy Murray **(Sykesville)** Michele Gillispie **(Takoma Park)** Sandra Fisher **(Temple Hills)** Teresa Cross, Ansylla Ramsey

MASSACHESETTS

(Boston) Mojisola Duval, Penny Hodge, Tammarrah Lee **(Dorchester)** Jacqueline Ashby, Eve Brade, Jenene Cook, Danielle C. Hines, Valena Lugay, Zenda Walker **(Jamaica Plain)** Penny Hodge, Mauryn Kkira **(Malden)** Yvonne Thomas; **(Randolph)** Zakiya Ife,Karen Preval **(Mattapan)** Audrey Aduama **(Medford)** Arndrea Wyche **(Roslindale)** Nadege Volcy
(Roxbury) Ernestine Washington **(Springfield)** Renee C. Anderson

MICHIGAN

(Buchanan) Sherridon Lyons **(Canton)** Lydia Woods-Gresham **(Detroit)** Steven Guy, Rosemary Honore, Phyllis Knight, Atoya Martin, Maia McKinney, Dena Reed, Melissa Ricks, Melzenia Scott, Airian M. Sharp, Janice M. Simmons, Ericka Taylor, Sheila Wade, Alena Waters, Flora N. Wilson **(Inkster)** Theresa Rodgers, Kathy L. Wade; **(Kalamazoo)** Brosie Somerville **(Macomb)** Jessica Rogers; **(Rochester)** Angela Sumpter; **(Shelby Twp.)** Gloria Butler **(Ypsilanti)** Lisa Pipkin

MISSISSIPPI

(Jackson) Angela F. Simpkins **(Tupelo)** Melony Armstrong, Nina Lyons

MISSOURI

(St. Louis) Mervina Burns, Eboni Bush, Vivian Gibson, Nicole Henry, Debra Martin Johnson

NEW JERSEY

(Bloomfield) Kitab Rollins **(Bound Brook)** Alissa Caldwell, Faatima Houston **(Camden)** Pandora G. Brown; **(Carney's Point)** Eartha Reavely **(Cherry Hill)** Wanda L. McCall **(East Brunswick)** Ms. Charles McCoy-eller **(Edgewater)** Rev. Dr. Wanda Lundy **(Galloway)** Paula Newby **(Glassboro)** Diane Hughes **(Hackensack)** Kelli Goodman, Terry Martinez **(Haskell)** Tori Mitchell **(Jersey City)** Lamonte Coles **(Lumberton)** Cynthia B. Jones **(Maplewood)** Fatimah Turner-Pryor, Kareemah Wood **(Metuchen)** Yvonne Varner **(Passaic Park)** Alethea Graham **(Plainfield)** JoAnne Appleton, Kudrat Gbadamosi **(North Plainfield)** Jameelah Curtis **(South Plainfield)** Betty Caines **(Teaneck)** Sheryl Martin **(Trenton)** Sonia Boone **(Union)** Ysenia Hernandez **(Vineland)** Tamika L. Garrett **(Willingboro)** Wanda A. Scott

NEW MEXICO

(Las Cruces) Fannie Kelley

NEW YORK

(Amityville) Darcel Colon **(Bronx)** L. Jamelliah Allen, Latoya Bancroft-Friday, Ruby DeLisser, Synade Jackson, Annetta Johnson, Edna McIntosh, Evadne McKay, Nene Ndiaye Thiobane, Deanen A. Toney **(Brooklyn)** Angela Brown

Sheila Foster, Geraldine Hyman, Khadijah Louis, Khady M'Baye, Judith Scott-Robinson, Carol Alcie Shaw, Saundra L. Sirmans, Stephanie Vincent **(Buffalo)** Rose Hussain, Glenda Martin **(Cambria Hgts.)** Carla S. Brown, Salkis Re **(Elmsford)** Lacie Redd **(Harlem)** Valerie Price **(Hempstead)** Allison Sylvestre **(Jamaica)** Kimberly Alao, Vanessa Benton, Louise Palmer, Deborah Tuggle, Patricia Wilburg, Marilyn Davis **(Mt. Vernon)** Donna Lambert, Yvette McGregor, Stacy-Ann Douse **(New York)** Cynthia Webb, Tracey Plaskett, Ethel Reed, Monique Stewart, Janie Washington, Debra Wilson **(South Ozone Park)** Tania L. "Abenaa" Veney **(Queens Village)** Barbara Maxwell **(Rockland)** Julianna Webb **(White Plains)** Deborah Howard **(Tarrytown)** Jacqueline Young

NORTH CAROLINA

(Charlotte) Fidelia Banson, Christine Beke, Bridget Brown-Kendall, Angela Carrothers, Ebony Funderburk, Stella Izundu, Renonia Lowery, Lauren McDonald, Kayle B. Mingo, Kimberly Seals, Tonka Vaughn, Sherry Williams; **(Claremont)** Mable Gibbs **(Denver)** Michelle Phinx **(Fayetteville)**: Lydia Green **(Mebane)** Rashida Walker; **(Raleigh)** Jamie Horton, Terry Paul **(Stanley)** Castina Johnson **(Winston-Salem)** Teretha Coe-Oaks

OHIO

(Akron) Theresa Boware (Canal Winchester) Jodi R. Spencer **(Cincinnati)** LaVerne T. Armstead Dwan Bass, Najla R. Salaam, Sheila Ree Smoot, Debra Stallworth **(Cleveland)** Patrisha Chism, Sharon Minter, Akila Muhammed **(Columbus)** Latanzia D. Clark, Chasrah Gomer, Delia Johnson, Athelia Lewis **(Dayton)** Trina Campbell, Gayle Cotton **(East Cleveland)** Rosalind Wilson **(Hilliard)** Taneka A. Adams **(Shaker Heights)** Safiyyah Muhammad **Toledo)** Donald Henderson, Shawyna Williams, Lauretta Satterfield, Lori Anne Christie **(University Heights)** June Moore **(Warrensville)** Theresa Delaney

OREGON

(Portland) Yvette Campbell, Robin Capers, Opal Chancler-Moore, Roslyn Davis-Holt, Iyabo Moore, Kenya Moore

PENNSYLVANIA

(Bala Cynwyd) Beverly B. Robinson **(Berwyn)**: Kimberly Nesmith **(Chalfont)** Shirlene D. **(Colwyn)** Robin R. Graham **(Harrisburg)** Desiree DeFoor, Elayne M. Smith **(Horsham)** Tracy E. Alailima **(Gettysburg)** Malethia Marconi **(Glen-**

side) Vera Vance **(Jenkintown)** Cheryle Jackson **(Media)** Michele **(Philadelphia)** Vivian Allen, Nadirah Barba, Sharon Beckett, Linda Bell, Yvonne Brown, Iris C. Burgess, Diana Carter, Vivian Carter, Synthia Davis-Russell, Ronay Dawson-Roberts, Stephanie DeVos, Clareath Foushee', Renee J. Hammett, Suzanne Henderson, Geraldine Holloman, Tanzania Hutchins, Wanda Johnson, Kathleen Johnson-Prillerman, Nadine Jones, Jeannine Lawson, Sharyn Madidi, Joan McAllister, Thelma Moore, Brenda Myrick, Knekeya Payne, Shimmella Payne, Najah Purnell, Trudy P. Randle, Olivia Shaw, Lustra Stone, Erika Thompson, Zanna Towns, Jenell Williams

SOUTH CAROLINA

(Charleston) Chavala Wilkerson **(Columbia)** Carmen Williams, Melissa Todd **(Rock Hill)** Shenedra Long **(N. Augusta)** Armeco W. Thomas **(Van Wyck)** Cassandra Howze

TENNESSEE

(Clarksville) Kimberly Dee Washington **(Knoxville)** Patricia Broyles **(LaVergne)** Rosalind Watkins **(Memphis)** Jarita Clark, Karla Clark, Grace Eweka, Theodore Jennings, Elizabeth, Venus Johnson, Deborah Key, Elizabeth Taylor, Sheryl Taylor, Ivana Thigpen, Barbara M. Thomas, Walter V. Turley Jr. **(Nashville)** Darrell Edwards, Linda R. Palmer, James Williams **(Ripley)** Carolyn Conley

TEXAS

(Arlington) Debrel Joseph **(Baytown)** Preth Charles **(Dallas)** Iris Brantley, Bridget Gopou, Rhea Hill, Shanda L. Malone, Dianne Mowoe **(Ft. Worth)** Tina Harrison, **(Grand Prairie)** LaTonya Jackson-Lott **(Houston)** Olohimai Alade, Gail E. Anderson, Uwimana Bupe, Sandra Cloud, TeLesha Ford, Vanessie Guillory, Barbara A.Harris, Annette Jackson, Sandra Kaye, Shmarilyn Lott-Cassel, Brenda Marshall, Patsia Moore, Cynthia Pierre, Tonya Reed, Vivian Richardson, Nicolette Roberson, Trudi Dockins, "AKEMI" **(Irving)** Starla Smith, Mary Jones **(Missouri City)** LaSharne Cotton, Eva Devore, Harriett Ellis, Brenda Hamilton **(Pasadena)** Diane Williams Maloy **(Pearland)** Kimberly Edwards **(Plano)** Brigitte Gopou **(Tyler)** Bessie Davis **(Wilmer)** Margie Burns

VIRGINIA

(Alexandria) Larry Hagan, Harriet Matthews, (Arlington) Chana Wells; (Culpepper) Vernelle Murray (Newport News) Sharon Tanner (Richmond) Teri (Cotman) Bolden, Janel Cotman, Pamela S. Pritchett, Dionne Eggleston (Stafford) Robin Mitchell (Warrenton) Renea Henry

WASHINGTON (State)

(Federal Way) P.J.Hadley Sammamish Saritza Stevens (Seattle) Deborah Chester, Tracy Perry (Spanaway) Miayona Jones (Spokane) Kim Conley, Naimah Jamison (Tacoma) Andrea Maxwell

WASHINGTON D.C.

Doroan Ambrose, Barbara Bennett, Ellen Collins, Kai D. DeRosa, Jennifer P. Edwards, Karen Hill, Denise Hinds, Duyan James, Jaamiah Kareem-Matthews, Tamara McDaniel, Sharon F. McGhee, Nadia McNeil, Queentari Nyasuma, Darlene M. Oliver, Amber Todd, Betty J. Tremble, Cynthia M. Wilkins, Elaine Scott-Williams

WISCONSIN

(Milwaukee) Latoya Arnold, Michele Barker, Marina Berry, Caroline Carter, Darcia Merritt Dillard, Symone Huley, Lisa Lewis, Dorothy McCollum, Ruth Morgan, Olivia Williams

INTERNATIONAL
BARBADOS (Christ Church)

Cathyann Morris, Victoria Sargeant, Beverley Shepherd (St. Michael) Suzanne Carlin Best; (St. James) Jennifer Boxill, Valmay Gibson

CANADA

ONTARIO

(Mississagua) Beverly Elaine Dixon; Gloria McLeod;(Scarborogh) Avalon Williams

QUEBEC

(**Montreal**)Erica Hernandez

ENGLAND

(**Birmingham**) Michelle Headlam (**Essex**) Mrs. Shirley V. Lloyd; Sonia Baptiste; (**London**) Carmen Hanna; Coral Hodges; Emelia-Jane Kazim, Gillian McKenzie, Delle Odeleye, Amba Mpoke-Bigg

FRANCE

(**Paris**)Ama Dadson

GRAND CAYMAN

Arliene A. Dawkins
ITALY (**Siena**) JoAnne Carnesciali

JAMAICA

(**Clarendon**)Yvonne Brown; (**Kingston**)Lurane Allen, Michelle Barrett, Valerie E. Bucknor, Yvonne Douglas, Ellan A. Edwards; Judith Emanuel-Dyke, Faith Hamer, Caren Nelson, Colleen Palmer, Stella A. Rwechungura, Diane Sharpe; (**St. Ann**) Sharon Cole, Mazie Luke-Watson, Marsha Smith, Sonia Thomas; (**St. Catherine**) Michele A. Bennett-Cummings, Colleen Campbell-Wellington, Sheena Murray

THE NETHERLANDS Rhylouise Hoogeveen-Hooi (**Almere**) Kory Pryor

ST. LUCIA, W.I. (**Castries**)

Daisy St. Rose

TRINIDAD, (**Caguanas**) Ruth Shirma Hewitt-Bartholomew (**Port of Spain**) Ruth Hewitt-Bartholomew

THE VIRGIN ISLANDS

(**Christiansted**) Colleen Liburd, Zahra Spencer (**St. Thomas**) Simone E. Martin

Bibliography

Sisterlocks Lifetime Journal

Essence Magazine

Journal of Pediatrics

Jewish News of Greater Phoenix

Slavery, Race and Ideology in the United States by Barbara Fields

Before the Mayflower by Lerone Bennett, Jr.

Johnson Products *Encyclopedia of African-American Culture and History*, vol. 3. 1972. Robinson, Greg

The Effects of Racism and Racial Discrimination on Minority by Silverman, Robert Mark Business Development: The Case of Black Manufacturers in Chicago's Ethnic Beauty Aids Industry

Journal of Social History 31.3 (1998): 571–597.

Confessions of a Video Vixen by Karrine Steffan

Trouble in Mind (1998) by historian Leon F. Litwack,

The Falsification of African Consciousness by Amos N. Wilson

http://www.biocrawler.com/encyclopedia/Cornrows

African Heritage Volumes

U.S.A. Today

Celebrity News

Holy Bible

Class Struggle and the Origin of Racial Slavery: The Invention of the White Race by Theodore Allen

Life on the Sea Islands by Charlotte Grimke

The Atlantic Monthly

Naomi's Guide to Aging Gratefully, (2006) by Naomi Judd

The Ugly Duckling by Hans Christian Andersen

The Story of Doctor Doolittle, by Hugh Lofting

Mary Poppins, by Pamela Lyndon Travers

Lost in a Sea of Hair Weaves

By Molara Wood | Published 11/21/2005 | Nigeria Matters | Unrated

New York Times Magazine

Complexions and Hairstories—*My Fair Friend Debra* (poem) by Eileen Carole

We Wear the Mask (poem) by Paul Lawrence Dunbar

A Dream Deferred (poem) by Langston Hughes

Hair Story—*Untangling The Roots of Black hair in America* by Ayana D. Byrd & Lori L Tharps

Story of Pride, Power, and Uplift—Anne Turnbo Malone (2003) by J.L. Wilkerson

African-American Inventors—Majorie Stewart Joyner (1996)—by Fred M.B. Amram

Styling Jim Crow: *African American Beauty Training during Segregation* by Julia Kirk Blackwelder

Rapunzel's Daughters—*What Women's Hair Tells Us About Women's Lives* by Rose Weitz

Trouble In Mind—*Black Southerners in the Age of Jim Crow* by Leon F. Litwack

Uncle Tom's Cabin

American Slavery, American Freedom—*The Ordeal of Colonial Virginia* by Edmund Morgan

"The Birth of a Nation"

Aunt Chloe

Britian's Sun Newspaper

Slave in a Box: The Strange Career of Aunt Jemima, by M. M. Manring.

The History of Black Business in America by Juliet E. Walker

Sketches of America by Henry Fearon

Up From Slavery by Booker T. Washington

Hair Raising by Noliwe Rooks 1996

Women's Wear Daily Magazine

That Hair Thing by Dr. Joanne Cornwell

Upscale Magazine

I Know Why the Caged Bird Sings by Maya Angelou

African American Poetry—*An Anthology* 1773–1927

Adoption Nation: How the Adoption Revolution is Transforming America

Nappy Hair by Carolivia Herron

The New York Times

American Society of Plastic Surgeons

Book of Ecclesiastes

The Daily Express

Nappy and Proud by Earl Ofari Hutchinson

The California Cryobank's website at www.cryobank.com.

Journal of Pediatrics

<u>Basic Books, 2001</u>

More Magazine

Pimp Hop Internet Magazine

New York Daily News

Pigmentation and Empire: The Emerging Skin-Whitening Industry by Amina Mire

978-0-595-42895-3
0-595-42895-9

Made in the USA
Lexington, KY
06 July 2012